I'm leaving you Simon, You disgust me...

A DICTIONARY OF RECEIVED IDEAS

I'm leaving you Simon, You disgust me...

A DICTIONARY OF RECEIVED IDEAS

William Donaldson

WEIDENFELD & NICOLSON

Cassell, an imprint of Weidenfeld & Nicolson
Wellington House, 125 Strand, London WC2R 0BB

A CIP record for this book is available from
the British Library

ISBN 0-304-36575-0

Designed by Gwyn Lewis

Printed in Great Britain by Clays Ltd, St Ives plc

Introduction

This book has been published by mistake (*see* PUBLISHING). Its author, William Donaldson, submitted it to our weekly New Title Acquisitions Meeting under the name of Ol' Dirty Bastard, the American hip hop star, whom he claimed to be representing. Editors (*see* EDITING) cannot be expected to read manuscripts due for publication – least of all those by Chart Toppers (*see* CELEBRITIES). These are fast-tracked straight to Marketing, their authors to Make-up and Wardrobe.

Mr Ol' Dirty Bastard was about to set off on a promotional tour of the UK for a book which he couldn't remember having written, when an 18-year-old student, enjoying a gap year working in Accounts, pointed out that it contained a joke based on a confusion between the philosopher, Sir Karl Popper, and the stimulant colloquially of the same name, popular with homosexuals (*see also* MOUSTACHES). This joke, it transpired, had already appeared in six previous books by Mr Donaldson, all remaindered within weeks of publication.

A search in Unrecovered Advances yielded the surprising information that Weidenfeld & Nicolson had been Mr Donaldson's publishers for 25 years – the last occasion being as recently as 2002, when *Brewer's Rogues, Villains and Eccentrics* enjoyed a modest success (it has to be admitted) with the critics, and, more relevantly, at point of sale.

By the time Mr Donaldson admitted that he was the author of *I'm Leaving You Simon, You Disgust Me* the book was already in the Production pipeline. Asked whether it was his customary mix of irreverent and wacky humour, further whether it would sit happily next to Dawn French's *Big Book of Boobs* in the Christmas Toilet Book Sector, he replied that it was, and that it would.

There was time to cut the print-run, but not to have the book edited. One can't do everything. It came as a surprise when the wife of someone in Key Accounts reported that, far from being wacky and irreverent, the book appeared to be a collection of perfectly sensible observations. Examples which struck her as being mere truisms included:

Asylum-seekers. Forever leap-frogging single mums-of-two in the council-house queue.

Ball, Zoe (1971–). Can Zoe juggle parenting and work? The debate continues.

Balzac, Honoré de (1799–1850). Though he served his apprenticeship writing potboilers in a Paris attic, his *Comédie Humaine* has been compared, in the grandeur of its architecture, to a great cathedral. Like so many French intellectuals, he died of coffee poisoning.

Baumes-les-Messieurs. One of France's best-kept secrets.
See also CONQUES.

Compton Pauncefoot. Either a picturesque village in Somerset or a West Indian fast bowler. The debate continues.
See also UPTON SNODSBURY.

Cosmetic surgery. You have to fix your life before you fix your nose.

Elephants. Forever sitting on pensioners and turning their dream holiday into a nightmare.

Genet, Jean (1910–86). French homosexual and writer. His turbulent life and early years spent in prison are reflected in his dramas, in which the characters act out bizarre and violent fantasies via elements of ritual, role-play and illusion.

See also VILLON, FRANÇOIS.

Glubb, John Bagot (1897–1986). British military commander and founder of the Arab Legion. Known as 'Glubb Pasha', he lost an arm in a skirmish with the Turks.

See also DE VIVAR, RODRIGO DÍAZ; MALLARMÉ, STÉPHANE; MAUPASSANT, GUY DE; RICHARD I; RIMBAUD, ARTHUR; VEGA, LOPE FELIX DE.

Judges, Booker Prize. The facetious rumour that the Booker Prize judges for 2004 were to be Ian Hislop, Mariella Frostrup, Jerry Hall, Linford Christie, Vanessa Feltz and Alan Titchmarsh was quickly scotched when it was announced that they were to be Sir Trevor MacDonald, Joanna Lumley, Ben Elton, Janet Street-Porter, Trevor Brooking and *Big Brother's* Nush.

Lennon, John (1940–80). We all experience pain, but John Lennon shared his with the world.

Lunchbox. Contrary to received opinion, Dr David Starkey has never said 'That's a very big lunchbox! Is it all yours?' when lecturing on Henry VIII.

Men, single. Debauched egotists who sleep with their maids.

77-year-olds. Forever passing away peacefully at home.

Toulouse-Lautrec, Henri (1864–1901). Like many people with a full address book, he found there were times when no one was in. Died of syphilis.

See also BYRON, LORD GEORGE; CASS, MAMA; HENDRIX, JIMI; JOPLIN, JANIS; MOON, KEITH.

Upton Snodsbury. Either a picturesque village in Worcestershire or a West Indian fast bowler. The debate continues.

See also COMPTON PAUNCEFOOT.

Welsh politicians. Forever fellating Rastafarians on Clapham Common.

I confess to being on all fours with Key Accounts: the joke eludes me. These entries appear to be statements of the obvious. *A Dictionary of Common Sense* would have been a more accurate title, in my opinion. It's too late now to make the change, so there you are. We offer you our apologies.

Simon King, PUBLISHER

Abierto. A good word – albeit Spanish – with which to open a Dictionary of Received Ideas set in an Islington Tapas Bar.

'Susan!'

Nothing.

'SUSAN!'

'Did you call?'

'Yes. They're *abierto*.'

'I can't hear you. I'm upstairs. In the twins' room.'

'We haven't got any twins.'

'No twins! How do we share the parenting?'

'We'll worry about that later.'

'What about the school run?'

'Ditto.'

'At least the Goya's *abierto*.'

'I can't hear you. I'm upstairs in the twins' room.'

'So you said.'

'Then I'm off to Waitrose. I'll fill up the Audi on the way back.'

'I can't hear you. I'm measuring the dining-room.'

Ablutions. A word that sits well in an occasional column.

See also ABODE; ALFRED; AMERICAN ACADEMICS; BUSTS; DANE, HAMLET THE MOODY; DUCK, DONALD; EATERIE; EMBONPOINT; HOSTELRY; INFELICITOUS; KEATS, JOHN; LIBATION; MEADOWS, MY POULTERER, THE ESTIMABLE MR; NOSHERIE; OCCASIONS; READER, GENTLE; REPORTER; THESPIAN; VARIETY, BIRDS OF THE FEATHERED.

Abode. Always 'modest', unless 'humble'.

'Simon! Long time no see! Well, well, well!'

'Plimsoll, is it? Platter? Parsnip? Pratley?'

'Plimmer. Vernon Plimmer. We were at Charterhouse together. For our sins!'

'Plimmer! Of course. Welcome to my modest abode! So – to what do I owe the honour?'

'At a loose end. Found myself in your neck of the woods. Thought I'd drop in on the off chance.'

'Good man! Take a pew, while I finish my ablutions! Sit ye down!'

'How's Susan?'

'Susan?'

'Your partner!'

'Of course! She's fine, I think. Odd weather for the time of year. Neither one thing nor the other.'

'Indeed. Autumnal one minute and quite mild the next.'

'Blustery, would you say, and bitterly cold?'

'Indeed. When I set out this morning I hardly knew whether to wear an overcoat or carry an umbrella.'

'And yet, "England with all thy faults, I love thee still – my country!"'

'Delightful! "I'd not exchange thy sullen skies ..."'

'"Friends, Romans, countrymen ..."'

'Pardon?'

'Sorry! I was miles away. Thinking of Tuscany, in fact.'

'You have a place there?'

'Well, yes. Nothing grand. But when on holiday one likes to mingle with people from Islington.'

'So one does. When in town, Daphne and I sometimes dine at the Goya in Islington High Street. You know it?'

'Indeed. We must meet there some time.'

See also CRAPS, A CROWD OF; 'FRIEND, IN A PIG'S ARSE'; LARKIN, PHILIP; MEET THERE SOME TIME, WE MUST; 'VERS DE SOCIÉTÉ'.

Abuse, verbal. Not the most serious of offences.

'Verbal abuse is one thing, Inspector; assault with a deadly weapon quite another.'

'Thank you, Headmaster. I think I know the difference. Come along, Sergeant.'

See also TOUCH OF FROST, A; MORSE, INSPECTOR.

Academics. Out of touch with the real world. Bill Shakespeare knew better than anyone what put bums on seats.

'Ah yes, but Shakespeare, like Keith Waterhouse in our own day, had the good fortune to have been educated at the University of Hard Knocks.'

See also AMERICAN ACADEMICS; BUMS ON SEATS; FRONT OFFICE, THE; GOLDWYN, SAM; KNOCKS, THE UNIVERSITY OF HARD; SHAKESPEARE, WILLIAM; TITS; WATERHOUSE, KEITH.

Accessible. The new celebrity historians have shown that accessibility of thought – an ability to illuminate without being solemn – is not inevitably accompanied by a lowering of academic standards.

'Or "dumbing down", to use the vogue expression!'

'Indeed, indeed. Surely it was Dr David Starkey who referred to Henry VIII as "having the hots for Anne Boleyn?"'

'Graham Norton, the squeaky-voiced Irishman, in fact, but the point holds.'

See also FERGUSON, PROFESSOR NIALL; GOOD TASTE; HISTORIANS, CELEBRITY; HISTORIANS, PHOTOGENIC; HISTORY, THE NEW; HUNT, DR TRISTRAM; STARKEY, DR DAVID.

Accessory. 'No, Daphne. That would make you an accessory.'

'I became an accessory when I married you, Vernon. Remember?'

See also PITY, AND MORE'S THE.

Accidents. Always 'unfortunate'.

See also ARISTOTLE.

Accountants. Always 'faceless'. The accountants have taken over.

'Argue me this, Susan. Was it a perverse irony that Orson Welles should have been deprived of the tools of his trade by the faceless accountants of Hollywood, or simply good housekeeping by the boys in the front office?'

'I can't hear you. I'm in the kitchen.'

'Oh. Parsnip dropped by today.'

'I still can't hear you.'

'I said, Parsnip dropped by today.'

'Who the hell's Parsnip?'

'I can't hear you, I'm in the den.'

'I said who's Parsnip?'

'Haven't the faintest idea. Married to someone called Doris. May bump into them at the Goya unless we're careful.'

'Forewarned is forearmed.'

'As they say.'

On any list of the ten greatest films of all time, at least two by Orson Welles would have to be included.

See also BOTTOM LINE; *CITIZEN KANE*; FRONT OFFICE, THE.

Accuracy. Usually 'nagging'. Derek Shackleton, of Hampshire and England, bowled at no more than a portly military medium, but such was his nagging accuracy that batsmen of international class were seldom able to get him by the collar.

See also CARTWRIGHT, DEAR OLD TOM.

Accused, the. The accused always hears the charges without emotion.

Act of God. Always a catastrophe. Something no reasonable man could expect.

Actors, English. The finest in the world. That said, on any list of the ten English actors who could mesmerize us by reading out the London telephone directory, it is unlikely that the name of Robin Askwith would appear.

See also ASKWITH, ROBIN; *UPS AND DOWNS OF A HANDYMAN, THE*.

Adams, Douglas (1952–2001). The best-selling author of *The Hitch-Hiker's Guide to the Galaxy* was famously afflicted by writer's block. What a tragic irony, then, that this arch-procrastinator should have met his final deadline early! At the age of 49, Adams suffered a fatal heart attack while riding an exercise bicycle in a Los Angeles gym.

See also AMBULANCES; ARRIVAL, DEAD ON; CONDITION, IN A STABLE; 49-YEAR-OLDS; 47-YEAR-OLDS.

Advertising. Paradoxically, there is now more advertising on BBC television than on the whole of ITV.

Aeschylus (*c*.525–456 BC). Greek tragedian. The story that he was killed by a tortoise dropped on his bald head by an eagle is probably apocryphal, but none the less significant for that.

Aesop (*c*.620–560 BC). Greek fabulist. His tale of the tortoise and the hare is only doubtfully a contribution to the Parmenidian debate on the impossibility of motion, but agreeable nonetheless.
See also PARMENIDES.

Affairs. Affairs are inevitable in the pressure cooker of politics.

Affairs, extra-marital. Always 'tawdry'. A cry for help. No need to explain why. *The Daily Mail* has not been deceived.
    'Nor, for that matter, has Mariella Frostrup. When defending shamed TV presenter Angus Deayton after his sacking from *Have I Got News For You*, the husky-voiced little Eskimo yet referred in her *Observer* column to his "tawdry love-life".'
    'As did Ian Hislop in *The Daily Telegraph*.'
    'That, perhaps, is less surprising.'

Again. 'We meet again! This must be fate! Plimsoll, is it?'
    'Plimmer.'
    'Of course! Vernon Plimmer?'
    'Guilty as charged!'
    'So – what brings you to the celebrated Goya *tapas*-cum-wine bar in the leafy environs of fashionable Islington? Have you relocated?'
    'Alas, no. As I told you yesterday…'
    'We've met before? You astound me! Terrible memory for faces.'
    'And names.'
    'Thank you, Susan. So Islington's not your patch?'
    'No – we're simply tourists from darkest Somerset! We try to get up to town twice a year at least.'
    'A visit to an art gallery, is it?'
    'Indeed. Today it was White Cube2. We scarcely knew what to think.'
    'I know what you mean. Damien Hirst? An artist who defies pigeon-holing, would you say?'
    'An interesting thought.'
    'And you take in a show, I imagine? Stoppard? The latest Simon Gray? Harold Pinter?'

'Ah, Pinter! I always say that Pinter's plays are poems.'

'I'd second that. When people ask me what a play by Pinter means, I reply, "It means whatever you think it means."'

'How true! So, what was it? *An Ideal Husband* at the Haymarket?'

'I don't think *An Ideal Husband* is on at the Haymarket at the moment.'

'Thank you, Susan, but I think I know what's on at the Haymarket. *An Ideal Husband* is *always* on at the Haymarket. As often as not with Dulcie Gray.'

'Binkie Beaumont used to refer to her and her husband, Michael Denison, as Dreary Michaelson and Gracie Dull, you know.'

'In that case I expect they'll be joining us later.'

'What was that, Susan?'

'Nothing.'

'On this occasion it was a visit to the Almeida with my better half. *Private Lives*. We roared with laughter.'

'I'm not surprised. The Master at his best. "Very flat, Norfolk…!"'

'Pray cease! I'll crack a rib!'

'So you still live in…'

'An agreeable little village not six miles from Taunton. I won't divulge its name. Don't want the world and his wife beating a path to its door! And you?'

'We were lucky enough to clamber aboard the property ladder before Islington became Islington, as it were. We weekend in Wiltshire, of course. Not far from Salisbury. I'm Simon, by the way. This is Susan, my significant other. Why don't you and…?'

'Daphne.'

'Why don't you and Daphne join us?'

'We'd be delighted!'

'That looks like an empty table over there. *HOMBRE!*'

'I do wish you wouldn't shout like that.'

'You have to attract their attention, dear. Shall I go first?'

'After you.'

'Age before beauty!'

'We're none of us getting any younger!'

'Lead on, MacDuff!'

'*Arriba!*'

See also COWARD, NOËL; *PRIVATE LIVES;* SECRETS, SOMERSET'S BEST-KEPT; TAUNTON.

Age. Takes us all by surprise.

Age, the endemic follies of the. *See* DAILY MAIL, THE; EVIL; MAN, THE PERFECTABILITY OF; NOOSE, THE; PENDULUM; PROGRESS, BELIEF IN THE ILLUSION OF; REAL WORLD, THE; UTOPIA, THE SEARCH FOR.

Age, the Victorian. Lytton Strachey got it right. He sometimes did. The history of the Victorian age can never be written because we know too much about it.

'That said, and apropos Andrew Wilson's *The Victorians* (Hutchinson, 2002), would it be fair to say that Wilson's picture – a view from a vicarage window – is a noble effort?'

'I'm afraid I can't help you there. I haven't read it.'

'I'm reading a good book at the moment. I can't put it down. What's it called, Susan?'

'What's what called?'

'That book I'm reading.'

'God knows. I'm reading an excellent book, however. It's...'

'Yes, Susan. I'm sure you are. This may interest you, Victor...'

'Vernon.'

'Of course. In AD 800, the Emperor Charlemagne used an asbestos tablecloth to impress his dinner guests. He surprised them by putting into the fire and then withdrawing it unharmed.'

'I confess I don't know what to say.'

'It's called *Y: The Descent of Men*.'

'What is, Susan?'

'The book I'm reading. It's by Professor Steve Jones. Really very interesting. Jones argues that the male sex – parasitic creatures in evolutionary retreat and a mutation from the basic model (female) – will one day cease to exist! And not before time, if you ask me.'

'Don't be silly, Susan. Tell me, Vernon, have you and Dolly...'

'Daphne.'

'Daphne. Of course. Have you and Daphne ever been to Conques?'

'Alas not. And you?'

'Not yet. Perhaps when the twins are a little older...'

'You have twins?'

'Indeed. Ben and Joanna. Aged nine.'

'The school run? You share it, I imagine?'

'Indeed. I do it on Mondays and Wednesdays. Susan on Tuesdays, Thursdays and Fridays. Anyway, as I said, we weekend in Wiltshire at the moment. And we have this place in Tuscany...'

'Yes, you told me.'

'I did? We've met before? Well I never! Anyway, on Friday nights we join a convoy of jeeps down the M4 – driven as a rule, I may say, by our inscrutable friends from the Land of the Rising Sun. Corporate bankers for the most part.'

'They'll be in Somerset next!'

'I dare say they will. Still, we all have a cross to bear!'

'"The slings and arrows..."'

'"When sorrows come, they come not single spies..."'

'"As flies to wanton boys, are we to the gods;/They kill us for their sport."'

'I'll have a consonant please, Carol!'

'I think I'll phone a friend!'

'Don't mention the war!'

'Ha! Ha!'

'Bad luck! Just behind on the buzzer there, Magdalene!'

'The Princess of Pop's love life is on hold!'

'Hardly surprising. Celebrities often need the space to find out who they really are.'

'Nothing daunts the hunting osprey.'

'Nor does it.'

'I wouldn't be a traffic warden in this weather!'

'No peace for the wicked!'

'Better days ahead!'

'If we're spared!'

'Anyway – Professor Jones argues...'

'Do what, Susan?'

'Steve Jones. He wrote this book I'm reading. *Y: The Descent Of Men*. He argues that, far from being an evolutionary step forward, the Y chromosome is in fact a rogue abnormality, a deformity which leads to distress, disease and early death.'

'A depressing picture, Susan!'

'Bollocks to that, Vernon. You wouldn't mourn the permanent

disappearance of other parasites, would you? The sheep tick, for instance?'

'Thank you, Susan. I'm sure we've all been thoroughly enlightened. In fact I'm reading the latest John Grisham. Can't remember the title, that's all.'

See also AVEYRON; BUZZER; CELEBS; CONQUES; DIVAS; ESKIMOS WORKING IN THE UNITED KINGDOM; JONSSON, ULRIKA; MAGDALENE COLLEGE, CAMBRIDGE; WALL, THE WRITING ON THE.

Age before beauty. *See* AGAIN.

Agenda. For Sir Alex Ferguson, coming second isn't on the agenda.

'Having said that, two goals down and just five minutes to go, Des. In fairness, that's a big ask, even for such experienced escapologists as Man U.'

'Thank you, Ron.'

See also ALBUMS; COMING SECOND; FERGUSON, SIR ALEX; MANCHESTER UNITED; OLD TRAFFORD; SCOTSMEN, STRAWBERRY-NOSED.

A great deal. 'You've been my partner for eleven years, Susan, and I never knew you didn't like the theatre.'

'That's hardly surprising, Simon. There's a great deal about me you don't know. Is this place without a licence or what?'

'It seems to me that you had more than enough to drink before we got here.'

'You're saying I've got a drink problem?'

'I'm saying nothing of the sort.'

'Well I have. I can't fucking get one. And they're drinking.'

'Who?'

'Those two men at the next table. I'm sure they arrived after us. The old one's come as Max Beerbohm. Usually a mistake. Cravat. Straw boater. Nasal plugs. Watery eyes. His toyboy looks Italian. Probably called Roberto. He's quite pretty, Roberto.'

'He is, isn't he?'

'Trust you to notice that, Daphne! Daphne has a slight weakness for the southern Mediterranean type!'

'I wouldn't go that far, Vernon. I don't know, though. He *is* cute.'

'And so are they.'

'And so are who what?'

'Drinking. The two men at the bar. Well dressed. Award-winning haircuts. Earrings. Celebrity stubble. Enhanced lips. Multi-studded. What do you think, Daphne? Life-style advisers? Loft converters? Pole dancers at Madame Jo-Jo's?'

'Lecturers in the New History, at a guess.'

'Of course! I think I'll join them.'

'You'll do nothing of the sort, Susan! They look to me as if they might have the Ecstasy concession at Caesar's Palace, Romford.'

'In that case I'll definitely join them. Damn. Too late. Here come their girlfriends.'

'Tracey and Sharon, unless I'm much mistaken.'

'And they're called Con and Marty, I suppose.'

'I wouldn't be at all surprised.'

See also BIMBO; SHOPPING MALL SLAPPERS; WATERHOUSE, KEITH.

Aguilera, Christina (1980–). She comes across as one of the sassiest babes in pop, but splitting from boyfriend Jorge Santos sent the pint-sized diva reeling.

'Just so. According to *The Sunday Times*'s lively new celeb column, 'Go Girl!', "The raunchy chart-topper is doing her growing up in public."'

'Always a mistake.'

'Indeed. *The Sunday Times* further reports that "The little disco madam has recently turned to celebrity hypnotist, Paul McKenna, for help – to stop her being so stroppy."'

'A lesson for wannabes everywhere!'

'I'll second that. *HOMBRE!*'

See also DIVAS.

Airey, Dawn (1962–). Television executive. An unashamed pop-ulist. A major player. One of those refreshing people who doesn't suffer fools gladly.

'What you see is what you get?'

'In a nutshell.'

'Firm but fair?'

'Absolutely.'

'A human bio-hazard, would you say?'

'That's going a little far, perhaps!'

'Stern but stupid, then?'

'Thank you, Susan. I hardly think Rupert Murdoch would have signed her to a multi-million golden handcuff deal if she was stupid!'

'On the contrary. That's exactly what he'd do.'

'Don't be silly, Susan. Susan's an intellectual, you see. She teaches Classics at University College London.'

'How interesting. That will explain her earlier references to Aeschylus and to Aesop, the fabulist.'

'Indeed. However, Dawn Airey, was it?'

'The very same!'

'She understands television. I read in the paper the other day that she's turned scheduling into an art form.'

'My point precisely, Vernon. Who but Dawn Airey would have dared to schedule Barbara Bedworthy in *Lesbo Love Romps* (1973) against *The Disappearing Barn Owl* on BBC2?'

'David Liddiment, in fact.'

'I'm obliged to you, Susan. I'm temporarily confounded. An apéritif, do you think? While we're waiting?'

'About fucking time.'

'Thank you, Susan. I think you've made your feelings clear. What about you, Victor?'

'Vernon.'

'Good God! Where? Don't say he's joined us. A colossal bore, if memory serves.'

'No, no. I'm Vernon.'

'So you are. I meant a different Vernon, of course. Vernon Plimmer.'

'That's me.'

'Really? I had you down as Pratley. Small world. How's your glass, Doris?'

'Daphne.'

'Of course. Daphne. How's your glass?'

'Empty. The same as mine. We haven't bloody ordered yet.'

'Nor we have. Thank you, Susan. *HOMBRE!*'

See also BEDWORTHY, BARBARA; POPULISTS.

Akram, Wasim (1966–) and **Younis, Waqar** (1971–). The finest opening partnership in fast-bowling history.

'I don't hope to see a better in my lifetime.'

See also BOWES, BILL and LARWOOD, HAROLD; DONALD, ALLAN; HALL, WESLEY and GRIFFITH, CHARLIE; HOLDING, MICHAEL and ROBERTS, ANDY; LILLEE, DENNIS and THOMPSON, JEFF; LINDWALL, RAY and MILLER, KEITH; MCGRATH, GLENN and LEE, BRETT; TRUEMAN, FREDDIE and STATHAM, BRIAN.

Alas. One doesn't go to the theatre as often as one should, alas.

Albatross. When it comes to collecting airmiles, the albatross is in the major league.

'Sir David Attenborough?'

'The very same.'

'A consummate professional.'

See also ATTENBOROUGH, SIR DAVID; PROFESSIONALS.

Albums. Some albums set the agenda (*see* COBAIN, KURT).

Alcohol. One should always apologise for not drinking at lunchtime.

'Adam's ale for me, if you don't mind. Is that very boring of me? A long afternoon at the office looms. I'm behind with my e-mails.'

'Which of us isn't! That said, we all know where prohibition leads.'

'We certainly do, thanks to America's doomed experiment.'

'I'd go further. I'd point out that Our Lord's first miracle was to turn water into wine.'

'And a very tolerable plonk at that, from all accounts!'

'It's a shame he's not with us now, in that case.'

'Thank you, Susan.'

'I think I'll join the celebrity historians at the bar. Con and Marty is it?'

'You'll do nothing of the sort, Susan. Tell me, Vernon. The Queen Mother. The nation's favourite gran. Was there a touch of arsenic in the marshmallow, do you think?'

See also MOTHER, THE QUEEN; PROHIBITION.

Alcoholic. What the alcoholic is after, of course, is not the drunkenness but the hangover. He wants to feel guilty.

'For real! Care for another, Marty?'

'Just the one, then, Con.'

'Cheers!'

'Brilliant!'

'The nuts!'

'Yo!'

'Word up!'

'Hullo hullo! Top totty one five! The real deal, Marty.'

'She's boff, mine!'

'Straight between the uprights!'

'Hole in one!'

'Top babes, Marty!'

'Well fit!'

'Totally toned!'

'Awesome!'

'Way to go!'

'Arsenal!'

'As the man said!'

'The main man!'

'He wrote the book!'

'Game on!'

'Hi! Is u 'avin a private or g or can n e 1 join in?' Im tracey. Hers my frien' sharon. Ill hav a spritzer, me.'

'And Sharon?'

'Ill hav a spritzer 2.'

'Two spritzers coming up.'

'Feel these, babe, feel these! How do you suppose I got those? In the gym? I don't think so! Horizontal jogging!'

'Tel u wot, shar. Wot a hunk! He pumps my gas, this 1!'

'What's your star sign, darling?'

'I is virgo, me. Wots urs?'

'Oh, thank you very much. I'll have a large vodka!'

'Arf! Arf! Ur brill, u. I luv a bloke wot makes me larf!'

'What do you do, then, you and Sharon?'

'Hav a gess. Go on, gess!'

'Commissioning editors at Channel 4?'

'No!'

'Bubbly wannabes?'

'No!'

'Hairdressers? Airline personnel?'

'No!'

'Editors-at-large, *The Independent on Sunday*?'

'No!'

'Table dancers?'

'No!'

'Sales and Marketing, Hodder Headline?'

'No!'

'Shop assistants?'

'Naaah! Wes in Media Studies, us. Wot about u?'

'Academics, me and Con. The New History. That's our dodge. I lecture at Keele. Con's at Birkbeck.'

'Cool. Us on da tv i spose.'

'We have projects under consideration. "100 Kings and Queens of England Who Were Killed in Shark Attacks." To date we haven't found one. It's back to the drawingboard *pro tem*. So. What is it? Rock or pop?'

'Pop – its gr8 4 shackin' out 2.'

'OK. Fave club?'

'The Wellington. Gr8 for c n soccer tossers b n b 10 up by bad rs dormen.'

'Fav disco?'

'Click – fab 4 throwin' shapes on de dance flor.'

'Got you. Moyles or Evans?'

'Moyles.'

'The best bum in pop? Kylie or J–Lo?'

'Kylie. Shes the fittest babe on the planet.'

'Flash or trash?'

'Trash.'

'OK. Who'd you do? Mark Lawson or Andrea Dworkin?'

'Andrea Dworkin. If i woz off me tits like.'

'Trinny and Susannah or Abbott and Costello?'

'Abbott and Costello. There icons, Abbott and Costello. Seen all there movies. *Abbott and Costello Meet Frankenstein. Abbott and Costello in High Society. Abbott and Costello Meet Captain Kidd.* I told u. Wes in Media Studies, us.'

'We're in luck here, Marty.'

'Bombs away, Con!' (*See also* BIMBO; WATERHOUSE, KEITH.)

'You know what, Vernon? It beats me why they let such people into a place like this. I'm referring to Con and Marty over there. To say nothing of their new friends, Tracey and Sharon.'

'Small wonder Tony and Cherie have stopped coming here.'

'I think they look like fun.'

'Tony and Cherie?'

'Hardly! No, Tracey and Sharon. I'll definitely join them later. Oh look. Tracey's off to the Ladies. I think I'll follow her.'

'Susan, I positively forbid you!'

'Only teasing. And don't look up. I think we're about to be joined by the sad old boy who's come as Max Beerbohm.'

See also CHRISTMAS, GETTING A NEW NOSE FOR; WALL, THE WRITING ON THE; WESTBROOK, DANIELLA.

Aldeburgh. 'They'll be in Aldeburgh next.' (*See also* THEY.)

'I beg your pardon? Were you speaking to us?'

'How remiss of me. I should have introduced myself. Jolyon De'ath. Fifty years with Basil Blackwell.'

'Simon Wigglesworth. My significant other, Susan. Our good friends, Vernon and Doris Pratley.'

'Daphne.'

'Of course.'

'This is my companion, Roberto. Alas, he has to be back in Italy on Tuesday.'

'How sad. Tell me, Vernon...'

'Florence to be precise.'

'So I see. You'll miss him.'

'I certainly shall. He's in the navy.'

'You surprise me. Tell me, Vernon. Welsh rugby. Where does it go from here?'

See also AT SEA; FLORENCE.

Alexander (the Great) (356–323 BC). Conqueror of the Persian empire. Alexander's tutor was no less an academic than Aristotle himself – though what the good professor taught the murderous Greek general we may well pause to query.

'One is inevitably reminded, is one not, that Plato was tutor to Dionysius, Despot of Syracuse, that Seneca, the old Stoic, was tutor to the young Nero, and that Socrates tutored the treacherous Alcibiades.'

'So much for formal education!'

See also ACADEMICS; EDUCATION, FORMAL.

Alfred (849–99). Anglo-Saxon King of Wessex. In an occasional column it might be amusing to refer to his 'legendary lack of culinary skills!'

See also ABODE; AMERICAN ACADEMICS; BUSTS; DANE, HAMLET THE MOODY; DUCK, DONALD; EATERIE; EMBONPOINT; HOSTELRY; INFELICITOUS; KEATS, JOHN; LIBATION; MEADOWS, MY POULTERER, THE ESTIMABLE MR; NOSHERIE; OCCASIONS; REPORTER; THESPIAN; VARIETY, BIRDS OF THE FEATHERED.

Ali, Muhammad (1942–). Pound for pound the greatest boxer ever to pull the gloves on.

'I don't hope to see a better in my lifetime.'

See also ARMSTRONG, HENRY 'HANK'; DURAN, ROBERTO; HAGLER, MARVIN; HEARNS, THOMAS 'THE HITMAN'; LEONARD, SUGAR RAY; LOUIS, JOE; MARCIANO, ROCKY; MOORE, ARCHIE; PEP, WILLIE; ROBINSON, SUGAR RAY.

All, the need to get away from it. The Inner Hebrides is a good place to go when you feel the need to get away from it all.

'I have heard it said that the Outer Hebrides is even better.'

'It's a point of view. That said, and for those who don't want to be a boat-ride away from cinemas and pizzerias, the best compromise in the Western Isles is Oban, on the mainland.'

All ears. *See* INTELLECTUAL, LIBERAL.

Allegri, Gregorio (1582–1652). Close your eyes when listening to Allegri's *Miserere* and you can smell the incense in the Sistine Chapel.

Alma Mater. In an occasional column, an amusing way to describe one's old school or university.

Am, I want to discover who I really. *See* AUTOBIOGRAPHY; CELEBRITIES; JONSSON, ULRIKA.

Ambiguity. Always 'teasing'.

Ambition. Today's wannabes understand that if you want it enough you can achieve your ambition. You can be whatever you want to be.
   'But what if you're completely without talent?'
   'I'm sorry? I don't think I understand the question.'
See also BECKHAM, VICTORIA; BUBBLY PERSONALITIES; WATERMAN, PETE.

Ambrose, Curtley (1963–) and **Walsh, Courtney** (1962–). The finest opening partnership in fast-bowling history.
   'I don't hope to see a better in my lifetime.'
See also AKRAM, WASIM and YOUNIS, WAQAR; BOWES, BILL and LARWOOD, HAROLD; DONALD, ALLAN; HALL, WESLEY and GRIFFITH, CHARLIE; HOLDING, MICHAEL and ROBERTS, ANDY; LILLEE, DENNIS and THOMPSON, JEFF; LINDWALL, RAY and MILLER, KEITH; MCGRATH, GLENN and LEE, BRETT; TRUEMAN, FREDDIE and STATHAM, BRIAN.

Ambulances. Always rushing people to hospital.
See also ARRIVAL, DEAD ON; CONDITION, IN A STABLE; 49-YEAR-OLDS; 47-YEAR-OLDS.

American academics. Often 'bearded'; always 'boring'. In an occasional column it might be amusing to speculate on the most absurd research project ever undertaken by an American academic.
   'Surely it was Sue Arnold...'
   'The matchless Sue Arnold?'
   'The very same...'
   'She's never less than readable.'
   'May I continue?'
   'Pray do.'
   'Surely it was Sue Arnold who referred in her *Independent* column

to "The Golden Fleece award for the looniest thesis produced by an American academic".'

'I'm laughing already!'

'The winner – wait for it! – was a PhD from a psychology graduate...'

'It *had* to be a psychology graduate!...'

'...who produced a treatise to show why people don't like queueing!'

'Enough! You'll have me choking on the *entremeses*!'

'We haven't ordered the *entremeses*.'

'Nor have we. *HOMBRE!*'

See also DONS, OLD-STYLE BACHELOR.

American girl, the big. 'Whatever the outcome, the big American girl will know she's been in a match.'

See also BRAZILIAN, THE GAP-TOOTHED; BULGARIAN GIRL, THE UNFANCIED; GHANAIAN, THE LIPPY; GLASWEGIAN, THE CHIRPY; IRISHMAN, THE EASY-GOING; INDIAN, THE WRISTY LITTLE; LANCASTRIAN, THE GRITTY; SPANIARD, THE MERCURIAL; TURKEY, THE CRUDE SLUGGER FROM.

Americans. *See* IRONY.

Amorous, overly. A construction that might sit well in a speech by the Prince of Wales.

See also BUSTS; VARIETY, BIRDS OF THE FEATHERED.

Amsterdam, the latest figures from. They support the proposition that the decriminalization of soft drugs yields a reduction in addiction to hard drugs. They equally support its contradiction. A mystery.

'Either way, who'd want to live in Amsterdam? That's what I always say.'

'I would, for a start.'

'I might have expected you to say that, Susan.'

Ancients, the. 'The ancients, wiser than us in this respect...' No need to explain why.

'Sounds like one for *The Oldie*, Richard.'

Anderton, Sophie (1979–). Lingerie model. The former Gossard girl has been to hell and back, but she's looking more relaxed now that she has discovered who she really is.

See also CHRISTMAS, GETTING A NEW NOSE FOR; HALLIWELL, GERI; MCCALL, DAVINA; WESTBROOK, DANIELLA.

Anfield boot room, the. *See* HARD-LUCK STORIES GALORE.

Animal-rights activists. The majority of members of animal-rights groups are infiltrators from the Special Branch.

Animals. 'Interestingly enough, Vincent...'
  'Vernon.'
  'Of course. Interestingly enough, Vernon, the temperature on the London Underground exceeds that which would be permissible by law were it animals that were being transported.'
  'There's food for thought!'
  'Talking of which ... *HOMBRE!*'

Animals, party. Forever letting their hair down in glitzy new clubs and sharing a giggle with their celebrity pals.

See also VIPs, BUSTY.

Animals, wild. How ironic that wild animals should behave so much better than so-called *homo sapiens*! Rape is unheard of in the jungle.
  'To say nothing of social security fraud and the whole range of inner-city violence!'
  'Delightful! Ah! He's seen us at last!'
  'Wonders will never cease!'
  '*Bon tarde*, Antonio.'
  'For real, bro. In fact, I'm Miguel. Antonio's off tonight.'
  'If you say so. Another menu, *por favor*. *Gracias*. Give us time to make our minds up.'
  'You're the man. Stay gold.'
  'Now – let's see.'
  'Decisions, decisions!
  'I like oysters but they don't like me!'
  'It scarcely matters since oysters don't feature on the menu.'

'It was a brave man who first ate an oyster! That's what I always say.'

'On the other hand, talk of the grit in the oyster remains a useful metaphor for the creative process.'

'Indeed it does. How about *pulpo en su tinta*, then? For the unenlightened, that's octopus cooked in its own ink.'

'Hm. I'm not sure.'

'I expect you noticed that a little earlier I said, "*Bon tarde*", when you would have been expecting me to say, "*Buenas tardes*".'

'I did think that was a little unusual, yes.'

'Perhaps – but on this occasion correct. *Bon tarde* is Ibicenco. Antonio is from the Balearics. Isn't that right, Antonio?'

'Miguel. Like I told you. Funk up your act, John, or we'll be here all night. Antonio's off. And he was born in Stoke-on-Trent.'

'Be that as it may, Susan and I usually have *sopa de picadillo*...'

'You've lost me there, I'm afraid...'

'Sorry. It's a typical Alpujarran soup...'

'As you would expect to find in Islington...'

'Please, Susan. I'm trying to explain to Vincent and Doris...'

'Vernon and Daphne.'

'Of course. I'm trying to explain to Vernon and Daphne what *sopa de picadillo* is. It's a chicken broth seasoned with *jamon serrano* and chopped egg, and, I may say, quite delicious.'

'Actually, Simon, I think I'll have crabcakes.'

'On second thoughts, so will I. And what about you and Dolly?'

'Daphne.'

'Of course. What will you and Daphne have?'

'We might go for gazpacho, I think.'

'Actually, Vernon...'

'So – that will be two crabcakes and two gazpachos. After that, Susan and I usually have have the *trucha de Poquiera*...'

'You've lost me again, I fear.'

'Sorry! It's baked trout from the local Poquiera river, wrapped in slivers of cured mountain ham.'

'Actually, Simon, I think I'll have the duck.'

'I don't see duck.'

'Top right.'

'Oh yes. Duck for us, then. And Vernon?'

'We'll go for the duck too.'

'Actually, Vernon, I think...'

'So. Four ducks. And for starters, two gazpachos and two crabcakes...'

'Actually, Simon...'

'That sounds fine.'

'And after that we'll have fritters.'

'I wouldn't be at all surprised.'

'Thank you for that, Miguel. Don't encourage him, Susan. It's like having Barry Cryer as a waiter.'

'Never heard of him.'

'One of the great unsung heroes of British comedy.'

'Indeed. And Graham Stark's another.'

'Thank you, Vernon.'

'I've never cared for Graham Stark.'

'Nor have I. So! We're ready to order. Damn me! Where's he gone? MIGUEL!'

See also COMEDY, UNSUNG HEROES OF BRITISH.

Anne of Cleves (1515–57). Contrary to popular opinion, and when lecturing on Henry VIII, Dr David Starkey has never pointed to a portrait of Anne of Cleves and said: 'That is *so* not a good look.'

See also ACCESSIBLE; AS IF!; BELLY UP; COMPLETE TOSSER; ELIZABETH I DIDN'T LIKE TO HAVE HER PERSONAL SPACE INVADED; FERGUSON, PROFESSOR NIALL; GETTING HIS LEG OVER; GOOD IN THE SACK; HAVING IT OFF; HISTORIANS, CELEBRITY; HISTORY, THE NEW; HOW SAD IS *THAT!*; HULLO SAILOR!; JAMES I HAD THE HOTS FOR CHARLES VILLIERS, 1st DUKE OF BUCKINGHAM; LEGS, FOR CHARLES II NELL GWYN WAS VIAGRA ON; MARY TUDOR WAS HAPPY TO FROCK UP OCCASIONALLY BUT IT WASN'T REALLY HER STYLE; PEAR-SHAPED; PRINCESS CAROLINE OF BRUNSWICK THE BELLE OF THE BALL? I DON'T THINK SO; SIR WALTER RALEIGH FLEW INTO ONE OF HIS HISSY FITS; STARKEY, DR DAVID; 'THAT'S A VERY BIG LUNCH BOX! IS IT ALL YOURS?'; TOTALLY TOILET; UTTERLY PANTS; WELL TROLLEYED.

Antonioni, Michelangelo (1912–). A film-maker who evokes the crisis of identity in modern life. In any list of the ten greatest films of all time, at least two by Antonioni would have to be included. Whether David Bailey was the model for the photographer played by

David Hemmings in *Blow-Up* arouses interest in some quarters, but not as often as it once did.

'That said, the scene in which Jane Birkin – who later married Serge Gainsbourg, the Gitane-smoking balladeer – wrestled in the nude with another actress is imprinted on some people's memories.'

'I dare say it is on yours, Simon. Some of us are too young to remember it, I'm glad to say.'

'Thank you, Susan.'

'I haven't finished. It's a well-known fact that, for some men, watching nubile young women wrestling in the nude is a "safe" way of working out their own homosexual desires.'

'Yes, we won't go into that, thank you, Susan. I don't...'

'I agree with Susan. I think it's very interesting. Do you have any brothers, Simon?'

'Yes, Daphne. Four. I'm the youngest. Why do you ask?'

'A recent study by Canadian psychologist, Ray Blanchard, has shown that the chances of a man being gay increase by a third with every older brother.'

'Well there you are!'

'And what are you suggesting, Susan?'

'I'm suggesting nothing, Simon.'

'I'm with *you*, Susan. For sure.'

'Ah! Miguel. We're ready to... Damn me! He's gone again! Why Tony and Cherie come here – not that they do any more – I'll never know.'

Anybody's language, in. *See* £1M; VAN NISTELROY, RUUD.

Anything, if men believe that they'll believe. 'I don't care what you do, Simon, as long as I don't know about it.'

See also CHELSEA GIRL ESCORTS; IF YOU MUST DO IT, AT LEAST HAVE THE DECENCY TO DO IT WITH A PROSTITUTE.

Apollo. The God of reason. He could make men mad. The ancients recognized no such distinction. Good name for a theatre.

Appellation contrôlée. 'If our cheese-eating friends don't wise up soon it'll be not so much *appellation contrôlée*, as *appellation terminée*!'

'Who the hell said that?'

'Not me.'

'Nor me.'

'Must have been Max Beerbohm. Or Dr Death, as he likes to call himself. Keep your voice down or he'll be joining us.'

'At least he's got a drink.'

'And Roberto's ever so cute.'

'Yes, Daphne. You've made that point.'

'Sorry, Vernon.'

Aquinas, St Thomas (1225–74). *Doctor angelicus*. He wrote that one of the pleasures of Heaven would be watching the damned suffer.

'Certainly a more robustly Christian view than the fashionably liberal pronouncements on social justice we get from today's so-called caring clergymen.'

'Really Susan! I'm quite shocked!'

'Oh dear. I was being ironic.'

'Ever a two-edged sword!'

'Well said, Vernon.'

'I'll second that. A really original contribution.'

'Now you're being silly, Susan.'

See WALL, THE WRITING ON THE.

Ariège. One of France's best-kept secrets (*see also* AUDE; AVEYRON; BAUMES-LES-MESSIEURS; CONQUES; COURSEGOULES; GORDES; LOT; LOUBRASSAC; LOZÈRE; MOSTUÉJOULS; RIEUX VOLVESTRE; SAINT-GUILHEM-LE-DÉSERT; SOLOGNE; VIEILLE-BRIOUDE).

'Tell me, Vernon, when it comes to "the great escape", is it a medieval must-have in East Sussex for you and Daphne – or the dramatic landscapes of the unspoilt Ariège?'

'We are considering a barn in Foix, southeast of Carcassonne. That said, a question suddenly occurs.'

'And what might that be? Speak now or forever hold thy peace!'

'Just this. If Ariège is one of one of France's best-kept secrets, how come that it features in what purports to be a Dictionary of Received Ideas set in an Islington wine bar? It's not possible surely to be both a secret and a received idea. There seems to be some sort of contradiction here, if not a paradox.'

'I'm temporarily nonplussed! May I come back to you on this one, Vernon?'

Aristophanes (*c*.449–380 BC). Greek playwright preeminent in the comedy genre. No party, class, sex, age-group or profession in ancient Athens was exempt from his satire.

'Were he alive today there is little in his work that he would feel the need to change.'

'A sobering thought indeed.'

Aristotle (384–322 BC). Greek philosopher, who, in his *Poetics*, distinguished tragedy from other literary forms such as comedy and epic poetry. As defined by Aristotle, a tragedy constituted an object lesson in the interplay of fate and behaviour. A man of heroic stature is led to catastrophe through a flaw in his otherwise admirable character.

'Thank you for that, Susan.'

'Excuse me.'

'Oh dear. Dr Death seems to have something to add.'

'Dr *De'ath*, in fact. Just a small detail. I read in the *Telegraph* the other day of an accident which had befallen a hill-climbing librarian in Glen Coe. I rather think his name was Tomlinson. Or perhaps it was Wilkinson. Whichever, the unhappy man's obituarist described his death as "a terrible tragedy". Would I be being intolerably pedantic, do you think, were I to suggest that "misfortune" or "mishap" would have been a happier description of the ill-fated Mr Tomlinson's demise?'

'No. I'll drink to that, Dr Death. Not that we can, since we haven't ordered yet! MIGUEL!'

'*De'ath*.'

See also ACCIDENTS; COMEDY; MISFORTUNE.

Armstrong, Henry 'Hank' (1918–81). Pound for pound, the greatest boxer ever to pull the gloves on.

'I don't hope to see a better in my lifetime.' His famed bolo punch – an uppercut to the solar plexus – had intensive care written all over it.

See also ALI, MUHAMMAD; DURAN, ROBERTO; HAGLER, MARVIN;

HEARNS, THOMAS 'THE HITMAN'; LEONARD, SUGAR RAY; LOUIS, JOE; MARCIANO, ROCKY; MOORE, ARCHIE; PEP, WILLIE; ROBINSON, SUGAR RAY.

Arrival, dead on. *See* AMBULANCES; 49-YEAR-OLDS.

Art, conceptual. A grey area.
   'Talking of conceptual art...'
   'Not that we were!'
   'May I?'
   'Pray do.'
   'In conceptual art, the artist is trying to address the unaddressable.'
   'In my opinion they should save themselves the trouble. On my last visit to the Tate Modern I hung my hat on one of the exhibits!'
   'Delightful! I recall that fine columnist, the late lamented John Junor...'
   '"The Man Who Said What Others Scarcely Dared to Think!"'
   'Precisely. I recall him doing the very same thing in 1979.'
   'However, even as we wipe away the tears of laughter, might it not be fair to allow a few words from that wise man, Sir Nicholas Serota? He said, you may remember, that to understand modern art you first have to understand its rules. Just as with football, say. You can't understand a game of football until you understand its rules.'
   'But it's precisely football's silly rules which guarantee that watching it is a boring and pointless exercise.'
   'Don't be ridiculous, Susan. Playing football to Premiership standard requires skill of the highest order.'
   'So does Chinese plate-spinning, but who'd want to watch that?'
   'Thank you, Susan. In fact I was going to say that I may have a perfect grasp of football's rules, but this will tell you nothing about whether I'm as skilled as David Beckham...'
   'A grossly overrated player, a speechless fop with legs as bandy as a northern jockey's...'
   'Thank you, Susan. Whether I'm as skilled as Beckham – my significant other's reservations notwithstanding – or as ungainly as a carthorse.'
   'So for once you and Susan seem to agree! It turns out that Sir Nicholas has said nothing of interest.'
   'I wouldn't go quite that far, Vernon.'

'Dear God, it's Max Beerbohm again. Yes, Max?'

'Jolyon. *Jolyon De'ath*. As I think I said. Anyway – a word on behalf of Sir Nicholas Serota. He has at least suggested – some way after Wittgenstein (*Lectures on Religion, Psychology and Aesthetics*, Blackwell 1967, General Editor, Jolyon De'ath) – that value judgements are objective. He appears to have grasped that there is such a thing as "educated taste", which depends, as a first step, on knowing the rules.'

'Yes, thank you, Max...'

'Jolyon. As Wittgenstein pointed out, we wouldn't call a suit well-cut if one sleeve was longer than the other, or a dog musical just because it wagged its tail when a certain piece of music was played. In sum, Sir Nicholas has made a small, but unoriginal, contribution to aesthetics, while telling us nothing about the merits or otherwise of conceptual art. Or association football, come to that.'

'Thank you for that, Max.'

'Jolyon.'

'Of course. Tell me, Vincent...'

'Vernon.'

'Of course. Tell me, Vernon. Guy de Maupassant. The unrivalled master of the short *conte*, would you say?'

Articulate. Women have earned the right to articulate their needs in bed, but are they any happier?

'Tracey and Sharon certainly seem to be. Oh look – they're off to the Ladies again. Lucky old them! I think I'll join...'

'Susan...!'

See also HAPPINESS; JET TO SPAIN.

As ever. 'As ever, you've been messaging *Five News* with your views on the big stories of the day. Denise, a hairdresser from Chingford, e-mailed us to say that:

'"We av msg 4 tony blair. Sort out gr8 briton b4 tryin 2 sort out da rest o the planet. Stop takin crap from asilem seekers n stick up 4 ur peeple."

'Thank you for that, Denise. Dan-e-Boy, a part-time scaffolder from Gateshead, picked up his mobile to say that:

'"All killers shd b strung up. R laws r 2 week."

'Thank you, Dan-e-Boy. Jinx from Stoke had this to say:

'"2 da idiot who say Mel C look like Jacko get ya i's tested!"'

'Thank you, Jinx. Yodler from Brum e-mailed us this:'

'"In reply 2 Caz about tax credits. If no 1 had kids it wud b the end of the human race, bimbo. Wud u prefer all tax credits 2 go 2 smackheads and asylum seekers?"'

'And finally Mad Max from Cricklewood messaged us to say:'

'" Good riddance 2 S Club. They woz crap."'

'Thank you for that, Mad Max.'

'Thank you, Kirsty.'

See also AIREY, DAWN; *FIVE NEWS*; MIDLANDS, SHELL-SUITED WORKING-CLASS WOMEN FROM THE; OPINIONS; PEOPLE, ORDINARY.

Ash Priors. A little village a mere six miles from Taunton, yet one of Somerset's best-kept secrets.

'Not any more!'

'Nor it is! Well, there you are!'

See also BISHOPS LYDEARD; CORFE; MILVERTON; SECRETS, SOMER-SET'S BEST-KEPT; TAUNTON.

Ask, a big. *See* AGENDA.

As if! Contrary to received opinion, Dr David Starkey has never said, 'Lady Emma Hamilton one of the great beauties of her time? As if!' in any of his refreshingly unstuffy television shows.

See also HOW SAD IS *THAT!*; JAMES I HAD ONE OF HIS HISSY FITS; HULLO SAILOR!; 'THAT'S A VERY BIG LUNCH BOX! IS IT ALL YOURS?'

Askwith, Robin (1950–). Actor (*see* ACTORS, ENGLISH; *UPS AND DOWNS OF A HANDYMAN, THE*).

Assassin, the Baby-Faced. *See also* OWEN, MICHAEL.

'Excuse me.'

'Yes, Susan?'

'Michael Owen isn't known as "the Baby-Faced Assassin". The sobriquet has been awarded to Ole Gunar Solskjaer, the curly-haired Eskimo.'

'Well I never! I thought you disliked football and knew nothing about it.'

'All the more surprising that I knew that and you didn't.'

'Ahem! Excuse me. Ahem!'

'You should do something about that cough, Max.'

'Jolyon.'

'Of course.'

'Jolyon De'ath. I couldn't help overhearing your wife...'

'Partner, to be accurate.'

'Your partner's observation about Mr Solskjaer. Apropos, have you noticed that it's always a "late winner" that's scored by the Baby-Faced Assassin. You never hear about an "early winner", do you?'

'Is that it?'

'Er – yes.'

'Staying long, are you? You and Ronaldo?'

'Roberto. And no we aren't. He leaves early in the morning. Alas.'

'I think he's ever so pretty.'

'Yes. Thank you, Daphne. You've made that perfectly clear. *HOMBRE!*'

'Now you're shouting, Vernon. And he does have a name, you know.'

'Of course. *MIGUEL!*'

See also ESKIMOS WORKING IN THE UNITED KINGDOM.

Astaire, Fred (1899–1987). His real name was Frederick Austerlitz, yet he was the quintessence of style in motion.

'He was incapable of a graceless movement, would you say?'

'Indeed.'

'And to whom do we owe that felicitous tribute? Michael Parkinson?'

'Barry Norman, in fact, but I take your point.'

'And Ginger Rogers?'

'So I've heard.'

'Yes, thank you for that, Miguel. A somewhat uncalled-for comment, but since you've decided to take our order, perhaps... Damn it! The fellow's buggered off!'

Asylum-seekers. Forever leap-frogging single mums-of-two in the council-house queue or living in the lap of luxury in guest houses across Britain.

'At the taxpayer's expense.'

'That's you and me.'

'They'll be in Norfolk next.'

'And Somerset. Mark my words.'

See also BENDING OVER BACKWARDS TO HELP SCROUNGERS; BRITAIN; MUMS OF TWO, SINGLE; OLD FOLK, OUR AILING; TOUCH, A SOFT.

Atkinson, Ron (1942–). Football manager and television commentator. It is not generally known that English is 'Big Ron's' first language.

'That said, I have seen him described by an Oxbridge professor as an innovator at the cutting-edge of linguistic development.'

'A sobering thought. Talking of which... *MIGUEL!*'

'Excuse me.'

'Dear God! It's Dr Death again.'

'Do keep your voice down, Susan. The man means no harm. Yes Max?'

'Jolyon.'

'Of course. I do apologise.'

'Your mention of the Oxbridge professor who has produced corpus evidence to suggest that Big Ron's unusual coinages are slowly but surely creeping their way into wider usage prompts a thought: consider the vile, and increasingly ubiquitous, term "uni". No one who had been to one of our older universities would commit such a disagreeable solecism, surely?'

'I dare say not. Wake up, Daphne...'

'Fascinating, don't you think, these little social signifiers tossed out in otherwise humdrum discourse?'

'Did someone say "intercourse"? Roberto's ever so...'

'*No*, Daphne. *Discourse*. Pray continue, Dr Death.'

'Dr *De'ath*.'

'If you say so.'

'What we need, it seems to me, is a new *Noblesse Oblige* for the third millenium: a post-Saussurian Mitford schooled in Derrida and Foucault.'

'We've drawn a bit of a brainbox here, Vernon.'

'An egghead, would you say?'

'Indeed.'

'Roberto's cute, though.'

'Thank you, Daphne. Tell me, Simon. Geri Halliwell. Looking less relaxed, would you say, now that she hasn't the faintest idea who she really is?'

'Indeed. But still every inch a pop totty.'

Atmosphere. Should always be 'unique'.

'From a pint in a pub to a tasty tapas, Gibraltar offers a fascinating blend of the flavours of Britain and Spain. See the famous apes, go dolphin-watching, or just soak up its unique atmosphere.'

'Sounds like one for the Travel section, Toby.'

See also ARIÈGE; AUDE; AVEYRON; CONQUES; CULTURE; HARROGATE; LOT; LOZÈRE; ORANGE; PORVOO; SALAMANCA; SIDI BOU SAID; SOLOGNE.

At sea. 'The Welsh forwards were so much at sea as to constitute a shipping hazard.'

'Thank you, Jerry. So where exactly does Welsh rugby go from here, Jonathan?'

'Good question.'

See also CHOKED; DEFENCE, THE WELSH; WALES.

Attenborough, Sir David (1924–). A consummate professional.

'Indeed! Unfortunately, the same cannot always be said of the inhabitants of the natural world around him!'

'Nor it can! Who can forget the time when the orang-utan relieved itself into Sir David's hat and ...'

'Pray cease! At least until we've eaten! Miguel!'

Attorney, power of. While it has been reliably estimated that 97% of married women no longer allow their husbands to exercise power of attorney over their opinions, are they any happier?

'Well, I am for one.'

'Thank you, Susan.'

See also HAPPINESS; JET TO SPAIN.

Attractive. As that wise woman Virginia Ironside recently said in her always readable *Independent* column, to attract today's woman you have to listen to her. To listen to someone is to validate them as a person.

'Was Miss Ironside suggesting that you could – excuse me – listen a woman into bed!'

'I wouldn't go that far! Yes, Susan?'

'I reckon Marty could. He's really *listening* to Tracey. Or it might be Sharon. Either way, it's immensely attractive.'

'Is that so? Tell me, Vincent…'

'Vernon.'

'Of course. Tell me, Vernon – your golf handicap. Coming down, is it?'

Aude. One of France's best-kept secrets (*see also* ARIÈGE; AVEYRON; CONQUES; LOT; LOZÈRE; SOLOGNE).

'Yes, Vernon?'

'I was wondering whether you'd come up with the answer yet to my small query lodged under Ariège? What are these best-kept secrets doing in a Dictionary of Received Ideas set in an Islington wine bar?'

'Ah yes. I've solved that one for you. It is the mistaken belief that Ariège and Aude are among France's best-kept secrets that is the received idea, not the places themselves.'

'You've syllogized your way to victory! I take my hat off to you!'

Auden, W.H. (1907–73). Life left its mark on his face rather than on his verse.

'I concur. That said, there is infinite sadness in the plight of the ageing homosexual.'

'Indeed. Yet Hugh of Lincoln's lyric voice sounded from the midden.'

'Christ! Who said that?'

'Not me.'

'Nor me.'

'Must have been Dr Death. I *told* you we'd never shake him off.'

'Roberto *is* cute, though. Don't you think?'

'Well, now you point it out, yes, I suppose he is. Excellent bone structure, and his skin has that soft, velvety overall bloom which…'

'I wasn't talking to you, Simon. I was talking to Susan.'

'Of course, of course. I was merely jesting…'

'Many a true word…'

'Yes. Thank you, Susan. Miguel!'

Augustine, St (354–430). Bishop of Hippo, but a convivial man for all that, and no enemy of pleasure.

'"Oh God! Make me chaste! But not yet!"'

'Delightful! Which reminds me. We haven't decided on a wine. What about a Costa?'

'And that is?'

'A dry rosado from the Sierra Nevada. It perfectly accompanies *sopa de picadillo* and *trucha de Poquiera*.'

'Neither of which we're having.'

'Thank you, Susan. What about an Alamos, then?'

'That's not one I'm familiar with, I must confess.'

'You surprise me, Vernon. It won the Chardonnay trophy at this year's International Wine Challenge. It comes from Catena. I can see I've confounded you.'

'Indeed you have. Catena?'

'In Argentina. Which proves that Argentina now has the potential to match Australia for affordable but complex Chardonnay in the tropically ripe but not too oaky spectrum of flavour.'

'I may have lost the will to live.'

'Thank you, Susan. I don't know what's come over you this evening. Anyway, Vernon, perhaps you and Doreen...'

'Daphne.'

'Of course. Perhaps you and Daphne might prefer a Terra Vitis from Corbières. As you'll be fully aware, it's open season at the moment for wild boar in the south of France...'

'I confess I wasn't.'

'Really? Anyway, it's a traditional, yet juicy, Mediterranean blend of Carignan, Syrah and Grenache, suffused with the herby scents of the Languedoc *garrigue*. It goes as well with a Toulouse or a Cumberland sausage as it does with boar.'

'Which none of us is having.'

'Pardon?'

'Wild boar. None of us is having it. Nor Toulouse sausage, come to that.'

'Thank you, Susan. Nor we are. It's the Alamos, then. And some Perrier water, do you think?'

'I read the other day that Perrier water makes a most effective spermicide...'

'Yes. Thank you for that, Susan. I'm sure Daphne and Vernon...'

'A fact that explains its popularity in California in the sixties.' (*See* SIXTIES, THE.)

'The decade when happiness was back in fashion!'

'I was afraid that someone might say that, but I assumed it would be Simon. No offence, Vernon.'

'None taken, I assure you.'

'What's the upshot of all this, then? Some water, is it? While we're waiting for the crabcakes?'

'Good idea!'

'We haven't ordered the crabcakes yet.'

'Nor we have! MIGUEL!'

Augustus (63 BC–AD 14). He found Rome a city of bricks and left it a city of marble. There may be a lesson here.

'Thank you, Susan.'

'Delighted to be of assistance.'

Austen, Jane (1775–1817). In spite of academic talk about 'moral sensitivity', Jane's books remain popular because they are about what interests the general reader: sex and money. In our attitudes to Jane, we ourselves are judged.

'I can see I've upset you, Susan.'

'No, no – do carry on.'

'Do you have this problem with Doris, Vernon?'

'Daphne.'

'Of course. Susan and I have been together for eleven years. I think I know her well enough by now to recognize signs that I've upset her! So – significant other of mine! – read out the charge!'

'OK. Your habit of referring to distinguished writers by their Christian names, as if they were personal friends, really irritates me. It makes you sound like an occasional essayist in a middlebrow weekly rather than a trader in fine wines with a whiff of Jermyn Street about him.'

'Thank you, Susan. My being a trader in fine wines is not something you've ever complained about when it comes to educating the twins, or weekending in Florence. I apologise, Vincent...'

'Vernon.'

'Of course. I apologise, Vernon. I expect Susan's had a hard day at work.'

'Nothing unusual, Simon. Just dealing with a collection of tossers like you. If you'll excuse me for a moment, I think I'll go to the Ladies.'

'I'll come with you.'

'Thank you, Daphne.'

'A word of warning, darling.'

'Yes, Miguel?'

'Ah, Miguel! We'd like to order. It'll be…'

'Hold up, John. I'm talking to your bird. Careful in the toilet, darling. The manager's put vaseline on all the surfaces, right? Stalwart of New Labour sat down last week, tobogganed across the restaurant with her knickers round her ankles. Only telling you.'

'Thank you for that, Miguel. Back in a moment, everyone!'

'Susan! Where do you think… Oh well. Now then, Miguel, we'd like… Damn me, he's gone again!'

'Well, well, well! What was all that about, Simon?'

'We'll never know, Vernon. Women! Can't live with 'em! Can't live without 'em! What did she mean by "a whiff of Jermyn Street" about me, do you think?'

'Well, Simon – how can I put this? The hair, the complexion, the aftershave…'

'Yes, thank you, Vernon, I…'

'The trousers newly pressed to an Executive Standard, the pink shirt…'

'The voice pitched to compete with the insistent jocose hum of a Berkshire snug bar, the almost visible mist of a Gentleman's Cologne rising from…'

'Eh? Who the hell said that?'

'Must have been Dr Death, John. So do you want to order or what?'

'Thank you, Miguel. Actually, we have a slight problem here. Not quite ready after all.'

'Catch you later, then. When your birds are back from the toilet. Stay corked.'

'Extraordinary!'

'Indeed. Anyway, what Susan said about a whiff of Jermyn Street. I'm sure she meant it as a compliment.'
See WALL, THE WRITING ON THE.

Australian women. The gratitude of Australian women brought to a climax is famous throughout the world. It is often possible for an entire visiting English cricket team to form a sexual connection with the same domestic air hostess in the Nothing to Declare queue before setting foot in Australia proper.

Authors. In a very real sense, authors do not create their books but are created by them. When interviewing an author be sure to ask him what gave him the idea for his latest book. He may say:
'Books nestle in the unconscious. I wait for one of them to insist that I write it.'
If it's a work of fiction, seek to discover whether the main character is based on the author.
'Surely it was that wise man Graham Greene who had it that at a certain point in any novel the characters take over?'
'Indeed. And yet he was more appreciated in France – where he went under the agreeable name of "Grim Grin" – than in his own country.'
'A great writer must find a capacity to be both at home and on a journey.'
'I'd go further. On a list of the ten greatest films of all time you'd have to find a place for *The Third Man*.'
'How true! And *Citizen Kane*, of course.'
'What's that got to do with it?'
'I'm not entirely sure. It's taking the devil of a time for the crab-cakes to arrive.'
'Hardly surprising since we haven't even ordered yet!'
'Nor have we. MIGUEL!'

Autobiography. Some authors write their autobiographies to clear their heads, others to set the record straight.
'Or to sell the serialization rights for £1m to *The Daily Mail*!'
'Delightful! Surely it was Ulrika Jonsson, the sex-mad Swede, who told *She* magazine that she needed space to discover who she really was.'

'Indeed it was. "I felt like a grey area between the stories written about me and the things that actually happened," claimed the raunchy Eskimo.'

'That said it all.'

'No it didn't. I've just had an idea.'

'And what might that be, Susan?'

'What might what be?'

'The idea you've had.'

'Oh yes. It came to me in the Ladies. A good alternative title for a Dictionary of Received Ideas set in an Islington wine bar. "I'm Leaving You, Simon. I Want To Discover Who I Really Am." Is that good, or what?'

'What is the woman talking about? Tell me, Vernon. Con and Marty over there. The celebrity historians. In touch with their feminine sides, would you say?'

See also CELEBS; ESKIMOS WORKING IN THE UNITED KINGDOM; JONSSON, ULRIKA; MAN, THE NEW; PARSONS, TONY.

Avedon, Richard (1922–). American photographer. From Marilyn Monroe and Lauren Hutton to migrant workers and carnival roustabouts, the portraits of Richard Avedon are a testament to human beauty and vulnerability.

'I've always said that the photographs he took of fairground drifters from 1979 to 1985 are symptomatic of the bleakness he has perceived in the late 20th century.'

'I agree. Would it be going too far, do you suppose, to call them the younger American cousins of Beckett's gentleman tramps – elegantly ravaged anti-heroes suspended somewhere between tragedy and comedy?'

'A most elegant comparison, Vernon. And yet, paradoxically, Avedon's idol as a young man was Fred Astaire, of whom he remarked, "He made love with his feet."'

'That said it all.'

'Michael Parkinson couldn't have put it better. Dear God! Don't look up!'

'Why?'

'I think they're going to sit at the next table.'

'Who?'

'That common foursome from Essex or somewhere of the sort. Marty and Tracey and the other two.'

'Oh good!'

'Never mind "good", Susan. Ignore them, for heaven's sake.'

'Pardon me.'

'Yes?'

'Is this table taken?'

'Yes, I think it is.'

'No it isn't.'

'Well done, Susan. Max Beerbohm and his Italian catamite on one side and celebrity historians on the other. What could be nicer than that?'

'We'll park ourselves here, then. I'm Con. And this is Marty.'

'How do you do?'

'Can't complain. We're lecturers in the New History, us. These are our friends Tracey and Sharon. They're in Media Studies, as you can see.'

'Plezd 2 meet u. He 8 a hamster, right?'

'Who?'

'Freddie Starr. u woz talkin' about him b4. i woz earwiggin'. Hope u dont mind.'

'In fact, we were talking about Fred Astaire. Tell me, Vernon...'

'Whos he wen hes at home? u herd of Freddie Stair, shar?'

'Cant say i hav, trace.'

'Tell me, Vernon. Billy Crystal. See the point of him, do you?'

See also ASTAIRE, FRED; PARKINSON, MICHAEL.

Aveyron. One of France's best-kept secrets. The picturesque village of Conques nestles by its northern border with Cantal.

See also ARIÈGE; AUDE; CONQUES; LOT; LOZÈRE; SOLOGNE.

Avignon. The city has attracted not only great painters but many writers too. Dickens and Henry James were just two of the celebrated writers who wandered its cobbled streets and wrote about the famous Papal Palace. Frédéric Mistral founded a literary movement here which, through *Le Petit Journal*, tried to revive the ancient language of Provence, but his attempt was only partially successful.

Ayer, A.J. *See* SARTRE, JEAN-PAUL.

Aznavour, Charles (1924–98). Singer.

'This will interest you, Vernon. It's not generally known that, because of the vast sums he owes the French government in back taxes, the little Armenian balladeer will have to go on singing until the year 2076.'

'No he won't. He died in 1998.'

'Thank you, Susan.'

B

Babes, *Brookie*. Record companies are queuing up to sign them.
'For at least one soap babe there'll be life after *Brookie*, then!'
'It's beginning to look that way.'
'And to whom are you referring?'
'Jennifer Ellison.'
'I confess I've never heard of her.'
See also ELLISON, JENNIFER; OPTIONS.

Babes, stressed-out pop. Forever sending shock waves through
the showbiz world by announcing a break-up with their fellas, thereafter issuing a statement through a spokesman to say that their jet-
set lifestyles are at the root of the problem.
See also COUPLES, FAIRY-TALE; DIVAS.

Babes, troubled soap. Forever checking into expensive clinics after
'cry for help' suicide bids.

Baby, having a. A baby isn't a sticking plaster with which to mend
a dysfunctional relationship. We forget this at our peril.

Bach, Johann Sebastian (1685–1750). 'Allow me to run this one
past you, Vernon. If his contemporary, Antonio Vivaldi, was the
Rolling Stones of his day, was Bach the Beatles?'
See also BEST, GEORGE; LOUSSIER, JACQUES; VIVALDI, ANTONIO.

Bachelor, *The* (Gary Sinyor, 1999). A jilted lover is offered the chance
to inherit a multi-million-dollar fortune – but only if he can find a
bride within 24 hours! Light-hearted romantic comedy starring Chris

O'Donnell, Renée Zellweger, Edward Asner and Artie Lange.
  'Sounds like one to miss, Vernon.'
  'I was quite looking forward to it, Daphne.'

Back yard. *See* GAMES, THE OLYMPIC.

Baddiel, David (1961–). Comedian and writer (*see* HUMOUR, A SENSE OF).

Badger, The Disappearing. See FRENCH COOKING.

Bainbridge, Beryl (1940–). She has a black vision, certainly, but who can better fashion dismay into comic acceptance? That said, she lives with a stuffed fighting bull in her front hall.

Bald men. All have pointlessly high testosterone levels.

Ball, bodies behind the. A tactic which only works in the hurly-burly of the Premiership.
  'At this level, getting bodies behind the ball isn't good enough. Liverpool are being taken apart by the skilful little Spaniards.'
  'Thank you, Ron.'
See also EUROPEANS, SOUTHERN.

Ball, the. An early touch of the ball settles the nerves.

Ball, Zoe (1971–). Can Zoe juggle parenting and work? The debate continues.
  'Your opinion on this one, Vernon. Yesterday on *The Moral Maze*, Dr David Starkey opined that Zoe's husband, Mr Fatboy Slim, had given Zoe the space to discover who she really was. A wise decision on Mr Slim's part, would you say?'
  'Indeed. I read in the *Telegraph* that Zoe had been staring into the abyss, but that she returned from a sunshine break in the Seychelles looking tanned and relaxed.'
  'Was she whisked through customs by burly security guards before speeding to an undisclosed destination?'
  'Indeed – if my copy of the *Telegraph* is to be believed. Either way, I take my hat off to Mr Slim for giving troubled Zoe the space she needed.'

'I'll second that! *Chapeau* Mr Slim!'

See also BEAUTIES, SHATTERED; JUGGLING WORK AND KIDS; PALS, SHOWBIZ.

Balls, little. *See* HOLE, THE; NOUS; SHERINGHAM, TEDDY.

Balzac, Honoré de (1799–1850). Though he served his apprentice-ship writing potboilers in a Paris attic, his *Comédie Humaine* has been compared, in the grandeur of its architecture, to a great cathedral. Like so many French intellectuals, he died of coffee poisoning.

Bankers. 'Do bankers ever loan their daughters out without security?' An amusing way to ask a bank manager's daughter for a dance.

Barbarians, the. 'Goths, Vandals, Huns ... No, not a Sisters of Mercy concert in a rundown quarter of Leipzig!'
   'What, then?'
   'A roll-call of infamous tribes from Eastern Europe and beyond – history's Hell's Angels, as it were!'
   'Delightful! Simon Schama?'
   'Dale Winton, but the point holds.'

Bard, TV Tracey's Shaw (!) To Be. Good headline for a story in *The Sunday Times*'s arts pages about Tracey Shaw's début in *Hamlet*.
See also CARMEN DUVAL, THE CELEBRITY'S PAL; SHAW, TRACEY.

Bardot, Brigitte (1934–). French film actress. Though she repre-sented freedom to others, Bardot herself came from a fiercely repres-sive, petit-bourgeois background. On her wedding night (after the civil ceremony, but before the religious one), her father stood outside her bedroom with a shotgun, ready to shoot Roger Vadim if he attempted to enter the bridal suite. BB – or the Sex Kitten, as she was known to a generation – now devotes herself to animal rights. It has been argued that her lips made Mick Jagger's lips possible (*see also* JAGGER, MICK).
   'BB? U herd o' bb, trace?'
   'Cant say i hav, shar.'
   'I still half fancy her.'
   'Ah, Miguel! Back at last. Well done. We're ready to order. To start... Damn, he's gone again!'

Barn Owl, The Disappearing. *See* FRENCH COOKING.

Barnsley. They're not daft in Barnsley.
See also CLEETHORPES, THE MAN FROM; PARKINSON, MICHAEL.

Barrie, Amanda (1935–). Actress. 'My Love for Women as well as Men. Hilarious, Heartwarming and Utterly Honest – Amanda Barrie's Own Story.'
    'Sounds like one for *The News of the World*, Rebekah.'
    '*The Daily Mail*, in fact, but I take your point.'
See also NEWS OF THE WORLD, THE; WADE, REBEKAH.

Barriers between disciplines, a good port breaks down all. *See* BOWRA, SIR MAURICE.

Bars. Should be 'lively' (*see also* BUDAPEST; FLORENCE).

Bash, showbiz. Always 'glittering'.

Beatles, the. If the Beatles wrote the soundtrack for the Sixties, then George Best did the choreography.
See also BACH, JOHANN SEBASTIAN; BEST, GEORGE; SIXTIES, THE; VIVALDI, ANTONIO.

Beauties, big-screen. Forever expressing their determination that any media coverage of their weddings should be discreet, reflecting their desire that these should remain private occasions.
    'Small wonder, then, that Welsh stunner, Catherine Zeta Jones, having sold her wedding rights to *OK!* magazine for £1.2m, should have felt "violated" when *Hello!* gate-crashed the ceremony, thereafter publishing unauthorized images!'
    'Small wonder indeed. As my copy of *The Daily Telegraph* pointed out, the "Cardiff Cracker had no option but to take *Hello!* to court".'
    'Indeed. And while she may not have been wearing a curly wig or have a degree in law, the "Virago from the Valleys" – as the *Telegraph* went on to report – "was very much the star of that particular courtroom drama! She even managed to get the better of Mr James Price QC, appearing for *Hello!* Mr Price sought to

establish which precise moment of her wedding day Miss Zeta Jones considered to be private! Quick as a flash…"'

'Pray cease. Already tears of laughter are coursing down…'

'Wait for it, Vernon! "Quick as a flash, and with her dark eyes twinkling mischievously, the Tiger Bay Temptress replied, "There is embracing … and there is embracing!"'

'Enough! Another such mischievous riposte and I'll choke on my crabcake. Not that it's arrived yet.'

'Nor has it. MIGUEL!'

Beauties, shattered. Often wearing dark glasses as they are whisked through customs at Heathrow after an 11-hour flight from LA.

See also BALL, ZOE; DIVAS; UNDISCLOSED DESTINATION, SPEEDING TO AN.

Beauties on the brink. *See* BABES, TROUBLED SOAP; BALL, ZOE; BEAUTIES, SHATTERED; LOVE-SPLIT CHART-TOPPERS; STRESSED-OUT SUPERMODELS.

Beauty, great. A blessing and a curse. No need to explain why (*see* BOGARDE, DIRK; KELLY, GRACE; LEIGH, VIVIAN).

Beauty contests. They degrade women. No need to explain why.

'Surely it was Kirsty Young who described them as an antediluvian concept.'

'That's a big word for a very pretty lady!'

Beckham, David (1975–). Attention-seeking soccer player admired by children for the accuracy of his corner kicks (*see also* BLING-BLING).

Beckham, Victoria (1976–). Former pop babe with the Spice Girls singing group. Contrary to received opinion, her husband, the celebrity soccer player, David Beckham, really was quoted in the Murdoch press as saying: 'I'd like Victoria even if she worked in Tesco's.'

'Just as well, since Tesco's is exactly where you'd think she worked.'

'That's so crap.'

'Hullo! Who said that?'

'I did. Want to order, then?'

'Ah, Miguel. Back again! And you have a point to make?'

'Sure have, John. You're being unfair to the wretched woman. I'm talking about Posh Spice, yeah? I'd place her in Boots the chemist. Unguents and vulva irritations.'

'You're the expert, no doubt. OK, I think we're ready to... Damn me! He's gone again!'

'He'll be back. Talking of Posh Spice, I read in the *Telegraph's* cutting-edge new gossip column – *Eye-Spy*– that "The total babe and style icon is a Hollywood wannabe. She has been seen in swanky nosheries seeking advice from best pal, Liz Hurley, on how to make it big in Tinsel Town."'

'Well there you are. MIGUEL!'

See also AMBITION; *FIVE NEWS*; NOSHERIE.

Bedworthy, Barbara (1960–). Actress (*see* AIREY, DAWN; *LESBO LOVE ROMPS*).

Bellamy's veal pies. *See* CHARLES I; EDWARD II; LAST WORDS; WILLIAM I.

Belly up. Contrary to popular opinion, Dr David Starkey has never used the expression 'belly up' in any of his television programmes.

See also ACCESSIBLE; ANNE OF CLEVES; BUCKS, LORD HOWARD OF EFFINGHAM GOT PLENTY OF BANGS FOR HIS; CASE, ON THE; CHARLES I, THINGS WENT TOTALLY PANTS FOR; CHECK, REALITY; COMPLETE TOSSER; ENVELOPE, PUSHING THE; FERGUSON, PROFESSOR NIALL; GAME ON, FOR CARDINAL WOLSEY IT WAS; GETTING HIS LEG OVER; GOOD IN THE SACK; HOW SAD IS *THAT*?; HISTORIANS, CELEBRITY; HISTORY, THE NEW; OWN GOAL, THE SPANISH KICKED AN; PEAR-SHAPED; SAUSAGE, MORE SIZZLE THAN; SHOPPING, ELEANOR OF AQUITAINE DIDN'T KNOW SHIT FROM; STARKEY, DR DAVID; THAT IS *SO* NOT A GOOD LOOK; WAY TO GO; WELL TROLLEYED.

Ben, Dan, Jeremy, Josh, Will, Charlie, Julian, Martin, Danny, James and Jonny. Good names for rugby players – Corinthian, devil-may-care chaps with big hair, vintage sports cars, two tickets for *Anything Goes* in the top pockets of their dinner jackets and with a pretty girl on either arm. In an earlier era, of course, the speedy little winger James Simpson-Daniel might have been a Battle of Britain pilot, shooting down Jerry by day and breaking hearts by night – but it's the French who will find him hot on their heels at the Stade de France on Saturday.

'Oh dear.'

'What's the matter, Susan?'

'Frankly, Vernon, I had hoped that no one would mention rugger.'

'Really? Why's that?'

'It has a very bad affect on Simon.'

'Yeah, I can see that, darling. OK, ready to order?'

'Thank you, Miguel. May I continue?'

'Go on then.'

'Ta. The thought of very large men running into each other at 30 miles per hour causes Simon to rear up and sweat like a racehorse in the paddock.'

'Now you're being silly, Susan! I like the game, of course, but to say that I can't think of Jonny Wilkinson's bronzed, perfectly toned thighs without ... without ... without ... excuse me a minute ... I think I dropped the car keys on the way in. I'll go and have a look for them. Won't be long.'

'There you are, you see.'

'Extraordinary.'

'I'd better come back, then.'

'If you would, Miguel.'

'Stay gold, sweetheart.'

'Once we were having dinner here and Simon thought he saw Jason Leonard, the burly English loose-head prop, on the other side of the room. He asked him for his autograph! I was so embarrassed. "Could you sign my menu, Mr Leonard?" he said. "It's for my nephew." Turned out to be Pauline Quirke. Easy mistake to make.'

'Indeed. He'd not have been the first.'

'Oh dear. Here we go again. Yes, Max?'

'Jolyon.'

'Of course. Yes, Jolyon?'

'Your earlier reference to the Corinthian attitude reminds me of the great athlete, C.B. Fry. My father, a Corinthian Casual in his youth, told me that Fry jumped for his country on the morning of his finals (in which he was awarded a double first), rowed in the Boat Race in the afternoon, had energy enough left over to dance the night away at the dear old Café de Paris and was up and about the next morning in time to score a double hundred against Australia at the Oval, still wearing his penguin suit and dancing pumps.'

'Well, there you are. Hard to imagine the gritty Lancastrian arriving at the crease in a DJ and disco shoes. Ah – here's Simon! Back with his car keys. You found them, then?'

'Yes, thank you, Vernon. I had them on me all the time! MIGUEL!'

See also DEAN, RIO, LEE, ALAN, GARY, JASON, ROY, DWIGHT, DION AND WAYNE; LANCASTRIAN, THE GRITTY.

Bench, the. Always telling the big Ghanaian to calm down and cut out the lippy stuff.

See also HISTRIONICS.

Bending over backwards to help scroungers. *See* ASYLUM-SEEKERS; WE BRITISH.

Bentham, Jeremy (1748–1832). Inventor of the felicific calculus, but like all very clever men Bentham was at bottom shallow. He failed to perceive that Utilitarianism is not a creed that man can live by. *The Daily Mail* has not been deceived.

Bergman, Ingrid (1919–82). In a long career she stubbornly fought for the right to be herself both as an actress and a woman. An unnecessarily turbulent private life tended to obscure the fact that her only real love affair was with the camera.

'Ingrid Bergman? U herd o her, trace?'

'Cant say i hav.'

See also BOGARDE, DIRK; KELLY, GRACE; LEIGH, VIVIEN.

Berkeley, Busby. *See* MOSS, KATE.

Berlioz, Hector (1803–69). One of the most likeable personalities in the history of Romantic music. Opium dreams and Shakespearean bombast.

Bernard, Jeffrey (1932–98). Soho's saloon-bar Socrates. He had the great merit of not taking himself too seriously.

'He had a saving sense of humour, would you say?'

'Indeed, but it was advisable to think twice before having a drink with him!'

'So I believe! The story has it that Keith Waterhouse, another saloon-bar Socrates, once agreed to meet him in a Soho pub. He woke up three days later in Carlisle!'

'Even as I wipe away the tears of laughter may I quote one of Jeffrey's immortal one-liners?'

'I wish you would.'

'"In my experience," he wrote in his incomparable *Spectator* column, "the light at the end of the tunnel invariably turns out to be an oncoming train!"'

'Pray cease! Another such one-liner and I'll choke on my gazpacho!'

'Not that it's arrived!'

'Nor has it! MIGUEL!'

Besides. 'Besides – isn't this exactly what I've been grooming you for, Daphne?'

'You think I'm ready then, Vernon?'

'I *know* you are!'

Best, George (1946–). Was he destroyed by the media, or by the intolerable demands of his own talent? The debate continues.

'Surely it was chat-show legend Michael Parkinson who observed that, "It's the life he chose to lead and if anyone wants to make a tragedy out of it that's their problem."'

'I confess I'm baffled, Vernon. I can't see that Best's life is my problem whether I see it as a tragedy or not.'

'You're right, of course. For once the King of Chat has got it wrong!'

'Even Homer nods!'

'I'm not so sure. The King of Chat further observed that, in Best's day, players of his skill received far less protection from referees – frequently being kicked into the stands by the likes of Tommy Smith of Liverpool and Chelsea's Ron "Chopper" Harris. Parkinson compared Best's performances to Michelangelo painting the Sistine Chapel during an air-raid!'

'A delightful analogy! The King of Chat at his very best! Yes, Susan?'

'They didn't have air-raids in Michelangelo's day.'

'Nor they did. We got it right originally. Even Homer nods!'

See also BEATLES, THE; HOMER.

Best television in the world, the. Contrary to received opinion, it is not the case that at 8.30 p.m. on Friday 7th September 2003 all five terrestrial channels simultaneously broadcast relocation programmes, one of which offered a villa in Andalucia to any viewer who could correctly answer the question: 'Which is the national dance of southern Spain? The flamenco or the cha cha cha?' In fact, BBC1 showed a repeat of *The Vicar of Dibley*.

'In fairness, as from 3rd November this year Channel 4 are to broadcast the new series of *The Sopranos* at 4.30 a.m. on alternate Mondays.'

'A cheap debating point, if I may say so, Vernon.'

'I withdraw.'

See also CHANNEL 4, THE CHIEF EXECUTIVE OF; DEBATING POINTS; *PLOPPIES, THE*.

Better half. *See* AGAIN; COWARD, NOËL; HOMER; MONKEYS; SPINOZA, BARUCH; TAPPING, TELEPHONE.

Beuvron-en-Auge. No village has any right to be as pretty as Beuvron-en-Auge.

See also CONQUES; DOMME; LOUBRASSAC; MARCILHAC-SUR-CÉLÉ; SAINT-CIRQ-LAPOPIE; SAINT-MEDARD-DE-PRESQUE; VIEILLE-BRIOUDE.

Big clubs. Always 'sleeping giants'.

'Leeds United are overdue some silverware, Ray.'

'Thank you, Ron.'

Big-match temperament. *See* EVANS, DAME EDITH.

Bill Oddie's Best of British. BBC2, 8 p.m. The former Goodie looks at barn owls.

'Sounds like one to miss, Vernon.'

'I was rather looking forward to it, Daphne.'

See also TAWNY PIPIT, THE.

Bimbo. Good title for a comic novel by Keith Waterhouse.

See also POTTERS BAR; WATERHOUSE, KEITH.

Birds. A fine opportunity, in a speech by a prince of the British royal family, for amusing clarification.

'When I say birds, I am, needless to say, referring to those of a feathered variety!'

See also BUSTS.

Birmingham. Formerly something of a black spot in terms of that most indefinable of qualities, 'style', Birmingham has in the last few years experienced a cultural renaissance. A branch of Harvey Nichols has recently opened, a new four-star hotel is being built, and top chef Gordon Ramsay...

See also BRADFORD; BRISTOL; CANALS; GLASGOW; LEEDS; MANCHESTER; NEWCASTLE; SHEFFIELD.

Bishops Lydeard. No more than six miles from Taunton, yet one of Somerset's best-kept secrets.

See also ASH PRIORS; CORFE; MILVERTON; SECRETS, SOMERSET'S BEST-KEPT; TAUNTON.

Björk. *See* ESKIMOS WORKING IN THE UNITED KINGDOM.

Black, Cilla (1945–). Much-loved family entertainer. How ironic that the new series of *Blind Date* in 2002 should have coincided with the anniversary of the death of Cilla's adored husband, Bobby. She has denied that she's lonely, though.

'"How could I be?" she has said. "Bobby is always with me."'

'That said it all.'

'So it did. However, it must have been a steep learning-curve for the Liverpool lass. Yes, Susan?'

'She recently claimed to have been the Madonna of the Sixties. That suggests that the caterwauling old busybody has learned sod all.'

'There's no need to be coarse, Susan. There's a time and a place for everything, and this isn't one of them.'

'I is with u, simon. Shes an icon 2 young wannabes, is cilla.'

'Well, thank you, Sharon.'

'Tracey. We is in Media Studies, us.'

'Yes. So you said. Tell me, Vernon. The old waterworks. Having trouble with them yet?'

Blackmail. Contrary to popular opinion, the following exchange really did occur in an episode of *Inspector Morse*.
 'Blackmail's an ugly word, Inspector.'
 'Blackmail's an ugly crime, headmaster.'
See also ABUSE, VERBAL; BLOCKHEAD; BRIDE; FACETIOUSNESS; *TOUCH OF FROST, A*; HORNBY, MRS.

Black men. Always a surprise to hear them speaking French.

Blackpool. 'I see that reality has once again overtaken the comedians!' An amusing remark to make during a party political conference held in Blackpool.

Bleasdale. 'Everyone says you're destined for great things, Bleasdale. It would be a shame to see a promising career cut short so prematurely. I'll bid you goodnight.'
See also MI6.

Blessing in disguise. *See* CUP, THE.

Bling-bling. Because of his 'bling-bling' lifestyle – the clothes, the music, the chunky jewellery, the bone-me-up-the-arse Ferraris in the drive – the soccer player, David Beckham, has become a black icon.
 'Apparently so. And by getting in touch with his feminine side, an excellent role model for today's young people, whatever their ethnic origins.'
 'Yeah, for real, John. Better to wear your wife's knickers than to smoke crack cocaine. Ready to order yet?'
 'Ah, Miguel! You've decided to honour us with your presence!'
 'Get on with it, John.'
 'Right – for starters it's... it's... hullo! Would you credit it? The confounded fellow's buggered off again! Yes, Doris?'
 'Daphne actually.'
 'Of course. Daphne. You have a comment to add?'
 'Well, yes. In fairness, and in spite of what Miguel said, it's not all dressing up in Victoria's knickers and painting his toenails pink. I'm talking about David Beckham. You've only got to read *Hello!* magazine to see photographs of him doing a lot of private work for charity.'
 'That's right. I gather that this Christmas he's to be seen in

a peak-time televised snowball fight with heart-swop toddlers.'

'Speaking for myself, I'll be watching *The Great Escape* for the twenty-second time.'

'I never tire of it.'

Blitz, the. There was a fellowship in the air-raid shelter which the doodlebug could never know.

See also DAYS, THOSE.

Blockhead. Contrary to popular belief, the line 'I may be one of the brutal and licentious military, Inspector, but I'm not a complete blockhead!' really did occur in an episode of *Inspector Morse*.

See also ABUSE, VERBAL; BLACKMAIL; BRIDE; FACETIOUSNESS; *TOUCH OF FROST, A*; HORNBY, MRS.

Blonde bombshells. *See* JONSSON, ULRIKA; JORDAN.

Blonde bombsites. *See* FELTZ, VANESSA.

Blondes. Always 'mystery'. Often 'frolicking' on beaches in the Caribbean with pot-bellied pop supremos.

'At his holiday hideaway in Barbados, Simon Cowell (TV's Mr Nasty!) relaxes by the pool with a mystery blonde.'

'Are brunettes ever "mystery", I wonder?'

'I think not. Nor do they "frolic".'

'I concur. They are sometimes "attractive", however.'

'Indeed. As my copy of today's *Telegraph* reported, "Even by his own impressive standards, popular crooner Jay Kay has been busy recently. On Thursday, the 4ft 8in Cat in a Hat rocked up in his Bentley to current fave club, Rouge, with a mystery blonde. But just two hours later he emerged with an attractive brunette whom he whisked off into the night."'

'That says it all.'

Blood, in the. *See* RACING.

Blues, the. Even Celebs get the blues. Just like the rest of us!

'Hold hard. I can scarcely believe my ears!'

'I speak the sober truth. I read it in the *Telegraph*. They're rich, famous and have hectic lifestyles, but, just like Real People, celebs sometimes suffer from depression.

'You could knock me down with a stage weight!'
See also CELEBS.

Bluthal, John (1932–). One of the unsung heroes of British comedy.
See also CHALLIS, JOHN; CRIBBINS, BERNARD; CRYER, BARRY; JACQUES, HATTIE; LE MESURIER, JOHN; LLOYD PACK, ROGER; LODGE, DAVID; MAGEE, HENRY; SMITH, LIZ; STARK, GRAHAM; TODD, BOB; WHITFIELD, JUNE.

Bodies, women's. Women have learned that they own their bodies, but are they any happier?

'Well, I am for one.'

'Thank you, Susan.'

'I've got this electric toothbrush, Daphne, and when Simon's gone to sleep, I...'

'Susan! I positively forbid you...'
See also HAPPINESS; JET TO SPAIN; LUGGAGE; WALL, THE WRITING ON THE.

Body. If all the chemical substances in a grown man's body were sold over the counter at Boot's the Chemist's they would fetch £3.47 at today's prices.

Body, a woman's. A woman's body keeps its secrets.

Body bags. Always coming home from war zones.

Body language. Body language says it all.

'In fairness, he didn't like that, the little Romanian. You can tell by his body language.'

'Thank you, Ron.'
See also ATKINSON, RON; HISTRIONICS.

Bogarde, Dirk (1919–96). Too sensitive a talent to be accommodated by the faint-hearted British cinema industry. Like all great film actors, he always knew exactly where the camera was.
See also BEAUTY, GREAT; BERGMAN, INGRID; FILM ACTING.

Bombers, suicide. Always 'cowardly'. A mystery.

Bones. You can mend broken bones. Broken hearts take longer.

Bonker, the Bombay. *See* HOT CELEBS!

Book. When you read a good book it should be like having an agreeable friend to dinner.

Bookings. Always 'down on last year', unless 'up'.

'Travel agents are reporting record bookings this year for skiing holidays at Chamonix in the French Alps.'

'Hardly one of France's best-kept secrets, then!'

See also ARIÈGE; AUDE; AVEYRON; BEUVRON-EN-AUGE; CONQUES; LOT; LOZÈRE; SOLOGNE.

Boost, a major. 'What do you make of this, Vernon? Today's *Eye-Spy*, the *Telegraph*'s new cutting-edge Diary, reports that D.J. Dan Peppe, Fatboy Slim's rival for Zoe's heart, has been given his own Radio 1 slot. A major boost to his profile, would you say?'

'Indeed I would. And I read the story too. According to the *Telegraph*, Mr Slim is absolutely "gutted".'

'As well he might be.'

See also BALL, ZOE.

Boot, left. Always 'educated', or 'cultured'.

See also COLE, THE YOUNG LAD.

Borg, Björn (1956–). When Borg played McEnroe the only real winner was tennis itself.

Borges, Jorge Luis (1899–1986). Blind Argentinian writer. He saw the world as a great library, or alternatively as a detective story, or even as an infinite recurrence of memories. An amusing anecdote is told of a meeting between Borges and Anthony Burgess in 1972. Though both of these great polyglots could speak each other's language better than a native, they found it more agreeable on this occasion to converse in ancient Norse.

Bosomy disco babes. Forever having a wild night out with soccer bad boy, Dwight Yorke.

See also JORDAN; SOCCER BAD BOYS.

Botham, Ian (1955–). Cricketer. If Beefy's heroics with bat and ball had appeared in a work of fiction no one would have believed them.

'If they'd appeared in a work of fiction no one would have been required to believe them.'

'Pah! Enough of your logic-chopping, Susan! Tell me, Vernon. For *après-piste* facilities, which gets your vote: La Plagne or Vale?'

See also INTELLECTUAL, LIBERAL.

Bottom line. At the end of the day it's all about bottom line.

See also ACCOUNTANTS; DAY, AT THE END OF THE.

Bowes, Bill (1916–87). With Harold Larwood he formed the finest opening attack in fast-bowling history.

'I don't hope to see a better in my lifetime.'

'And, as that wise man John Arlott had it, one of the most humorous and companiable of cricketers; a man of jokes – none richer than his batting.'

'Delightfully put! He was of that era, of course, when the Nottinghamshire selectors – in need of a new fast bowler – simply summoned up a fit young man from a local colliery.'

'But Bill Bowes played for Yorkshire.'

'I dare say he did, but my point holds nonetheless.'

'You're probably thinking of Bill Voce. He opened the bowling with Larwood for Nottinghamshire and England, I believe.'

'Thank you, Susan, I'm much obliged.'

'Don't look now, but I think Dr Death's clearing his throat. We're about to hear from him again, unless I'm much mistaken.'

'At least his Florentine catamite doesn't say much.'

'Perhaps he doesn't speak English.'

'I think he's ever so pretty.'

'Yes, Daphne. You've made that abundantly clear.'

See also AKRAM, WASIM and YOUNIS, WAQAR; AMBROSE, CURTLEY and WALSH, COURTNEY; DONALD, ALLAN; HALL, WESLEY and GRIFFITH,

CHARLIE; HOLDING, MICHAEL AND ROBERTS, ANDY; LILLEE, DENNIS and THOMPSON, JEFF; LINDWALL, RAY and MILLER, KEITH; MCGRATH, GLENN and LEE, BRETT; TRUEMAN, FREDDIE and STATHAM, BRIAN.

Bowra, Sir Maurice (1888–1970). The finest conversationalist of his time, though some have disputed this claim on behalf of his erstwhile colleague, Sir Isaiah Berlin. What he taught, nobody knows.

'I beg to differ. His field was civilization itself. No doubt a much despised subject these days.'

'Ah! Dr Death! It's you again!'

'I should apologise for yet another interruption.'

'Don't mention it. And I agree with you about Sir Maurice. Learning cannot be compartmentalized. A good port breaks down all barriers between disciplines. You and your young friend? Hasn't he got a ship to catch? *Tempus fugit!*'

'Indeed. We shall have to leave quite soon now.'

'What a shame.'

'Thank you, Daphne.'

'Sorry, Vernon.'

See also DONS, OLD-STYLE BACHELOR; JOHNSON, SAMUEL; PIPE-SMOKING SODOMITES; SPARROW, JOHN.

Bowyer, Lee. *See* HADDOCK, MAD AS A.

Boycott, Geoff. *See* GET, WHAT YOU SEE IS WHAT YOU.

Boys. Invariably 'in forensic'.

'Get this along to the boys in forensic, Jack.'

'But, Guv...'

'That will be all, Jack.'

See also SCIENTISTS.

Bradford. Formerly something of a black spot in terms of that most indefinable of qualities, 'style', Bradford has in the past few years experienced a cultural renaissance. A branch of Harvey Nichols has recently opened, a new four-star hotel is being built and top chef Gordon Ramsay...

See also BIRMINGHAM; BRISTOL; GLASGOW; LEEDS; MANCHESTER; NEWCASTLE; SHEFFIELD.

Brahe, Tycho (1546–1601). Astronomer and patient observer of the heavens, but a convivial man for all that. He lost his nose in a duel and thereafter wore a false one fashioned out of gold.

'I confess I never read it.'

'What?'

'*Wallpaper*.'

'Xscuse me...'

'Oh dear. Yes, Tracey?'

'I's Sharon. u's thinkin o Tyler Brule.'

'Do what?'

'The man wot edits *Wallpaper*. Its a stile mag.'

'Well, thank you for that. We learn something new every day. However, I was talking about Tycho Brahe.'

'Never herd o him. u herd o Tycho Brahe, trace?'

'Cant say I hav. Were in Media Studies, me 'n' shar.'

'You surprise me. Answer me this, Vernon...'

'Wot u say u 'n' me get 1 on in da toilet, shar?'

'Gr8 idea.'

'I think I'll join you.'

'SUSAN! I absolutely... Damn. Too late. Women!'

See also CHRISTMAS, GETTING A NEW NOSE FOR; WALL, THE WRITING ON THE; WESTBROOK, DANIELLA.

Brain, a good cricketing. There is all the difference in the world between having a good brain and a 'good cricketing brain'.

'A fellow with a good cricketing brain may not have an exceptional so-called IQ, but he always knows where his off-stump is.'

'Thank you, Richie.'

'They're taking the devil of a long time in the Ladies. I wonder what they're doing.'

'Women's talk, I shouldn't wonder.'

Brain, a good footballing. *See* BALLS, LITTLE; HOLE, THE; NOUS; SHERINGHAM, TEDDY; SHIRT, THE BIG LAD IN THE NUMBER 9.

Brain, the. 'This will interest you, Vernon. I read recently in *The Daily Telegraph* that there are two sides – or lobes – to the brain, each with its discrete function.'

'Is that so?'

'Indeed. The left-hand, or masculine, lobe is rational and logical.'

'Of course.'

'It concerns itself with what men know about. Distances. Lawns. Motorway junctions. Fences. Spatial relations. Corporate structures. Asset allocation...'

'What's to be gained by promoting Denise in Bought Ledger!'

'Excellent, Vernon! If I may continue? With the right-hand lobe those of a feminine persuasion...'

'God bless them...!'

'God bless them indeed! With the right-hand lobe, the ladies grope their way to some sort of imagined truth. Needless to say, feminists argue that throughout history we have exalted the former over the latter.'

'Yet, pound for pound, a dolphin's brain is 20 times heavier than Professor Stephen Hawking's. A sobering thought.'

'*A Brief History of Time*? Have you read it?'

'Please! Surely it was Les Dennis on *Family Fortunes* who wagered a week's wages that no one had got past page 23!'

'In fact it was Keith Waterhouse in *The Daily Mail*, but the point holds.'

See also POTTERS BAR; WATERHOUSE, KEITH.

Brainbox, a bit of a. Good name for an intellectual.

See also ATKINSON, RON; EGGHEAD.

Branagh, Kenneth (1961–). He's only 5ft 4in.

'But every inch an actor!'

'Surely it was Branagh who said: "The cinema is a director's medium. That's why I prefer the theatre. In the theatre I get the final cut."'

'Yet Branagh himself has directed many films.'

'A delightful conundrum, if not a paradox!'

'We'll trouble it out while the girls are in the powder room.'

Branch, the Special. Too big for their boots.

'Look, sunshine! You may be Special Branch but that doesn't make you Lord God Almighty!'

'All right, Jack – I'll see to this.'

'But, Guv...'

'That will be all, Jack.'

See also BRASS, THE TOP; *TOUCH OF FROST, A.*

Brass, the top. Always incompetent.

'The top brass won't like it, Jack.'

'The top brass don't need to know, Sergeant.'

See also BRANCH, THE SPECIAL; CASE; CURIOSITY; *TOUCH OF FROST, A.*

Breakfast. Always 'hearty'. In a humorous column say of an erring husband, 'The condemned man ate a hearty breakfast!'

Bremner, Rory (1961–). Impressionist and comedian. Will the real Rory Bremner please step forward!

See also SATIRE.

***Brewer's Dictionary of Phrase and Fable*, my copy of.** In an occasional column, always 'well-thumbed'.

See also CHAMBERS BIOGRAPHICAL DICTIONARY, MY COPY OF; *ROGET'S THESAURUS*, MY COPY OF.

Bride. Usually 'blushing' (*see also* SARCASM).

Briefs, silk floral. Not everyone knows that silk floral briefs, in classic cami-knicker styling and with the John Galliano stamp of approval, can be bought at Browns, 26 South Molton Street, London W1, for just £240.

'Sounds like one for a "Ten Best Knickers" feature, Susannah.'

See also BECKHAM, DAVID; FRANKEL, SUSANNAH; FRUMP.

Brightwell Baldwin. Either a picturesque village in Oxfordshire, or a West Indian fast bowler. The debate continues.

See also STEEPLE BUMPSTEAD.

Brillat-Savarin, Jean Anthelme. *See* CHEESE.

Bristol. Formerly something of a black spot in terms of that most indefinable of qualities, 'style', Bristol has in the past few years experienced a cultural renaissance. A branch of Harvey Nichols has recently opened, a new four-star hotel is being built and top chef Gordon Ramsay...

See also BIRMINGHAM; BRADFORD; GLASGOW; LEEDS; MANCHESTER; NEWCASTLE; SHEFFIELD.

Britain. Currently being flooded with asylum-seekers whom evil Russian vice lords put to work as sex slaves in sordid Soho brothels.

'Excuse me.'

'Yes, Tracey?'

'I thought u said they was 4 ever leapfroggin housing qs.'

'Who? Evil Russian vice lords?'

'No. Asylum seekers.'

'And so they are. Those lucky enough not to be working in sordid Soho brothels.' Either way, *The Daily Mail* has not been deceived.

See also ASYLUM-SEEKERS; BENDING OVER BACKWARDS TO HELP SCROUNGERS; WE BRITISH.

Britain in bloom. Harrogate, in North Yorkshire, has earned the title 'England's Floral District'. With its splendid array of parks and gardens, it often features in the 'Britain in Bloom' competion. But it's not all tea rooms and floral festivals. Lee Bowyer, formerly of Leed United FC, and several members of the cast of the popular soap opera *Emmerdale* are among the town's high-profile residents.

Britain's nuclear secrets. Always turning up in a skip in Stevenage.

'Or in the gentlemen's lavatory at the Gay Hussar in Greek Street!'

'Good old Tom!'

See also DRIBERG, TOM; PERSONAL MEDICAL RECORDS, OUR.

British, we. We British are thought to despise the intellect. What an agreeable irony, then, that *Chambers Biographical Dictionary* should contain no mention of Sir Alf Ramsey – the hero of England's 1966 World Cup triumph – but a lengthy article on Frank Plumpton Ramsey (1903–30), a Cambridge mathematician who was a contemporary there of Russell and Wittgenstein!

'That said, there is an even longer article on Esther Rantzen (1940–), the popular television entertainer.'

'Well, there you are.'

See also INTELLECT; RANTZEN, ESTHER; WE BRITISH.

Brits. Always 'heroic'.

See also LADS, OUR.

Britten, Benjamin (1913–76). The most English of composers. Sea songs and boy sopranos.

See also ALDEBURGH.

Brontë, Emily (1818–48). The second of the Brontë sisters. Her characters are buffeted by passions they can no more control than they can the storms that buffet the Yorkshire moors.

Bruckner, Anton (1824–96). He wrote nine, ten or eleven symphonies, depending on how you count. A German writer has said that he was half-Caesar, half-village schoolmaster. In art, as in life, such men are difficult to place.

See also LOUSSIER, JACQUES.

Brunel, Isambard Kingdom (1806–59). The Leonardo of his time, he once invented a machine to extract a sixpence which had got stuck in his throat. How it had got there history does not record.

Brunelleschi, Filippo (1377–1446). Florentine architect whose celebrated domes were supposedly modelled on his mistress's bosoms.

Bruno, Frank. *See* FRANK, BRUNO.

Brush, Basil. Contrary to received opinion, and on taking over the distinguished house of John Murray – Byron's publishers – Hodder Headline's managing director, Roland Philips, really did say:

'New Publishing Director Gordon Wise has been tasked with placing Murray in a relevant context, where subject and saleability meet.'

Philips had previously been media books supremo at Pan

Macmillan, where his authors had included Bruce Forsyth, Ulrika Jonsson and Basil Brush.

See also BYRON, LORD GEORGE; JONSSON, ULRIKA; PUBLISHING.

Brussels bureaucrats. Always 'unelected'.

See also BUREAUCRATS.

Bubbly personalities. Today's wannabes display bubbly personalities, but are they any happier?

'Probably not. In our parents' day, of course, discovering a "personality" in the family was an occasion for embarrassment, rather like an unwanted pregnancy.'

'How true. As I recall, anyone displaying a "personality" was bundled off immediately to work at a Butlin's holiday camp.'

See also HALLIWELL, GERI; PAROS, LARDY GIRLS WITH BUBBLY PERSONALITIES ON HOLIDAY IN; PERSONALITIES.

Budapest. Locals are justly proud of Budapest's musical heritage: Franz Liszt (1811–86), Béla Bartók (1881–1945) and Zoltán Kodály (1882–1967) are favourite sons. But it doesn't rest on its musical laurels. Budapest is a city of two halves: on one side of the Danube you'll find a historic castle and an Art Nouveau spa; on the other, lively bars and clubs.

See also FLORENCE.

Buddha, Gautama Siddharta (*c*.563–483 BC). It is surely more than an agreeable coincidence that Buddha was a contemporary of Confucius, though there is no evidence that the two men ever met.

See also GREAT IRONIES OF HISTORY.

Budget, a flexible. Today's young woman may have a flexible budget and an open mind but, after she's kicked off her shoes at the end of a hectic day, does she know what she really wants?

'Bugger Bognor!' *See* MOTHER, THE QUEEN; WILLIAM I.

Buildings, old. Forever being restored to their former glory.
See also LIKE STEPPING BACK IN TIME.

Bulgarian girl, the unfancied. 'The unfancied Bulgarian girl
doesn't seem to have read the script.'
   'Thank you, Mark.'
   'Virginia, actually.'
   'I do apologise.'
See also AMERICAN GIRL, THE BIG.

Bullies. Always 'cowardly'. No need to explain why.
See also BOMBERS, SUICIDE.

Bullitt. *See* CAR CHASES.

Bumblebee. *See* COMIC IMAGINATION; COOK, PETER; RIMSKY-
KORSAKOV, NIKOLAI.

Bums on seats. *See* ACADEMICS; FRONT OFFICE, THE; GOLDWYN,
SAM; MONKEYS; WATERHOUSE, KEITH.

Bunton, Emma (1977–). Former member of the Spice Girls pop
group, appearing under the cognomen 'Baby'. Contrary to received
opinion, Dr David Starkey has never likened Emma Bunton to 'a fat
girl from Luton on holiday in the wrong part of Ibiza' in any of his
ground-breaking television shows.

Bureaucrats. Always 'faceless'. Thunder against them.
See also BRUSSELS BUREAUCRATS; HEDGE, A.

Burglaries. 83% of all burglaries take place between 3 and 4 in the
afternoon. There may be a lesson here.

Burn-out. 'I worry about the fixture pile-up, Ray. The lads will be
burned out by the time they are 30.'

Burst out laughing. *See* CELEBS.

Business dinner. A cause for suspicion.

'You're looking very glamorous for a business dinner, Daphne.'

'He's a very important client, Vernon. Don't wait up.'

See WALL, THE WRITING ON THE.

Busts. A fine opportunity for amusing clarification in a speech by a prince of the British royal family.

'Unaccustomed as I am to unveiling busts...!'

'Delightful!'

Bust size. Unimportant.

'Surely it was that wise woman Irma Kurtz who said, "Don't worry about the size of your bust, love. It's the chick behind the tits who does the living."'

'Anna Raeburn, in fact, but the point holds.'

See also QUALITY; TITS.

But. 'But don't you see, I love you, Susan.'

'Well, Simon, all I can say is you've got a funny way of showing it.'

See WALL, THE WRITING ON THE.

Buttons, pressing those tender female. *See* MAN, THE NEW; PARSONS, TONY.

Buzzer. 'Fingers on the buzzers!'

'Very bad luck, Magdalene. Just behind on the buzzer there. So, it's New College, Oxford, 230; Magdalene, Cambridge, –5. But don't worry, Magdalene. Still plenty of time to catch up.'

See also MAGDALENE COLLEGE, CAMBRIDGE.

Byatt, A.S. (1936–). Novelist and critic. When reading Antonia Byatt's quartet of novels, begun in 1978 and charting the progress of Frederica Potter, is it just fatigue that leads one to wish that the 2000-odd pages had been more ruthlessly edited for excess and elaboration?

'I'd go more than half way with you on this. The virtuoso cleverness and self-mocking solemnity beget a recurrent sense that the story has not yet got under way.'

'Just so. It would be fair to say – would it not? – that instead of this airy soufflé of highbrow talk one wants a packet of fish and chips.'

'Indeed. With vinegar. And salt.'

'Speaking of which... MIGUEL!'

Byng, Jamie (1973–). Publisher.

'Byng does dude like he's read up on it in a body language manual. A near-perpendicular slouch, incessant tousling of hair and a deep drawl featuring some mid-Atlantic consonant distortions.'

'Love him or hate him, you can't be ambivalent about Byng!'

'Sounds like one for the Media pages, Libby.'

Byron, Lord George (1788–1824). Like many people with a full address book he found there were times when no one was in.

See also CASS, MAMA; EPSTEIN, BRIAN; HENDRIX, JIMI; HUTCHENCE, MICHAEL; JONES, BRIAN; JOPLIN, JANIS; MONROE, MARILYN; TOULOUSE-LAUTREC, HENRI.

Bystanders. Always 'innocent'.

'It's the innocent bystander who ends up in the morgue, that's what I always say.'

See also PROHIBITION.

Caesar, Gaius Julius (100/102–44 BC). Roman general, statesman and dictator. In spite of his many conquests in the field, Caesar was made to sit up and think by Cleopatra, an absolute monarch with whom he famously enjoyed many hours of rumpty tumpty on the Nile.

'Dr David Starkey?'

'Barbara Windsor, but I take your point.'

See also ACCESSIBLE; HISTORIANS, CELEBRITY.

Cagney, James (1899–1986). American film actor. There's an engaging irony in the fact that this legendary tough guy of so many classic *films noirs* should in real life have been a cultured, sensitive man who wrote agreeably unpretentious verses and assembled the finest private collection of French impressionists outside France.

See also EASTWOOD, CLINT; MARVIN, LEE; PESCI, JOE; ROBINSON, EDWARD G.; WIDMARK, RICHARD.

Caine, Sir Michael (1933–). Film actor. If Caine is still haunted by his working-class background, perhaps that says as much about us as it does about him.

Calderon de la Barca, Pedro (1600–81). Spanish dramatist and poet. Like so many writers of Spain's 'golden age', he lost an arm in a skirmish with the Turks.

See also DE VIVAR, RODRIGO DÍAZ; GLUBB, JOHN BAGOT; MALLARMÉ, STÉPHANE; MAUPASSANT, GUY DE; RICHARD I; RIMBAUD, ARTHUR; VEGA, LOPE FELIX DE.

Caligula, *properly* **Gaius Julius Caesar Germanicus** (AD 12–41). Roman emperor. Historians have found it difficult to separate fact from fiction in his brief but traumatic reign, but the well-known saying 'Caligula's horse must be above suspicion' leaves food for thought.

Call-girls. Always 'high-class' (*see also* PROSTITUTES).
  'Angus Deayton's Sordid Antics with a High-Class Call-Girl! Pages 2, 3, 4, 5, 6, 7, 8, 9,10, 11, 13, 14, 17, 18, 22, 23, 24, 32, 33, 34, 41, 42, 43, 44, 66, 67, 68, 69, 72, 73, 74...'
  'Sounds like one for us, Rebekah!'
See also AFFAIRS, EXTRA-MARITAL; *NEWS OF THE WORLD, THE*; WADE, REBEKAH.

Calypso cavaliers. 'All the talent in the world, Dermot, but...'
See also PLAYERS, FRENCH RUGBY; VOLATILE.

Camels. A Bactrian camel has two humps and a Dromedary one, or the other way round. People become confused. That said, either could walk from Sidi Bou Said to Bishops Lydeard without taking water on board.
See also BISHOPS LYDEARD; MOTSON, JOHN; SIDI BOU SAID.

Camera. If you respect the camera you can make it your friend.
  'Thank you, Sir Anthony.'
See also FILM ACTING; HOPKINS, SIR ANTHONY.

Campaigns. Always 'orchestrated', unless 'whispering'.

Camus, Albert (1913–60). Philosopher, novelist and playwright. Like so many French intellectuals, Camus kept goal for Algeria and died in a car crash.
  'And if that isn't absurd you tell me what is!'
  'Michael Parkinson?'
  'Jonathan Ross, but I take your point.'

Canals. Contrary to received opinion, Birmingham has more miles of canal than Amsterdam.
See also BIRMINGHAM.

Candour. Always 'disarming'.

Cannabis. A gateway drug. Causes long-term memory loss. The reason why, since the early 1960s, each generation, on reaching the age of 43, has to be reminded by helpful articles in *The Independent* and *The Guardian* why their 15-year-old children might be lighting joss-sticks in their bedrooms.

'That said, legalizing cannabis would be the first step on a slippery slope.'

'Legalizing what?'

'I can't remember. The twins?'

'What about them?'

'Lighting joss-sticks in their bedroom, are they?'

'I rather think they are. Why would that be?'

'I haven't the faintest idea. I'm a *Telegraph* man myself. Care for another?'

The Daily Mail has not been deceived.

See also CHOCOLATE; HEROIN; SLIPPERY SLOPES.

Canonization. Always 'belated'.

Capital offence. *See* MAN, ISLE OF.

Caption. A good caption writes itself. Yet a good photograph provides its own caption. There may be a lesson here.

Caravaggio, *properly* **Michelangelo Merisi da Caravaggio** (1573–1610). For Caravaggio, trouble was always just around the corner, yet he changed the way we look at the world. His pictures had the impact of early cinema – but his life was *film noir*. Mention 'high drama and heroic nudity'. He died of coffee poisoning and left no school.

Car chases. It is not generally known that the 77-minute car chase round San Francisco in *Bullitt* failed to win Channel 4's 'The 100 Most Boring Car Chases Ever Filmed' competition in December 2002. The prize was won by the slightly shorter, but even more tedious, car chase in *The French Connection*. The endless silly business with the fleet of Mini Coopers in *The Italian Job* was thought to be too facetious to qualify.

Cardiff crackers. *See* BEAUTIES, BIG-SCREEN.

Career woman. *See* LUXURIES, LIFE'S LITTLE.

Caring clergymen. *See* AQUINAS, ST THOMAS.

Carmen Duval, The Celebrity's Pal. Good byline for the Arts Editor of *The Sunday Times*.
See also BARD, TV TRACEY'S SHAW (!) TO BE; SHAW, TRACEY.

Caroline and Toby. *See* HUGO; HUMPHREY; MELISSA; NEWLY PAIRED-OFF THIRTYSOMETHINGS.

Carpenter, John (1930–). Film director. Carpenter's films are a reminder that we can be besieged from within as well as from without. Where evil is concerned the walls are porous.
'The French were the first to perceive this?'
'I think not.'
'I stand corrected.'

Carrots. Eat one carrot and you can see in the dark.

Carry On At Your Convenience (1973). British screen comedy at its best.
'The French were the first to perceive this?'
'Indeed.'

Cartwright, dear old Tom (1926–). With dear old Derek Shackleton he formed one of the most innocuous opening attacks in fast-bowling history.
'I hope to see many better in my lifetime.'
See also ACCURACY; AKRAM, WASIM and YOUNIS, WAQAR; AMBROSE, CURTLEY and WALSH, COURTNEY; BOWES, BILL and LARWOOD, HAROLD; DONALD, ALLAN and POLLOCK, SHAUN; HALL, WESLEY and GRIFFITH, CHARLIE; HOLDING, MICHAEL and ROBERTS, ANDY; LILLEE, DENNIS and THOMPSON, JEFF; LINDWALL, RAY and MILLER, KEITH; MCGRATH, GLENN and LEE, BRETT; TRUEMAN, FREDDIE and STATHAM, BRIAN.

Casablanca (1942). A classic.
'This will interest you, Vernon. Contrary to popular belief, the

line, "From now on, Rick, you'll have to do the thinking for both of us," really *does* occur in *Casablanca*.'

'You astound me. That said, there was no script, you know. Famously – and in common with so many great films – the actors received their lines from the director, John Huston, written on scraps of paper...'

'...breakfast menus...'

'...the backs of envelopes...'

'...old shopping lists...'

'...out-of-date electricity bills...'

'...unread bank statements...'

'...thank you Doris, I think we've got the point – just seconds before the cameras were about to roll.'

'"Here's looking at you, kid!"'

'"Of all the gin joints in all the towns in the world..."'

'Truly a classic!'

'Excuse me.'

'Ah Susan! Back from the Ladies at last. You have a point to make?'

'John Huston didn't direct *Casablanca*.'

'I dare say he didn't. My point holds nonetheless.'

'You're probably thinking of *The Treasure of the Sierra Madre*.'

'Quite possibly, but...'

'Or *The Red Badge of Courage*. That famously didn't have a script.'

'On any list of the ten greatest films of all time you'd have to include *The Magnificent Ambersons*.'

'And *Rear Window*?'

'I think not, Doris.'

'Daphne.'

'Of course. Apropos *The Treasure of the Sierra Madre*, it was famously the director John Huston's gift to his father, the great actor, Walter Huston.'

'I dare say it was. Tell me, Vincent...'

'It is the only time in cinema history when father and son both received Oscars for their work in the same film.'

'I'm not in the least surprised. Tell me, Vincent. Port Bou. Have you and Dolly ever been there?'

'I confess we haven't.'

'Dali lived there, you know, with Amanda Lear, the celebrated transsexual.'

'Trust you to know that! Simon's *fascinated* by ladyboys! Once I found him downloading *Chix with Dix* from...'

'*Nonsense!* I ...'

'My mistake. *Sluts with Nuts*, was it? Anyway...'

'That's enough, Susan! I'm not in the least *fascinated* by transsexuals. I merely... *MIGUEL!*'

Casanova, Giacomo (1725–98). Italian adventurer whose racy memoirs, written in an imperfect but lively French, describe his agreeable rogueries and amours in most countries in Europe.

'That can't have been bad! – as I once heard Michael Parkinson remark.'

'What a delightful observation!'

'On the other hand, his incessant womanizing is strong evidence in itself that he was impotent, probably homosexual.'

'That can't have been good!'

'Michael Parkinson?'

'Indeed. The King of Chat at his very best!'

Case. 'You're off the case, Jack. You're emotionally involved.'

'But, Guv...'

'That will be all, Jack.'

See also BRANCH, THE SPECIAL; BRASS, THE TOP; CURIOSITY; *TOUCH OF FROST, A.*

Case, on the. It is not generally known that Professor Simon Schama really did say, 'With Sir Francis Walsingham on the case, plotters at the court of Elizabeth I knew there was no hiding-place,' in one of his popular television shows.

See also HISTORIANS, CELEBRITY; HISTORY, THE NEW; STARKEY, DR DAVID.

Cass, Mama (1940–69). Like so many pop superstars it was all too often her sad destiny to have entertained a stadium packed with 80,000 adoring fans and to have then gone home alone. Her life lacked a third act.

'We're all guilty?'

'In the cases of Lord Byron and Mama Cass I wouldn't wish to take any personal responsibility.' (*See also* BYRON, LORD GEORGE; COBAIN, KURT; EPSTEIN, BRIAN; HENDRIX, JIMI; HUTCHENCE, MICHAEL; JONES, BRIAN; JOPLIN, JANIS; MONROE, MARILYN; MOON, KEITH; TOULOUSE-LAUTREC, HENRI; WALES, DIANA, PRINCESS OF; YATES, PAULA.)

'Excuse me.'

'Yes, Susan?'

'The Princess of Wales was hardly a pop superstar.'

'On the contrary, I'd argue that – love her or hate her – that's precisely what she was.'

'If you say so.' (*See also* MARGARET, PRINCESS.)

Casus belli. 'Hurumph, hurumph.'

'Oh dear. Yes, Julian?'

'Jolyon.'

'Of course. So? Your point?'

'Just this. The Butcher of Baghdad's invasion of Kuwait in 1990 constituted a clear and unambiguous *casus belli*. On that occasion, one was – if you'll excuse a slight excursion into the Horatian mode! – on the side of the Romans rather than Wilfred Owen. "*Dulce et decorum est pro patria mori.*"'

'I've lost the will to live.'

'Please, Susan. Allow Jolyon to continue.'

'Thank you. Here's my point. Where is the *casus belli* this time round? Rumsfeld and his hawkish associates can be as insolent as they wish about "old Europe", but the French and the Germans have a point. What's your view, Mr Pinfold?'

'Pratley. Call me an unreconstructed fence-sitter, Dr Death, but on this occasion I'm less interested in a decent *casus belli* than a decent Beaujolais!'

'A shame, in that case, Mr Parsnip, that your host, Mr Wagglewater...'

'Wigglesworth.'

'I apologise. That your host, Mr Wigglesworth, appears to have ordered an Argentinian Chardonnay!'

Categorization. Should be defied (*see* BRUCKNER, ANTON; LOUSSIER, JACQUES).

Cats. Loyalty is not a word you will find in the average cat's vocabulary.

'This will interest you, Vernon. I read somewhere that a cat, having stowed itself away on an aeroplane, can find its way home over a great distance – from Miami in Florida, for example, to Stansted in Essex.'

'On the other hand, 78% of all calls made by the Fire Brigade are to rescue cats which are stuck up trees.'

'Is there a connection?'

'I think not.'

'If I may be allowed a telling postscript, then?'

'The floor is yours.'

'It is not generally known that the distinguished publishing house, Faber and Faber, would have long since been conglomerated – under a thin, ambitious woman previously from Marketing – had it not been for income derived from a popular Andrew Lloyd Webber musical, itself derived from Tom Eliot's *Old Possum's Book of Practical Cats*.'

'A sobering thought.'

'Indeed. However, may I put in a word for sensible housekeeping at a corporate level?'

'Pray do.'

'There are still too many people in this country who think there's something indecent about making a profit.'

'That was well said. Had it not been for profits accruing from Jeffrey Archer's much-derided thrillers, Hodder Headline would not have been able to publish Amy Jenkins.'

'Amy Jenkins? I don't think I've heard of her.'

'Well, there you are.'

'In fact, Jeffrey Archer until recently has been published not by Hodder Headline but by HarperCollins.'

'My point precisely. Still no sign of the crabcakes.'

'That's because the waiter's southern European – if one's allowed to make such remarks in this politically correct day and age!'

'I concur. There's something in the southern European temperament which makes them prone to indiscipline.'

'And to neglect the simple prosecution of their duties. MIGUEL!'

'They're usually jolly attractive, though. Take Roberto...'

'Yes, thank you, Daphne. This may interest you, Simon. Did you know that the Austrian composer, Franz Schubert, wrote 606 songs?'

'I confess I didn't.'

'That's an output equal to about 60 modern-day pop albums!'

'A jaw-dropping achievement!'

See also CHARACTER, THE ITALIAN. EUROPEANS, SOUTHERN; MEN, SPANISH.

Catullus (*c.*84–54 BC). Roman poet and master of the love lyric, he knew better than most that love and hate are but two sides of the same coin. Died of dropsy.

Celebrities. Forever arriving at Heathrow Airport surrounded by burly bodyguards, being whisked through customs and thereafter speeding to undisclosed destinations (*see also* BEAUTIES, SHATTERED). Alternatively, giving the media the slip by leaving police stations by a side entrance.

'All the more surprising, then, that in spite of their hectic lifestyles, some celebrities manage to stay "relaxed", even "down to earth".'

'Surprising indeed. May I cite an example?'

'Pray do.'

'According to *The Daily Telegraph*, super-cool Ulrika Jonsson smiled and joked with fans yesterday as she signed copies of her new book, *Honest*, at the Brent Cross shopping centre!'

'Did the busty Eskimo look relaxed?'

'She did indeed! The sex-mad weathergirl even took a cheeky swipe at former lover Sven-Göran Eriksson's partner when she was asked to sign a copy "to Nancy". "What?" said the TV stunner. "Not Nancy Dell'Olio!?!"'

'Pray cease! Another such cheeky swipe and I'll crack a rib!'

'Perhaps we could allow Bert Sanders of Hendon to have the last word.'

'And who might he be?'

'Bert is one of the raunchy Swede's biggest fans. He'd walked 30 miles before breakfast to join the book-signing queue.'

'So what was Bert's verdict?'

'"She was lovely," Bert reported. "Really down to earth. I got the impression she was very relaxed."'

'That says it all.'

See also CELEBS; ESKIMOS WORKING IN THE UNITED KINGDOM; JONSSON, ULRIKA; LOVE-LIVES.

Celebs. They often burst out laughing at one another's zany antics.

'Even in posh nosheries?'

'Particularly in posh nosheries.'

'During her split from Fatboy Slim, did Zoe Ball continue to burst out laughing?'

'No, showbiz insiders report that the raunchy jockette momentarily lost her bubbly personality.'

See also BALL, ZOE; BUBBLY PERSONALITIES; LOVE-LIVES; NOSHERIE.

Celebs, stressed-out. Often in hiding, trying to save their three-year marriages.

See also BALL, ZOE; COUPLES, FAIRY-TALE.

Celibacy. 'This will interest you, Vernon. I read recently that, by the year 2015, eight out of ten women between the ages of 28 and 35 will have chosen celibacy as the most viable option.'

'Make that nine out of ten'

'Thank you, Susan. MIGUEL!'

See WALL, THE WRITING ON THE.

Centre Court, the. 'So, Lleyton. You won the US Open at Flushing Meadows. You won the Australian Open in your home town of Sydney. What does it mean to you, winning here at Wimbledon on the most famous court in the world?'

'Fuck all, mate. 'Scuse I, I'm off for a tinny.'

'Back to you, Sue.'

'Thank you, Barry.'

Cervantes, Miguel (1547–1615). At an age when most people would be applying for their pensions, Cervantes sat down in his lonely attic and wrote *Don Quixote* in eleven days to pay off his debts. The lesson is as timely now as it was in the 17th century.

Challis, John (1945–). One of the unsung heroes of British comedy.

See also BLUTHAL, JOHN; CRIBBINS, BERNARD; CRYER, BARRY; JACQUES, HATTIE; LE MESURIER, JOHN; LLOYD PACK, ROGER; LODGE, DAVID; MAGEE, HENRY; SMITH, LIZ; STARK, GRAHAM; TODD, BOB; WHITFIELD, JUNE.

***Chambers Biographical Dictionary*, my copy of.** In an occasional column, always 'well-thumbed'.

See also BREWER'S *DICTIONARY OF PHRASE AND FABLE*, MY COPY OF; *ROGET'S THESAURUS*, MY COPY OF.

Champion, a great. The sign of a great champion is that he wins even when he's playing badly.

'How true. Take "Pancho" Gonzales at Wimbledon in 1949.'
'What happened?'
'He lost.'
'Well, there you are.'

Chances, half. Have to be put away.

'At this level, if you don't put the half chances away you get punished.'
'Thank you, Trevor.'

Channel 4, the Chief Executive of. Forever announcing 'a return to core values'. Nobody knows what these are. That said, *Boys and Girls*, a game show devised by Chris Evans in which young people break wind competitively, has proved a ratings disappointment.

See also BEST TELEVISION IN THE WORLD, THE.

Character, the Italian. There is something in his character which makes your Italian unamenable to discipline.

'I'd go further, Vernon. For "indiscipline" I'd substitute "lawlessness". Nor is this mere semantics. I read in the *Telegraph* on Tuesday that at Naples Central Criminal Court in August this year, 27 men faced charges of extortion, fraud, forgery, kidnapping, murder, arson, assault, blackmail, bombing and slander.'
'Hardly surprising in that part of the world!'
'Indeed not. On the occasion in question, the defendants were

a cardinal archbishop, nine monks, seven schoolmasters, five doctors, three senior policemen and the mayor.'

'And the outcome?'

'They were all acquitted.'

'Well, there you are!'

'The Chief Prosecutor lodged an appeal but before it could be heard he was arrested for running a brothel. MIGUEL!'

Charisma bypass. *See* DUNCAN SMITH, IAIN.

Charles I (1600–49). King of Great Britain and Ireland. Like so many English monarchs, his last words were, 'I could do with one of Bellamy's veal pies!'

See also COACHING INNS; EDWARD II; LAST WORDS; WILLIAM I.

Chart-topper. If we knew the ingredients that go to make a chart-topper we'd all be laughing.

Chaucer, Geoffrey (1340–1400). The father of English literature. His cheery and loquacious pilgrims are as much a part of the English scene today as they were in the 14th century.

Cheat. It is too often forgotten, perhaps, that it's only a short step from cheating on your wife to cheating on your country. *The Daily Mail* has perceived this.

Cheese. Causes nightmares. According to the French politician, gastronome and *belle-lettriste* Jean Anthelme Brillat-Savarin (1755–1826) – dubbed 'the philosopher of the kitchen' on account of his *Physiologie du Goût* (1825) – 'a dessert without cheese is like a beauty with only one eye'.

'I dare say he did, but at this rate we'll never get the crabcakes, never mind dessert. MIGUEL!'

It might be amusing in a humorous column to refer to cheddar cheese as 'the ubiquitous mousetrap'.

Chelsea Girl Escorts. *See* ANYTHING, IF MEN BELIEVE THAT THEY'LL BELIEVE; IF YOU MUST DO IT, AT LEAST HAVE THE DECENCY TO DO IT WITH A PROSTITUTE.

Chick behind the tits, the. *See* BUST SIZE.

Children. A short cut to the moral high ground.
'Ah yes. But perhaps you'd see it differently if you were a mother yourself.'
See also ABUSE; FASHION FUN; 42-YEAR-OLDS.

Children, women and. Always 'innocent'. A mystery.

Chingford, a disco slapper from. *See* AS EVER.

Chivalry. There was always a fine line between sexism and chivalry, and no doubt it was frequently crossed. The return of the British Gentleman, however, means no more going Dutch.
'Sounds like one for *Richard and Judy*.'

Chix with Dix. *See* CASABLANCA; PORT BOU.

Chocolate. 'This will interest you, Vernon. According to *The Daily Telegraph*, scientists have discovered that chocolate produces the same reaction in the brain as marijuana. They've discovered other similarities, too.'
'Really?'
'Indeed.'
'And what might they be?'
'They can't remember!'
'Delightful!'
See also GATEWAY DRUG.

Choked. 'I feel choked for the Welsh boys, Jonathan.'
'At least they showed some pride in the shirt, Jeremy.'
'Very much so, Jonathan. But we have to ask: where does Welsh rugby go from here?'
See also AT SEA; DEFENCE, THE WELSH.

Christie, Linford (1960–). Contrary to received opinion, *The Sunday Times* has never referred to Britain's 1992 Olympic 100 metres gold medallist as 'the generously beloined sprint supremo'.
See also JUDGES, BOOKER PRIZE.

Christmas. Always just around the corner. It gets earlier every year. That said, it's curtains for the traditional panto.

Christmas, getting a new nose for. *See* WESTBROOK, DANIELLA.

Church, Alonzo (1903–87). American logician. At a meeting of the Aristotelian Society it might be amusing to murmur: 'Like Catholics, logicians have an infallible Church!'

Churchill, Sir Winston Leonard Spencer (1874–1965). British statesman. Were the qualities that saw Churchill – and the nation – through the days of near-catastrophe less well suited to more peaceful times? The debate continues.
See also MOTHER, THE QUEEN.

Cimino, Michael (1940–). American writer and film director. At the age of 63, Michael Cimino is the latest French reclamation project. It was only to be expected. The French love Jerry Lewis. They love Mickey Rourke. How surprising is it that they love Cimino?
    'That said, on any list of the ten greatest films of all time you'll not find one by Michael Cimino.'
    'Nor will you.'

Circumstances. 'It's a funny thing, Inspector, but I can't help thinking that in different circumstances you and I could have become good friends.'
    'Not in this lifetime, sunshine. You're nicked.'

Citizen Kane (1941). On mention of *Citizen Kane* it is impressive to murmur, 'Sometimes when you see a film which invented the rules you are less aware of the fact than you should be. And why? Because now you take these rules for granted.'

Civilians. Always 'innocent'. Often gunned down at checkpoints.

Clarinet. 'Surely it was Flaubert who had it that "all blind men play the clarinet".'
    'A delightful attribution, Vernon, but will the man from Clee-

thorpes understand?' (*See* CLEETHORPES, THE MAN FROM.)

'I'm from Cleethorpes, Simon, and I don't know what you're on about.'

'My point precisely, Doreen.'

'Daphne.'

'Of course. This will interest you, Victor. Stocking manufacturers now have the technology to make pantyhose which doesn't ladder, but they don't use it because if they did their profits would decline.'

'They didn't get rich by throwing it about!'

'Nor they did. MIGUEL!'

See also FLAUBERT, GUSTAVE.

Cleethorpes, the man from. *See* CLARINET.

Cliché. In every cliché there is a grain of truth.

Closure. Sometimes it's too soon for closure, even though the healing process has begun.

'That wise woman Virginia Ironside has perceived this.'

'You took the words right out of my mouth.'

See also GRIEVE.

Clouseau, Inspector. Inspector Clouseau may be gone, but isn't there a bit of him alive in all our hearts?

See also SELLERS, PETER.

Coach, the. Always has to go. No need to explain why.

'Terry Venables? Magic as a coach, Barry, but of course he had to go.'

Coaching. We're in danger of coaching the natural talent out of our lads. We should never forget that Ronaldo had never kicked a football in his life until picked to play for Brazil in the World Cup at the age of 17, but had practised his skills by foot-juggling an orange on Copacabana Beach.

See also EFFECTIVE.

Coaching inns. Always have a room on the first floor where Charles I passed the night before the Battle of Naseby.

Cobain, Kurt (1967–94). American singer. Nirvana's second album, *Nevermind*, set the agenda. Ten years and eight million copies later, the ripples it set in motion on its release in 1991 extend further than ever.

'Interest in the troubled singer is at a premium.'

'Indeed. That said, his life lacked a third act.'

See also BYRON, LORD GEORGE; CASS, MAMA; DEAN, JAMES; EPSTEIN, BRIAN; HENDRIX, JIMI; JONES, BRIAN; JOPLIN, JANIS; MONROE, MARILYN; MOON, KEITH; TOULOUSE-LAUTREC, HENRI; WALES, DIANA, PRINCESS OF.

Cole, the young lad. English soccer player with Arsenal FC.

'The young lad Cole must have radar in his educated left boot.'

'It's got "back of the net" written all over it.'

'Thank you, Trevor.'

Coleridge, Samuel Taylor (1772–1834). Would 'Kubla Khan' ever have been completed had the person from Porlock not arrived? On the other hand, Coleridge's wholesale plagiarizing of German philosophers leads us into deep waters.

Collateral damage. *See* LIFE, LOSS OF.

Collective, the Gay Left. 'They don't look very gay to me!'

'Seen your boy lately?'

'Just a phase.'

Colonial façade. Who better than Michael Palin to peep behind Senegal's colonial façade for a glimpse of the reality underneath?

'He's never less than watchable.'

Columns, cookery. Always 'delightfully personal'.

Columns, gardening. Always 'lively', often 'delightfully quirky'.

Comedy. 'Surely it was Bob Mortimer, of the surreal duo Reeves and Mortimer...'

'Slapstick.'

'I beg your pardon? Con, is it?'

'No. Marty. Reeves and Mortimer. I'd call them slapstick rather than surreal. Surreal is when the furniture talks. Not when a middle-aged man jumps around pulling faces and making monkey noises. However, your point is...?'

'Merely that Bob Mortimer, of the – er – slapstick duo Reeves and Mortimer, had it that comedy is harder to write than tragedy.'

'How true!'

'Thank you, Vernon. However, we owe this insight to John Mortimer, in fact, the creator of the immortal Rumpole of the Bailey. It's *Steptoe and Son* which should be set for 'A' levels, not so-called Harold Pinter. That's what I always say. Isn't it, Susan? SUSAN!'

'Sorry, Simon. I was miles away.'

'Apropos comedy, I'm one of those odd bods who cry at weddings and laugh at funerals. Daphne says it's my silly sense of humour. Talking of which...'

'Not that we were!'

'Not that we were! Delightful! Talking of which, will you be attending the Courtly-Davenport nuptials in September?'

'For my sins!'

'Well, I think hes totally gr8. Hes an icon, is Vic Reeves. Hes off da wall! Hes totally bonkers!'

'Thank you, Tracey.'

'Sharon.'

Comedy, unsung heroes of British. *See* BLUTHAL, JOHN; CHALLIS, JOHN; CRIBBINS, BERNARD; CRYER, BARRY; JACQUES, HATTIE; LE MESURIER, JOHN; LLOYD PACK, ROGER; LODGE, DAVID; MAGEE, HENRY; SMITH, LIZ; STARK, GRAHAM; TODD, BOB; WHITFIELD, JUNE.

Comic imagination. Surely Peter Cook's incomparable comedic imagination was best demonstrated by Ian Hislop in a BBC2 documentary broadcast in December 2002.

'Never herd o' him, me. u herd o peter cook, trace?'

'Cant say i hav, shar. i reckon ian hislop, tho'. He's totally brill, ian hislop.'

'Yeah. Totally brill.'

'May I continue?'

'Go on, then.'

'Thank you. I was about to quote Ian Hislop on Peter Cook. "Peter used to come into the *Private Eye* offices from time to time," said Hislop. "After a while he'd be off on one of his surreal flights of fancy. It was sheer genius. 'One day,' he'd say, 'this enormous bumblebee flew straight up my left nostril…'".'

'What?'

'He was unable to continue.'

'Who? Cook?'

'No. Hislop.'

'Why?

'He was helpless with laughter!'

'Just as we are now!'

'That says it all!'

'Miguel!'

See also COOK, PETER.

Coming second. No one remembers the name of the man who came second.

'I do. Tim Henman.'

'Thank you, Susan. But in fact he doesn't usually get that far.'

'All right. Darren Campbell, then.'

'For a woman, you're surprisingly well informed!'

'Well thank you, Vernon. And what about Roger Black? And…'

'You've made your point, Susan.'

See also HENDRICK, MIKE.

Commonwealth Games, the. 'Congratulations, Shane. But tell me this. You won a gold medal at Atlanta and another gold medal in front of your home crowd in Sydney. But what did it mean to you to win a gold medal here at the Commonwealth Games in Manchester?'

'Fuck all, mate. 'Scuse I, I'm off for a tinny.'

'Er, back to you, Sally.'

Community stalwarts, 76-year-old. Forever falling down stairs and knocking themselves unconscious. 'Elsie will be sorely missed.'

See also PENSIONERS.

Commuters. Always 'long-suffering'.

See also GRIND TO A HALT; JEREMY; PUBLIC TRANSPORT; TAX-PAYERS.

Compromise. Compromise is often the name of the game, and never more so than when selling a property in the spring and buying one in the autumn.

Compton Pauncefoot. Either a picturesque village in Somerset, or a West Indian fast bowler. The debate continues.

See also UPTON SNODSBURY.

Conques. One of France's best-kept secrets. That said, it was once a staging-post on the pilgrims' route to Santiago de Compostela.

See also AVEYRON; PILGRIMS, MEDIEVAL.

Conrad, Joseph, *pen name of* **Teodor Josef Konrad Nalecz Korzeniowski** (1857–1924). Polish-born novelist who mastered a fluent and effective English prose. In his works he tended to study men put to the test in lonely places, expounding a view of human nature which was at bottom pessimistic. In sum, not a congenial man. His creative gifts enriched his readers, no doubt, but brought him only a partial solace.

Conran, Jasper (1961–). Dressmaker. No one knows better than Jasper Conran that, year after year, posh is the new posh.

Constable, John (1776–1837). English landscape painter. Is it possible to look at the work of John Constable without seeing in one's mind's eye inferior reproductions of *The Haywain*? Is there anything to be discovered about him that we don't think we already know? Perhaps not. Yet his work caused a sensation in French salons in the 1820s and was admired by Géricault and Delacroix, among others.

Constipation. Paradoxically, a sign of good health – except when it isn't.

See also PRESLEY, ELVIS.

Coogan, Steve (1965–). English comedian and actor.
   'Will the real Steve Coogan please step forward!'
   'Where does Steve Coogan end and Alan Partridge begin?'
   'Good question. Apropos, might it be fair to say that society created

Alan Partridge, Steve Coogan merely reported him?'

   'And your point is, Plimsoll?'

   'I just thought...'

   'MIGUEL!'

Cook, Peter (1941–95). Truly the godfather of modern comedy, yet how ironic that the man who had us all in fits of laughter with his off-the-wall humour should have spent the last thirty years of his life in a Hampstead drain in the company of an eccentric from Seattle. He would sleep during the day and at night play telephonic pranks on Norwegian fishermen. There may be a lesson here (*see also* MILLER, JONATHAN; MILLIGAN, SPIKE).

   'Surely it was Germaine Greer who perceived that when Cook, as "Pete", tried to make Moore, as "Dud", crack up (or "corpse", as professionals call it!) he was in reality making love to him.'

   'In fact Germaine was less mealy-mouthed, as you'd expect. What she said was that Cook, basically, wanted to fuck Moore...'

   'Well, yes, thank you, Marty.'

   'Con.'

   'Whatever. He was certainly touched by genius (*see also* COMIC IMAGINATION). I'm talking about Peter Cook. One typical flight of fancy I'll never forget. It was on a "Derek and Clive" record...'

   'Objection!'

   'Yes, Vernon?'

   'You assured us earlier that we'd not have to suffer one of them again.'

   'Indulge me for a moment. Cook was asked by Dudley what was the worst job he'd ever had. "Working for Jayne Mansfield," he replied. "I had to remove the lobsters from her arse."'

   'Enough! Another such flight of fancy and I'll split my sides!'

   'Jayne Mansfield? Never herd o her. U herd of jayne mansfield, Trace?'

   'Cant say I hav. Shall we?'

   'After u.'

Cooking. When you think about it, cooking is just like life. Often things turn out not quite how you wanted them to, but that isn't always a bad thing. Something can go wrong and, in fixing it, you come up with something better. Cooking is an improvisational act. In this sense it is no different from any part of life. Things go wrong. How you cope makes the difference.

'Thank you, Nigella.'

See also KITCHEN.

Coppers. 'We're coppers, George. Not social workers.'

'But, Guv...'

'That will be all, George.'

See also PSYCHOLOGY; PHILOSOPHY.

Corfe. An agreeable little village not six miles from Taunton, yet one of Somerset's best-kept secrets.

See also ASH PRIORS; BISHOPS LYDEARD; MILVERTON; SECRETS, SOMERSET'S BEST-KEPT; TAUNTON.

Cornwall. The theory that, because of centuries of inbreeding, 67% of adult males in Cornwall are their own grandfathers, is probably wide of the mark, but agreeable nonetheless. On the other hand, the widely held belief that only 17% of the indigenous population has ever travelled outside the county is probably true.

Correction. 'Correction, Jack! You *did have* leave coming to you.'

'But, Guv...'

'That will be all, Jack.'

See also FRENCH COOKING.

Cosmetic surgery. The debate continues.

'You have to fix your life before you fix your nose.'

'Anna Raeburn?'

'Jumping Jesus! Where?'

'No, no. Not here.'

'Thank God for that! Ghastly woman.'

'I meant did she say that?'

'Did she say what?'

'You have to fix your life before you fix your face.'

'How would I know? Still no sign of the crabcakes.'

See also NOSE, THE; TITS.

Cossington-Smith, Grace (1892–1984). Australian painter. Born in Neutral Bay, New South Wales, she studied art at Dattilo Rubbo's Art School, Sydney, and later in England and Germany. Credited with introducing Post-Impressionism to Australia, she was a pioneer of the Modernist movement and co-founded the Contemporary Group in 1926. Her paintings did not become popular until late in her career. They include *The Sock Knitter* (1915).

Cottage, the. 'Listen carefully, Daphne. This is important, so I don't want you to argue. Pack a bag, take my car and drive straight to the cottage. Wait for me there.'
See also CRAZY; DAPHNE.

Couple, the average. It has been calculated that after three years of marriage the average couple talk to one another for seven-and-a-half minutes a week.
'You were saying, Susan?'
'It's not important.' (*See* WALL, THE WRITING ON THE.)
'That's all right, then. Tell me, Vernon. Amanda Platell. See the point of her, do you?'

Couples, fairy-tale. Forever spending the day behind closed doors in an eleventh-hour attempt to save their rocky marriages.
'They need space and time to be alone.'
'Do they forget to burst out laughing?'
'Indeed they do.'
See BALL, ZOE; BURST OUT LAUGHING; CELEBS; VIPs, BUSTY.

Courbet, Gustave (1819–77). Painter. *Sans idéal et sans religion.* Died of dropsy.

Coursegoules. Although only a crow's flight from the 20th-century hum of the Côte d'Azur, Coursegoules remains one of France's best-kept secrets.
See also ARIÈGE; AUDE; AUTOIRE; AVEYRON; BAUME-LES-MESSIEURS; CONQUES; GORDES; LOT; LOUBRASSAC; LOZÈRE; MOSTUÉJOULS; RIEUX VOLVESTRE; SAINT-GUILHEM-LE-DÉSERT; VIEILLE-BRIOUDE.

Courts, full rigour of the. *See* SHOP-LIFTING.

Couture. It is in fashion's interest to keep couture alive and kicking. It allows designers to create the future.

'Sounds like one for "Fashion & Style", Susannah.'

See also FRANKEL, SUSANNAH; FRUMP.

Coward, Noël (1896–1974). His very name evokes a more agreeable age. In a hundred years time there still won't be a corner of the civilized world where the expression 'a very Noël Coward sort of person' isn't immediately understood.

'What a depressing thought.'

'Thank you, Susan. My better half's reservations notwithstanding, that is what is meant by "style".'

'Could that wise man *le Comte de Buffon* have had the Master in mind, do you suppose, when he remarked: "*Ces choses sont hors de l'homme. Le style est l'homme même*"?'

'It's an agreeable fancy, certainly. I take my hat off to you.'

'Having an affair with the Duke of Edinburgh doesn't strike me as very stylish.'

'Noël Coward had an affair with the Duke of Edinburgh? You astound me.'

'Don't concern yourself, Vernon. Susan's being facetious as usual. That was the little musical comedy actress, Can't remember her name.'

'The little musical comedy actress had an affair with Noël Coward? Oh *please!*'

'*No!* With the Duke of Edinburgh!'

'There you go again! It was the Duke of Kent who had an affair with Noël Coward.'

'What! The President of the All England Tennis Club? *Never!*'

'No! His father.'

'I thought that was Mountbatten.'

'You're confusing him with Hutch.'

'Don't tell me who I'm confusing him with, Simon. The Countess Mountbatten famously had an affair with Hutch: a big black man who played the piano at Quaglino's in the old days. My father used to dance there with Susan Clifford-Turner. She later married Colin Ingleby-McKenzie, an old Etonian who captained Hampshire at cricket. Susan Clifford-Turner, that is. Not the Countess Mountbatten.'

'I'm getting confused. Next you'll be telling us that Prince Andrew…'

'That's enough of that, Susan.'

'I met her once, the little musical comedy actress, in a hotel in Manchester. Didn't care for her.'

See also PRIVATE LIVES.

Cowell, Simon (1962–). TV's 'Mr Nasty.'

'What you see is what you get?'

'Quite the opposite, or so rumour has it.'

'We'll not go into that, if you don't mind. At least not until we've finished the crabcakes.'

'What crabcakes? We still haven't ordered.'

'Nor have we. Miguel!'

See also BLONDES.

Crabcakes. 'Interestingly enough, the best crabcakes Susan and I ever had weren't in Rick Stein's vaunted Padstow nosherie, but in a little pub well off the beaten track in darkest Bermondsey. I won't divulge its whereabouts. Don't want the world and his wife beating a path to its door.'

See also GAZPACHO; NOSHERIE.

Crack cocaine. One pipe and you are a dead man. (Needless to say, *une pipe* has a different meaning in France, and is more expensive, *see also* PROSTITUTES, FRENCH.)

Craps, a crowd of.

'My wife and I have asked a crowd of craps
To come and waste their time and ours: perhaps
You'd care to join us? In a pig's arse, friend.'

See also ABODE; 'FRIEND, IN A PIG'S ARSE'; LARKIN, PHILIP; MEET THERE SOME TIME, WE MUST; 'VERS DE SOCIÉTÉ'.

Crazy. 'You're crazy, Vernon!'

'It's a crazy world, Daphne! Or haven't you noticed?'

See also SUSAN.

Credit. *See* LADS, THE.

Crew. Always 'motley'.

Cribbins, Bernard. *See* COMEDY, UNSUNG HEROES OF BRITISH.

Cricketer, the natural. The natural cricketer always knows where his off-stump is.

See also BRAIN, A GOOD CRICKETING; INDIAN, THE WRISTY LITTLE.

Crime. There's no such thing as a victimless crime.

Crime, white-collar. 'Interestingly enough, Vernon, insurance frauds and Stock Exchange swindles carried out by respectable business-men in the City of London net more for the perpetrators each day than was stolen in the Great Train Robbery of 1963.'

'I can well believe it.'

'MIGUEL!'

Crisis meetings. Forever being held at St James's Palace.

See also LOVE-SPLIT CHART-TOPPERS; POP HOTTIES, HIP-SHAKING.

Criticize, it's very easy to. *See* FILM ACTING.

Crocodiles. Whenever a crocodile is captured in Australia's outback it is discovered to have a clock, still ticking, in its stomach, and a set of false teeth.

See also SHARKS, GREAT WHITE.

Cromwell, Oliver (1599–1658). British soldier and statesman. Far from being the dull dog of legend, Cromwell liked a drink and was rumoured to have danced a jig at his daughter's funeral.

See also CHARLES I.

Cross to bear! we all have a. *See* AGE, THE VICTORIAN.

Cryer, Barry (1936–). One of the unsung heroes of British comedy.

See also BLUTHAL, JOHN; CHALLIS, JOHN; CRIBBINS, BERNARD; JACQUES, HATTIE; LE MESURIER, JOHN; LLOYD PACK, ROGER; LODGE, DAVID; MAGEE, HENRY; SMITH, LIZ; STARK, GRAHAM; TODD, BOB; WHITFIELD, JUNE.

Cry for help. *See* BABES, TROUBLED SOAP; SHOP-LIFTING.

Cukor, George (1890–1983). As a film-maker he was decades ahead of his time. The French were the first to perceive this. His movies were synonymous with taste, wit, elegance and style.
　'He never married.'
　'You surprise me.'

Culture, the local. Should be 'soaked up'.

See also ATMOSPHERE; SALAMANCA.

Cup, the. There's a romance to the Cup, but at the end of the day it's the League that counts. Being knocked out of the Cup can be a blessing in disguise.

See also LEAGUE TITLE, THE.

Curiosity. 'So – sister of mine! – what brings you to a deserted barn on the outskirts of the village of Little Frampton-under-Widdle in Shropshire at 11.55 p.m. on a wet Sunday night in November?'
　'The same thing as brought you here – brother of mine! Curiosity.'
　'Sounds like one for Inspector Frost, Sergeant.'
　'Inspector Morse, in fact, but the point holds.'

See also MORSE, INSPECTOR; *TOUCH OF FROST, A*.

'Cut the crap, Luv!' Good headline for a story in the *Telegraph's* new cutting-edge 'Celebrity Diary'.

Cynicism. *See* SCEPTICISM.

Daily Mail, The. Say what you like about *The Daily Mail*, it is a brilliantly edited newspaper.

'I agree. When was *The Daily Mail* last deceived by one of the endemic follies of our age?'

See also BABY, HAVING A; EVIL; MAN, THE PERFECTABILITY OF; NATURE, HUMAN; PENDULUM; PROGRESS, BELIEF IN THE ILLUSION OF; REAL WORLD, THE; UTOPIA, THE SEARCH FOR.

Dane, Hamlet the moody. A construction that sits well in an occasional column.

See also ABLUTIONS; ABODE; ALFRED; AMERICAN ACADEMICS; BUSTS; DUCK, DONALD; EATERIE; EMBONPOINT; HOSTELRY; INFELICITOUS; KEATS, JOHN; LIBATION; MEADOWS, MY POULTERER, THE ESTIMABLE MR; NOSHERIE; OCCASIONS; REPORTER; THESPIAN; VARIETY, BIRDS OF THE FEATHERED.

Danno. 'Book him, Danno.'
'You've lost me, I fear.'
'Before your time.'

Daphne. *See* COTTAGE, THE; MYSTIC MEG.

Dare. 'How dare you, Simon! How bloody dare you! No! Don't touch me!'
See WALL, THE WRITING ON THE.

Darkness, The. Band. It's a long way to the top if you want to rock and roll, but The Darkness have the classic rock prerequisites: a bassist with a Charles Bronson moustache, a pathologically flamboyant frontman and a better-looking brother on guitar.

'Yeah, right. Heard their new track, "Get Your Hands Off My Woman, Motherfucker", have you, John?'

'Ah, Miguel! No, I confess I haven't. How nice of you to join us, however.'

'Ready to rock, are you? Your birds seem to be back from the toilet.'

'Yes – we're all present and correct, I think. So, for starters... Bugger me, he's gone again! MIGUEL!'

Darren in Finance. *See* DENISE IN BOUGHT LEDGER.

Date, up to. Paradoxically, nothing dates more quickly than the currently up-to-date.

'Well, how could it? Anything else is already out of date.'

'Thank you, Susan.'

Day, at the end of the. *See* ACCOUNTANTS; BOTTOM LINE; CUP, THE; DESCARTES, RENÉ; DISPOSAL; FERGUSON, PROFESSOR NIALL; KIDS, THE WIFE AND; MILLER, JONATHAN; SNOOKER.

Days, these. 'What passes for thinking these days...'

Days, those. 'It was three to a shirt in those days and the outside bucket.'

See also BLITZ, THE; DOODLEBUG.

Dead Ringers. Comedy show.

'Oddly enough, and in spite of the critical plaudits, I enjoyed it more before it transferred to television.'

'I concur. Paradoxically, and just because it allows your imagination to run free, radio paints a far more vivid picture than television ever can.'

'Weve drawn 2 tossers here, shar.'

'Not 1/2, trace.'

'Im off 2 the toilet. U comin, shar?'

'Mind if I join you?'

'Youd b welcom, Daphne.'

'Great. You coming, Susan?'

'I'll join you later, Daph.'

'DAPHNE! Damn, too late...'

Dealers, drug. Forever being arrested in 'dawn raids'.

See also FLYING SQUAD, THE.

Dean, James (1920–55). Had he lived he'd now be 83.

'Rather long in the tooth for a rebel without a cause!'

His life lacked a third act. There may be a lesson here.

See also CASS, MAMA; HENDRIX, JIMI; HUTCHENCE, MICHAEL; JONES, BRIAN; JOPLIN, JANIS; MONROE, MARILYN; MOON, KEITH; WALES, DIANA, PRINCESS OF.

Dean, Rio, Lee, Alan, Gary, Jason, Roy, Dwight, Dion and Wayne. Good names for soccer players.

'How true. Pomaded hooligans forever being beaten up by bar bouncers and sleeping with common women.'

'Hang on a minute.'

'Yes, Susan?'

'What about Robinson, the England rugby union back? He's called Jason. Rather ruins your theory, doesn't it?'

'Excuse me!'

'Good grief. It's the "Comparable Max" again!'

'I thought Roberto had a ship to catch.'

'He has a little time still, thank you, Mrs Wigglesworth.'

'Ms Crampton, actually. Simon and I aren't married.'

'I apologise.'

'You have something to say?'

'In fact, I was worried because I heard you say earlier that mention of rugby football has a most disturbing effect on your partner, Mr Wigglesworth.'

'How thoughtful! You all right, Simon?'

'Perfectly all right, thank you, Susan, and your point about Jason Robinson is factually accurate, but you failed to mention that the little Sale flyer began his career in rugby league and... and... and...'

'Are you sure you're all right, Simon?'

'Yes, yes. Perfectly all right. Just loosen my collar. That's better. Where was I? I have it. He started his career in rugby league, a sport as flat-capped and horny-handed as association football, and whose first name trends – for obvious sociological reasons – tend to be similar to those of soccer. Thereafter the differences are obvious.

The firm smack of young bodies meeting in the tackle, beer-barrel thighs pumping like pistons, the up and under in the scrimmage... I think I need a breath of fresh air... Small walk... I'll be all right...'

'I did warn you, Ms Crampton!'

'Thank you, Dr Death.'

See also BEN, DAN, JEREMY, JOSH, WILL, CHARLIE, JULIAN, MARTIN, DANNY, JAMES AND JONNY.

Death. Shouldn't be swept under the carpet.

'As a subject of conversation these days it's more taboo even than sex.'

'What is?'

'Death.'

'Let's not talk about that!'

'Indeed not. That said, however, we could learn much from the way the Pueblo Indians treat their old folk.'

'I dare say we could.'

'Tell me, Vernon. Did you notice that a moment ago I referred to the "Comparable Max"?. An agreeably deft allusion, I think you'll agree, to the fact that Max Beerbohm was known as the "In..."'

'Toilet everyone?'

Debating points. Always 'cheap'.

See also BEST TELEVISION IN THE WORLD, THE.

de Botton, Alain (1961–). Author and wine-bar philosopher. What matters to de Botton when he travels is the chance to 'consume' a place, to pay it enough unhurried attention to absorb a personal meaning.

'I recall that on one occasion, having travelled in Barbados, Provence and Madrid, he returned home to West Kensington, where he was able to infuse his walk to Hammersmith underground station with "renewed wonder and gratitude".'

'That says it all.'

'It would be fair – would it not? – to say that for de Botton, without a change of mind as well as a change of scene, travel means nothing but a burst of burning fuel?'

'You've put it better than I could, Vernon.'

Decisions, decisions. *See* ANIMALS, WILD; STARVING.

Decommissioning. 'You can decommission guns and bombs, but you can't decommission age-old sectarian hatreds rooted in Ireland's tragic past. Isn't that so, Vernon?'
'Come again, Simon? Nodded off for a moment there.'

Defence, a Third World. Always 'naïve'.

Defence, the German. Always 'well-organized'.

Defence, the Italian. Always 'cynical'.

Defence, the Welsh. A comedy of errors, but no one in a red shirt was laughing.
'So where exactly does Welsh rugby go from here, Jonathan?'
'Good question, Jeremy.'

Defence of any team managed by Kevin Keegan. Always 'leaking goals'.

Defenders, big English. Forever being left for dead by nippy little Nigerians.

Degas, (Hilaire Germain) Edgar (1834–1917). Renowned for scenes of ballet, café-life and laundresses about their business. Who but the French could have produced an Edgar Degas?

Delights. Often 'forbidden'.
'Having sampled the forbidden delights of Dakar, Michael Palin moves on to Nouakchott, capital of Mauretania and largest city of the Sahara.'

Dementia. *See* OVER-55s, THE.

Dench, Dame Judi (1939–). Even as a young actress, Dame Judi was never beautiful, but she became beautiful as soon as she stepped on to a stage.
'That says it all.'
See also EVANS, DAME EDITH; SMITH, DAME MAGGIE.

Denise in Bought Ledger. Forever having a word with Darren in Finance.

Derrida, Jacques and **Foucault, Michel**. *See* ATKINSON, RON.

Descartes, René (1596–1650). He brewed his own coffee in the Turkish manner, a habit he acquired when living alone in the bitter winter of 1619.

'Yet even in these disagreeable circumstances he never lost his Gallic urbanity!'

'Ah yes, but if only he had honoured feelings as much as thought!'

'I concur. At the end of the day, couldn't "*Cogito ergo sum*" be translated as "I'm all right Jack"?'

'Indeed, indeed. And how typically French! You all right, Susan? SUSAN!'

'Sorry! I was miles away!' (*See* WALL, THE WRITING ON THE.)

'At least she wasn't in the toilet.'

'Ah, Miguel! Thank you for pointing that out. Right. For starters... Damn me, he's gone again!'

Descriptions, Theory of. Bertrand Russell's only significant contribution to philosophy. 'The present King of France is bald. True or false?'

'You can put that where the monkey put its nuts.'

'Pete Waterman?'

'Keith Waterhouse, in fact, but the point holds.'

Design. All important. Publishers know this. The eyes consume a book before the brain (*see also* EYES).

'Get Dr A.C. Grayling's typescript down to Design, will you, Katie?'

See also EDITING; PUBLISHING.

Desirability stakes. *See* TAUNTON.

Detachment. Always 'Olympian'.

Details. Seldom welcome. 'Spare me the gory details, Inspector. Come along, Daphne.'

Detection. Television gives a false impression of what coppering is all about. It's 60% hard graft. Planting the evidence and questioning suspects round the groin? That's just the glamorous side.

'Evening all.'

Detectives, seasoned. Forever being shocked by what they see on Internet porn sites.

Developments. Always 'unexpected'.

Devil, the. 'Talk of the devil!'

'What?'

'Over there! In the corner. It's Dawn Airey!'

'So it is! Well I never!'

'I think I'll go and have a word – oh, oh! My mistake! It's not Dawn Airey. It's Mickey Skinner.'

'No! Not the big lad who played blind-side wing forward in England's grand slam-winning team of 1992?'

'The very same, Vernon. Will you ever forget his hit on his French opposite number, Marc Cécillon, in the World Cup quarter-final in Paris in 1991? The big Frenchman must have been knocked back ten yards at least.'

'If it had been Dawn Airey in the No. 6 shirt he'd have been knocked back twenty yards and the game would have been over.'

'Thank you, Susan. Well, well, well. I think I *will* go and have a word with him. I'm sure he won't mind. I won't be a moment.'

'Oh dear. Do you think you should? You remember what happened last time.'

'Don't fuss. I'll be fine.'

'Seems to be going all right. Mickey's offering him a drink.'

'Simon's refusing.'

'He's coming back.'

'You OK, Simon? You look a little shaken.'

'It wasn't Mickey Skinner. It was Dawn Airey after all.'

'What did she say about her tackle on the big Frenchman?'

'She can't remember it.'

'Probably got a touch of concussion. Channel 5?'

'Explains a lot.'

de Vivar, Rodrigo Díaz de (*c*.1043–99). Spanish soldier, nicknamed El Cid. In spite of losing an arm in a skirmish with the Turks, he fought against the King of Navarre and overcame the Navarrese champion in single combat.

See also CALDERON DE LA BARCA, PEDRO; GLUBB, JOHN BAGOT; MALLARMÉ, STÉPHANE; MAUPASSANT, GUY DE; RICHARD I; TURKS, A SKIRMISH WITH THE; VEGA, LOPE FELIX DE.

Diamond, Neil (1941–). American singer and composer of popular songs.

'Ah, Daphne! Back from the Ladies at last! In your lengthy absence we were discussing the work of Neil Diamond. One of the great back catalogues in pop, would you say?'

'You've got me there, Simon. Here's one, however: to be big in dance music for two decades – like Underworld, for instance – you'd need some luck, wouldn't you agree?'

'If you say so, Daphne. However...'

'Talking about luck, Daph...'

'Miguel! How thoughtful of you to notice us. Right, we're ready to order. For starters...'

'Hold up, John. I'm talking to Daphne. Ask yourself this, Daph: if Underworld hadn't got their break with a tampon ad in 1982, would their album *Dubnobasswithmyheadman* ever have happened?'

'Yeah, I take your point, but...'

'Most enlightening, Miguel, but I think...'

'Excuse me, John, but I'm still checking out Mr Pratley's bird, okay? So what is it, Daph? Pop or rock?'

'Pop that rocks.'

'Style?'

'Hm. Retro with a funky edge.'

'Beer or Bolly?'

'Bolly.'

'Fave club?'

'*Cake* in Bermondsey. "The Norty Niterie for Gals Only!"'

'For real. Moyles or Evans?'

'Evans. I rate his business sense.'

'Liam or Robbie?'

'Neither. I prefer Roberto. For sure!'

'If you say so. Best party trick?'

'Thanks to yoga I can put my legs behind my...'

'DAPHNE! That will be *quite* enough! I really can't imagine what...'

'I'd keep an eye on your bird if I was you, Mr Pratley. OK. Ready to order? I haven't got all night.'

'Yes. Now. Let's see. For starters... I can't believe it! He's gone again!'

Dickens, Charles (John Huffam) (1812–70). Like so many of our most sympathetic novelists, Dickens had no sympathy for his wife. His characters, like their creator, are searching for a vanished happiness. While the true nature of his relationship with Ellen Ternan, a young actress, is unknown, in later works, such as *Great Expectations*, themes of unrequited love begin to emerge.

Dibley, The Vicar of. *See* BEST TELEVISION IN THE WORLD, THE.

Die. 'Too old to rock. Too young to die.' Good headline for an obituary of Joe Strummer in a broadsheet.

See also STRUMMER, JOE.

Dietrich, Marlene, *originally* **Maria Magdalena Von Losch** (1901–92). Actress and cabaret performer.

'Give La Dietrich a lamp-post, a beret and a pair of fishnet stockings and she could make a trench coat sexier than a sequined brassière.'

'James Sherwood, *The Independent's* cutting-edge fashion guru?'

'A medicated out-patient from the Chelsea and Westminster Hospital, in fact, but I take your point.'

See also RAINWEAR.

Different, that's. Women have been known to behave badly too, you know.

'That's different.'

'I stand corrected!'

Dinner-party, an Islington. One of the endemic follies of our age is to confuse an Islington dinner-party with Real Life.

'And yet – ironically, perhaps – the chattering classes have as much right to be heard as Davina McCall or Jeremy Tarrant.'

'*Chris* Tarrant.'

'And him.'

'MIGUEL!'

See also NEWLY PAIRED-OFF THIRTYSOMETHINGS.

Diogenes (*c.*412–*c.*323 BC). Philosopher dubbed 'the Cynic'. Many anecdotes have attached themselves to his name, illustrating his exaggerated contempt for worldly matters: that he lived in a barrel; that when his contemporaries were preparing war against Macedonia he rolled in his barrel up and down the street in order, he said, that he might be busy too; that he got out of his barrel at midday and wandered around with a lantern, looking, he said, for an honest man; that when Alexander the Great asked whether he could do anything for him, he replied:

'Yes, you can get out of my way.'

Alexander countered by saying that had he not been Alexander he would have liked to have been Diogenes, a reply which, while graceful in the circumstances, raised difficult questions of transpersonal identity that the old Cynic chose not to take up on this occasion.

'Thank you, Susan.'

'Don't mention it. Happy to make a contribution.'

Disasters. Always 'unmitigated'.

Disasters, natural. God working out his purpose.

Disposal. At the end of the day, you can only use the players at your disposal.

See also BOTTOM LINE; DAY, AT THE END OF THE.

Distances. Excellent subject for a dinner-party conversation.

'Interestingly enough, Vernon, Susan and I have recently discovered that it's quicker these days to drive from the Cotswolds to Sloane Square than from Sloane Square to Belsize Park.'

'Except that it isn't.'

'Nor it is. Tell me, Vernon. Björk, the little Eskimo. Stacks up for you, does she?'

'I'm not sure if I'm familiar with her work.'

See also ESKIMOS WORKING IN THE UNITED KINGDOM; NEWLY PAIRED-OFF THIRTYSOMETHINGS.

Distinction. Often 'dubious'.

'If memory serves, it was your dubious distinction to have secured Anthony Worrall Thompson his first job in television!'

'Guilty as charged! That said, it was your boy Charlie, was it not, who had the dubious distinction of letting loose seventeen white rats among the dancing débutantes at Queen Charlotte's Ball in 1988?'

'*Touché!* I give you best!'

Divas. Always 'pint-sized'. Forever being sent reeling when their love lives go wrong.

See also AGUILERA, CHRISTINA; BABES, STRESSED-OUT POP; BEAUTIES, SHATTERED; FANS; GATES, GARETH; HALLIWELL, GERI; MINOGUE, KYLIE; PALS, SHOWBIZ; SHOWBIZ WORLD, THE.

Divorce. Always 'painful' or 'bitter'; often 'messy'.

'Time is the great healer, of course.'

'How true! You remember the Pilkington-Smythes?'

'I don't think I do.'

'Tubby and Prue?'

'I'm none the wiser.'

'Sadly they've split. However, I bumped into Tubby only the other day. "Since our divorce," he said, "Prue has become my best friend."'

'Well, there you are.'

'I read recently that when downsizing after a messy divorce, the average woman wants to buy a house for under £220,000, which keeps stamp duty down to 1%.'

'Very sensible.'

'Indeed. Ideally, she would like a two-bedroomed property on the outskirts of Chichester. Research shows that prime areas around Chichester include West Wittering, West Itchenor, Bosham and Emsworth.'

'How jaw-dropping. I have nothing to add to that, I must confess.'

Divorcées. Always 'attractive'.

Doctors. They should stop playing God.
'You can't find the soul with a scalpel.'
'Sounds like one for *The Oldie*, Richard.'

Doctor Zhivago (David Lean, 1965). In spite of a charming performance by Julie Christie as the woman torn by conflicting loves
in revolutionary Russia, the real star of Pasternak's masterpiece is
Freddie Young's Oscar-winning cinematography. Picturesque and
brutal, its eternal themes and tragic undertow perfectly express
the author's epic vision.
See also LAWRENCE OF ARABIA; LEAN, DAVID.

Dogs. There are no problem dogs, only problem owners.
See also LABRADORS.

Donald, Allan (1966–). With Shaun Pollock he formed the finest
opening partnership in fast-bowling history.
'I don't hope to see a better in my lifetime.'
See also AKRAM, WASIM and YOUNIS, WAQAR; AMBROSE, CURTLEY and
WALSH, COURTNEY; BOWES, BILL and LARWOOD, HAROLD; HALL,
WESLEY and GRIFFITH, CHARLIE; HOLDING, MICHAEL and ROBERTS,
ANDY; LILLEE, DENNIS and THOMPSON, JEFF; LINDWALL, RAY and
MILLER, KEITH; MCGRATH, GLENN and LEE, BRETT; TRUEMAN, FREDDIE
and STATHAM, BRIAN.

Dons, old-style bachelor. Eschewing arid specialization, the old-
style bachelor don was seen at his best in conversation.
'Or, in the case of Sir Isaiah Berlin, in the medium-length *éloge*.'
'How true! It was Sir Isaiah's agreeable habit, I believe, to take his
tutorials at the Ritz Hotel in London.'
'Where the service, I'm sure, was better than it is here! MIGUEL!'
See also BOWRA, SIR MAURICE; PIPE-SMOKING SODOMITES; SPARROW,
JOHN; SPECIALIZATION.

Don't mention the war. *See* AGE, THE VICTORIAN.

Doodlebug. *See* BLITZ, THE.

Doorstep, culture on your. *See* SALAMANCA.

Door-to-door encyclopedia salesmen. No one has ever seen one.
See also ISLE OF MAN.

Dordogne, the. *See* ENGLAND, MISSHAPEN MEN FROM THE NORTH OF.

Doubles. In tennis, singles and doubles are entirely different games.
In doubles, return of serve is all important, as it is in singles.
See also SET, THE SEVENTH GAME IN EACH.

Doubles, mixed. Always played in a marvellous spirit.
   'Oh I say! What a lovely moment of humour!'
   'Thank you, Mark.'
   'I'm Virginia, in fact.'
   'So you are. Back to you in the studio, then, Chrissie.'
   'In fact I'm John.'
   'Of course.'

Doubt. Not the opposite of faith but an important part of faith. No
need to explain why.
   'Faith without doubt is mere knowledge.'
   'Sounds like one for *The Oldie*, Richard.'
See also FAITH.

Draughts. One should never sit in a draught.

Dream on, pal. Contrary to popular opinion, Andrew Marr has
never used the construction 'dream on, pal' in any of his delightfully informal commentaries or chatty columns in *The Daily
Telegraph*.
See also GO FIGURE; MARR, ANDREW; SEX SYMBOLS.

Driberg, Tom (1911–89). British Labour politician. On mention of
his name, cry 'Good old Tom!' No need to explain why.
See also BRITAIN'S NUCLEAR SECRETS; HUSSAR, THE GAY.

Dry-cleaning, same day. 'They'll be ready on Thursday.'

Duck, Donald. In a humorous column, or in a speech by the Prince of Wales, it might be amusing to refer to him as 'that estimable fowl, Donald Duck!'

See also ALFRED; BUSTS; DANE, HAMLET THE MOODY; KEATS, JOHN; MEADOWS, MY POULTERER, THE ESTIMABLE MR; VARIETY, BIRDS OF THE FEATHERED.

Dumbing down. *See* ACCESSIBLE.

Dumped. Always 'unceremoniously'.

See also MATT, ELECTRICIANS CALLED.

Duncan, Isadora (1878–1927). Dancer in the modern mode. Self-taught, she based her technique on a study of Greek vases and of natural phenomena, such as the movement of birds wheeling in the sky. Thus in her best work she achieved an unusual kind of poetry in motion. She died tragically and left no school.

Duncan Smith, Iain (1954–). The 'Quiet Man' of politics.
  'Iain who?'
  'Pray cease! You'll have me in the aisles!'
  'He's had a charisma bypass, that's what I always say.'
  'Churchill he ain't!'

See also PERUGIA, UNIVERSITY OF.

Dunces' colleges. *See* MAGDALENE COLLEGE, CAMBRIDGE; PERUGIA, UNIVERSITY OF.

Duran, Roberto (1958–). Pound for pound the finest welterweight ever to pull the gloves on.
  'I don't hope to see a better in my lifetime.'

See also ALI, MUHAMMAD; ARMSTRONG, HENRY 'HANK'; HAGLER, MARVIN; HEARNS, THOMAS 'THE HITMAN'; LEONARD, SUGAR RAY; LOUIS, JOE; MARCIANO, ROCKY; MOORE, ARCHIE; PEP, WILLIE; ROBINSON, SUGAR RAY.

Dying art, a. *See* EDITING.

Ealing comedy. British film comedy at its best. The French were the first to perceive this. Warm without being sentimental, gentle without being funny. Refer to 'the great days of Ealing'.

Early days. *See* LEADS.

Early retirement, opt for. *See* HARASSMENT, SEXUAL.

Earth, down to. In spite of their hectic lifestyles, some celebs manage to stay 'down to earth'.
   'And "relaxed"?'
   'Indeed.'
See also CELEBS; JONSSON, ULRIKA.

Eastwood, Clint (1930–). American film actor and director. His name on a marquee still spells box-office bonanza.
   'Except that it doesn't.'
   'Thank you, Susan. That said, there's an engaging irony in the fact that this legendary hard man of so many classic westerns should in real life be a cultured, sensitive man who writes agreeably unpretentious verses and has assembled the finest private collection of French impressionists outside France.'
See also CAGNEY, JAMES; MARVIN, LEE; PESCI, JOE; ROBINSON, EDWARD G.; WIDMARK, RICHARD.

Easy mistake to make. *See* BEN, DAN, JEREMY, WILL, CHARLIE, JULIAN, MARTIN, DANNY, JAMES AND JONNY.

Eaterie. A word that sits well in an occasional column.

See also EMBONPOINT; LIBATION; MEADOWS, MY POULTERER, THE ESTIMABLE MR; NOSHERIE.

Economists. If they're so clever why aren't they rich? Michael Parkinson has perceived this.

'I wouldn't trust them to run a pie-shop in Barnsley!'

See also BARNSLEY; PARKINSON, MICHAEL.

Ecstasy. Interestingly enough, more teenagers have died from eating porridge in the UK since 1987 than from taking the dance-culture drug Ecstasy.

'A sobering statistic indeed. However, to publicize it widely would be to send out quite the wrong signals.'

'Indeed. It might persuade vulnerable young people to experiment with more dangerous drugs.'

'Like paracetamol?'

'There's no need to be facetious, Susan.'

See WALL, THE WRITING ON THE.

Editing. A dying art, needless to say. Should be 'discreet' or 'tactful'.

'These days we cannot expect the editors at Hodder Headline to know whether "*Je suis encore tout étourdie*" or "*Je suis toute étourdie*" is correct, but they might have suspected that if the two usages appear within two pages of each other, one of them is likely to be an error.'

'A delightful rebuke! Philip Howard?'

'No. I just thought of it myself.'

'I should have known.'

'Thank you, Susan.'

See also DESIGN; PUBLISHING.

Educated. *See* BOOT, LEFT.

Education, formal. There is more than one kind of wisdom. Some people, lacking a formal education, are yet wise in the ways of the world.

'I would cite my poulterer, the estimable Mr Meadows.'

'A true philosopher?'

'Indeed. And one of nature's gentlemen.'

'I have a sudden urge to hang myself.'

'Thank you, Susan.'

See also INTELLECTUAL, LIBERAL; MEADOWS, MY POULTERER, THE ESTIMABLE MR; WALL, THE WRITING ON THE.

Edward II (1284–1327). King of England from 1307.

See also BELLAMY'S VEAL PIES; CHARLES I; LAST WORDS.

Effective. Very effective, but you won't find it in the coaching manual.

'Thank you, Richie.'

Eggheads. *See* ATKINSON, RON; BRAINBOX, A BIT OF A.

Eggs. Six a week and you are a dead man.

Eisenstein, Sergei (1898–1948). Latvian-born Soviet film director. Eisenstein was the first film-maker to realize that the crowd could itself be the principal character in a film. In any list of the ten greatest films of all time, at least two by Sergei Eisenstein would have to be included.

'I've never seen one.'

Elephants. Forever sitting on pensioners and turning their dream holidays into a nightmare.

'In June 2002, a dream holiday turned into a nightmare for pensioner Albert Toggle when his wife, Effie, was sat on by an elephant.'

'*The Sunday Times's* hilarious new "Wacky Facts!" feature?'

'No. *The News of the World's* "Real Life" column, but I take your point.'

See also GRANNIES ON HOLIDAY; *NEWS OF THE WORLD, THE*; PENSIONERS.

Elfin American actress, the. *See* 45 IN APRIL.

Eliot, T.S. (1888–1965). American-born poet and critic. He usually floats like a cork on a sea of knowledge but *Old Possum's Book of Practical Cats* shows him in an agreeable light.

See also CATS; OPPOSITES.

Ellison, Jennifer (1979–). Actress. Jen is weighing up the options.
See also BABES, *BROOKIE*; OPTIONS.

El Tel. Contrary to received opinion, during the 2002 World Cup Finals the former England manager Terry Venables really did say: 'You would have thought that if any team could put up a decent wall it would be China.'
See also COACH, THE.

E-mails. One should always be behind with one's e-mails.
   'Agreeable lunch at the Ivy with Anthony, Susannah, Trinny, Michael and Katie. Then back to the office to catch up with my e-mails.'

Embonpoint. A word that sits well in an occasional column.
See also EATERIE; HOSTELRY; LIBATION; MEADOWS, MY POULTERER, THE ESTIMABLE MR; NOSHERIE.

Émigrés. They earn their living by giving guitar lessons and making salads.
   'I see that you are familiar with Flaubert's *Bouvard et Pécuchet*.'
   'Yes, thank you, Jolyon. Tell me, Vernon. This month's *Goose Fat and Garlic*. Read it, have you?'

Emotions. Today's new man has learned how to vocalize his emotions, but is he any happier?
   'I'd rather not discuss that, if you don't mind, Susan. Tell me, Vernon. Lulu. The little singer from the Gorbals. See the point of her, do you?'
See also MAN, THE NEW; PARSONS, TONY.

Empty-nesters. Empty-nesters no longer settle for a well-tended rose garden in the shires and the occasional weak sherry before dinner.
   'Nor do they. I gather that many are selling up for livelier locales and more exciting lifestyles.'
   'So stand aside, DINKS (*Double Income No Kids!*), the CLAMS (*City Living Active Matures!*) are coming to town!'

'What on earth are they talking about? You coming to the toilet, Trace?'

'I certainly am.'

'Susan?'

'After you. Come along, Daphne.'

'Lead the way.'

'So – to continue in the absence of the ladies. I gather that Robbie Fogden, a 56-year-old semi-retired businessman, has sold his house in Devon and has returned to his roots in West London with his wife Maureen, also 56.

'"Now we can enjoy what the capital has to offer," says Robbie. Highlights have included a recent boat trip down the Thames to Westminster, followed by a ride on the London Eye.'

'Your young friends, Con. They spend a lot of time in the Ladies.'

England, misshapen men from the north of. Forever treading warily through the Dordogne with their mountainous trouser-suited wives in search of farm houses to renovate.

'What do you think, Sidney?'

'It is quiet.'

'Yes, it is quiet.'

'Spacious lounge-room.'

'Nice bathroom.'

'Yes, nice bathroom, Elsie. Two toilets. That's unusual.'

'One of them's a *boudoir*, Sidney.'

'The French!'

'Good kitchen.'

'Quite a nice view.'

'All the amenities.'

'We should definitely think about it.'

'Yes. We should definitely think about it, Sidney.'

See also PAROS, LARDY GIRLS WITH BUBBLY PERSONALITIES ON HOLIDAY IN.

English. You can't get more English than runner beans.

'Thank you, Rick.'

See also BRITTEN, BENJAMIN; SAUSAGE, THE ENGLISH.

Entwistle, John (1944-2002). The quiet man of The Who; a gentle giant.

'Surely it was Pete Townshend who, when Entwistle died, observed: "The Ox has left the building."'

'That said it all.'

Envy of the world. *See* INSTITUTIONS, OUR.

Epstein, Brian (1932–67). Liverpudlian impresario. Like many people with a full address book, the troubled entrepreneur found there were times when no one was in.

See also BYRON, LORD GEORGE; CASS, MAMA; HENDRIX, JIMI; HUTCHENCE, MICHAEL; JONES, BRIAN; JOPLIN, JANIS; MONROE, MARILYN; TOULOUSE-LAUTREC, HENRI; WALES, DIANA, PRINCESS OF.

Equal parenting. We may have embraced equal parenting, but a male nanny will still raise eyebrows at the school gate.

Eriksson, Sven-Göran. *See* ESKIMOS WORKING IN THE UNITED KINGDOM.

Eroticism in the cinema. As that wise man Barry Norman has pointed out, what makes a scene erotic in the cinema is understatement, a mere suggestion of sexual tension – not naked bodies and buttocks going up and down. For Norman, the most erotic scene in cinema history is the moment in Hitchcock's *The Thirty-Nine Steps* when Robert Donat's hand almost brushes Madeleine Carroll's knee.

'You surprise me. I'd have thought he'd have chosen the scene in *The Thomas Crown Affair* in which Steve McQueen and Faye Dunaway play chess.'

'Yes, that *was* boring.'

'Susan! Back from the Ladies...'

'But not as boring as the scene in *Tom Jones* in which Tom Finney and Susannah York gnawed endlessly on chicken legs.'

'I think you mean *Albert* Finney, Susan.'

'If you say so, Simon. In which Tom Finney and Albert Finney ate chicken legs *al fresco*. Either way, it's Mrs Norman I feel sorry for.'

'Yes, thank you, Susan. Tell me, Vernon. Sigourney Weaver in *Alien*? She set a new template for the kick-arse heroine, would you say?'

'I'll take your word for it. You're the expert.'

'Indeed he is. He has this fantasy in which Sigourney...'

'We won't go into that, thank you, Susan. Miguel!'

See also HEROINES, KICK-ARSE; WALL, THE WRITING ON THE.

Escapologists, experienced. *See* AGENDA; MANCHESTER UNITED.

Eskimos working in the United Kingdom. *See* BJÖRK; ERIKSSON, SVEN-GÖRAN; FROSTRUP, MARIELLA; GUDJOHNSEN; EIDUR; GUD-JONSSON, JOEY; JONSSON, ULRIKA; MAGNUSSON, MAGNUS and MAGNUSSON, SALLY; SCHMEICHEL, PETER; SOLSKJAER, OLE GUNNAR; TOKSVIG, SANDI.

Estimable. A word that sits well in a humorous column. 'My poulterer, the estimable Mr Meadows...'

See also ABLUTIONS; ABODE; EDUCATION, FORMAL; EMBONPOINT; HOSTELRY; INFELICITOUS; LIBATION; NOSHERIE; THESPIAN.

Etruria. The source of all ancient vases.

Europeans, southern. Always 'mercurial'.

'I gather that the mercurial little Spaniard has already scored 20 goals in the current campaign.'

'An interesting observation, if I may say so, Vernon. I doubt whether a Scotsman could be mercurial. Or an inhabitant of the West Midlands.'

'Or a Canadian, come to that.'

'Definitely not a Canadian! The mercurial Canadian? The mind recoils. On the other hand, a Welshman might be mercurial. They called Lloyd George "the Welsh Wizard", after all.'

'Hurumph hurumph!'

'Goats and monkeys! It's Dr Death again. Yes, Jolyon?'

'Interestingly enough, the richly talented Welsh footballer Billy Meredith was also referred to as "the Welsh Wizard" and, by a deliciously deft verbal association with the snowy-maned Liberal premier, as "the Lloyd George of Welsh football"!'

'Thank you, Dr Death.'

'Don't mention it, Mr Wattlebotham.'

'Wigglesworth.'

'If you say so.'

Eurostar. *See* ROCKET SCIENCE.

Evans, Dame Edith (1891–1978). She was no great beauty, but she became beautiful as soon as she stepped onto a stage.

'Who else could have played the part of Juliet the age of 69?'

'I always say that Juliet is one of those problem parts. By the time an actress is old enough to play it, she is – cruel irony! – too old to play it!'

'In old Bill Shakespeare's day, of course, the part was taken by a boy.'

'What's that got to do with it?'

'I haven't the faintest idea. Tell me, Vernon. The big lad Flintoff. Do you think he has the big-match temperament?'

See also DENCH, DAME JUDI.

Evening all. *See* FLYING SQUAD, THE.

Events, forthcoming. 'Sat. 15th March. 10.30 a.m.–1.30 p.m. Lady Margaret School, Parson's Green, SW6. Indoor Car Boot Sale. Admission 50p. Concessions 30p. Refreshments available.'

'Sounds like one to miss, Daphne.'

'I'm with you there, Vernon.'

Evidence. Forever being tampered with (*see* MARJORIBANKS, MAJOR).

Evil. Sometimes 'takes on a human face'. *The Daily Mail* has perceived this.

'When evil takes on a human face the time has come to think think the unthinkable.'

'The return of the noose?'

'Indeed.'

See also DAILY MAIL, THE.

Exceptions that prove the rule. *See* IRONY; LOVE, FALLING IN.

Exterior. Always 'gruff'. Yet a gruff exterior may conceal a kind heart.

'Surely it was that robust jurist Mr Justice Melford Stevenson who said after a difficult case: "I must confess I cannot tell whether you're innocent or guilty. I'm giving you three years. If you're guilty, you've got off lightly. If innocent, let this be a lesson to you."'

'Wise words indeed.'

'Wot a total twat, that's wot I say.'

'Thank you, Sharon…'

'Tracey.'

'Of course. Nonetheless, a few more like Sir Melford on the bench and there might be less risk of being mugged at a cash machine by a coloured gentleman in a canary-yellow pumpkin hat.'

'He wouldnt b 2 clever as a mugger wearin' a canary yello pumkin hat.'

'I dare say he wouldn't, but that has nothing to do with the point I'm making.'

See also JUDGES, HIGH COURT.

Extremists. What all extremists fear most, of course, is the moderation of those who oppose them.

See also ROBESPIERRE, MAXIMILIEN.

Eyes. The eyes taste the food first (*see also* DESIGN). The Japanese were the first to perceive this.

'Surely on a list of the ten greatest films of all time at least two directed by Akira Kurosawa would have to be included.'

'You've lost me. Your point is?'

'Since we were discussing the Japanese I thought this was a good moment to mention their greatest *auteur*.'

'What's that got to do with the fact that the eyes taste the food first?'

'If it ever arrives!'

'Good point. MIGUEL!'

See also KUROSAWA, AKIRA.

Facetiousness. Contrary to public belief, the line, 'A man's been killed, Sergeant. This is no time for facetiousness,' really did occur in an episode of *Inspector Morse* written by Malcolm Bradbury, once Professor of Modern Literature at the University of East Anglia.
See also SARCASM.

Fairy tales. Often about to end.
   'For Whitney Houston, the fairy tale was about to end.'
See also HOUSTON, WE HAVE A PROBLEM.

Faith. Faith is the evidence of things not seen. It creates the truth to which it adheres.
   'Sounds like one for *The Oldie*, Richard.'
See also DOUBT.

False. 'Interestingly enough, Vernon, a false theory often yields more useful information than a true one.'
   'Could you give us an example?'
   'Indeed. Suppose you were now to ask me the time. I might say "It's between 12 noon on the 19th of November and 12 noon on the 20th – which would undoubtedly be true. However, were I to say, and without looking at my watch, that it's exactly 9.33 p.m. ...'
   'Extraordinary. It feels like 3 a.m. at least.'
   'Please, Susan. Allow me to continue. Were I to say that it's exactly 9.33 p.m., this would undoubtedly be false – albeit far more helpful than the true theory previously provided.'
   'Fascinating! Popper?'
   'Not when I'm drinking, thank you.'
See also POPPER, SIR KARL.

Fame, overnight. And yet, in an odd way, we've always been famous to ourselves.

Fame, the pain behind the. 'Davina McCall's Troubled Past.'
'Sounds like one for *Real Lives*, Rebekah.'
See also MCCALL, DAVINA.

Fame, the rise to. Often 'meteoric'.

Family, the victim's. Forever on the BBC's 6 o'clock *News* demanding justice.
See also MOTHER, THE VICTIM'S.

Fanfares. Always 'loud'.

Fans. Forever being sent reeling when a pint-sized diva or Tinseltown favourite hits the streets wearing mumsy slippers and baggy jeans. When 39-year-old single mum Jodie Foster appeared in public in flip-flops and a lambswool cardie, her fans were stunned. A Tinseltown insider explained:
'Jodie has really taken to motherhood. These days she often looks more like the local librarian than a Hollywood superstar!'
'We did it for the fans, Barry.'

Fantasies, sexual. Should never be satisfied in reality. Women know this. The indulgence of one's sexual fantasies leads to a craving for increasingly bizarre experiences. A lonely downward path to eventual insanity.
'This may interest you, Vernon. I read this morning in the *Telegraph* that Delta Goodrem, the Soap Stunner from Downunder, was "totally grossed out when chatted up by wrinkly rocker Gene Simmons".'
'I'm not surprised. I saw her in *Spartacus* and she didn't look too good even then.'
'No, no. You misunderstand me, Vernon. Not Jean Simmons, the film actress. *Gene* Simmons, of the rock group Kiss.'
'Of course. A silly mistake on my part.'
'The *Telegraph* went on to reveal that Mr Simmons had, as they

put it, "shagged 3,000 hot babes and enjoyed a steamy affair with soft-porn star Shannon Tweed".'

'I don't know what to say.'

See also RIMBAUD, ARTHUR.

Fantasy, Brazilian. 'Oh my word! A goal straight from the storehouse of Brazilian fantasy!'

'Thank you, John.'

See also MOTSON, JOHN; OLD TRAFFORD.

Fashionably liberal pronouncements on social justice. *See* CARING CLERGYMEN.

Fashion fun. Is it harmless fashion fun for kids – or another step on the road to loss of innocence?

'Sounds like one for *Richard and Judy*.'

Fatalism. A theory famously upheld by Ryle's paradox. 'The statement "You will die by drowning," is either true or false. If true, true now. If false, false now. Therefore there is no point in teaching sailors to swim.'

'There's no answer to that!'

'As Eric and Ernie would have said!'

'Yes their iz.'

'Oh dear. Yes, Sharon?'

'Tracey. Ryle woz refutin fatalism. Wot he went on 2 say woz that the statements about drowning in the future were tru or false just becoz people did, or didnt, take swimmin lessons. U thick or sumthing?'

'Yes, well, thank you, Tracey. This may interest you, Vernon. Did you know that the flatulence produced daily by a single sheep could provide sufficient power for a van to travel 25 miles?'

'I confess I didn't.'

'Please, Simon! Not while we're eating. Not that we are.'

'Nor are we. MIGUEL!'

See also RYLE, GILBERT.

Fate, this must be. *See* AGAIN.

Father. Always 'proud'. This is a mystery.
  'Seen your boy lately?'
  'Just a phase.'

Fat men. Always surprisingly light on their feet.

Faustian pact. *See* MOORE, DUDLEY.

Favourite sons. *See* BUDAPEST.

Feeding frenzy. *See* MEDIA, THE.

Feltz, Vanessa. *See* BLONDE BOMBSITES.

Feminine side, getting in touch with one's. *See* MAN, THE NEW.

Feminists, American. In the 1970s, the Irish influence in Boston caused feminists to booby-trap their genitals with industrial dynamite and then to incite rape attacks in crowded supermarkets.

Ferguson, Professor Niall (1965–). Celebrity historian. Contrary to popular belief, Professor Ferguson has never used any of the following words or constructions in his television programmes: 'At the end of the day, James I was a bit of a tosser'; 'Henry VIII executed a neat one-two with Cardinal Wolsey'; 'Fannying about'; 'Not if I see you first, sunshine'; 'George IV was well hammered at his wedding'; 'Pear-shaped'; 'Pushing the envelope'.
See also HISTORIANS, CELEBRITY; HISTORY, THE NEW; STARKEY, DR DAVID.

Ferguson, Sir Alex (1941–). Foul-mouthed soccer supremo. It has been said of Ferguson that he didn't create his own values. He inherited them from an engineering shop in his native Glasgow. They came with his toolbox and he could no more reinvent them than he could reinvent himself.
  'Toilet, trace?'
  'After u, shar.'
See also AGENDA.

Ferry, Bryan (1945–). Pop singer previously with Roxy Music. He has been described as the triumph of artifice. What he is about is that he isn't about anything.

Fever, chess. Chess fever gripped western Poland in 1739 to such an extent that the wheat harvest was not gathered and thousands of people starved to death in the cold winter of 1739–1740.

'As yet there is no computer in the world that can beat an International Master at chess.'

'Except that there is.'

'I stand corrected.'

Field day. *See* MEDIA, THE.

Film acting. More difficult than it looks. The great stars of the cinema are always themselves, but being yourself on camera is the hardest thing of all.

'Surely it was that wise man Barry Norman who pointed out that in this regard Olivier himself was ready to learn from Marilyn Monroe.'

'Either him or that other bollocky old film fan.'

'And to whom are you referring, Susan?'

'Michael Parkinson.'

'It's very easy to criticize, you know.'

'To coin a phrase?'

'I didn't say that.'

'You surprise me.'

See also MONROE, MARILYN; NORMAN, BARRY; PARKINSON, MICHAEL; WALL, THE WRITING ON THE.

Final, the Cup. It's all about pressure on the day.

'The lads have been playing out of their skins all season, Barry. Then they come to Wembley and their legs go. They freeze on the day.'

'Thank you, Ron.'

'On the other hand, some lads come of age during the Cup Final.'

See also CUP, THE; FORM.

Finalists, reality show. Forever revealed as having had sex across the bonnet of a Toyota Corolla.

'TV Popstars Finalist Sarah Harding Had Sex Romp Over Bonnet At The Jolly Roger!'

'Sounds like one for us, Rebekah!'

See also NEWS OF THE WORLD, THE; WADE, REBEKAH.

Finest, Fleet Street's. *See* REPORTER.

Finish. Always 'emphatic', except when 'disappointing'.

Fit. There's all the difference in the world between being fit and being match fit. Why this should be, nobody knows.

'A thought occurs. Is that why Denis Bergkamp, the skilful little Dutchman, so often picks up a niggle in the opening exchanges?'

'I haven't the faintest idea.'

Five News. Forever sending its cameras into the street and asking hairdressers and bar staff for their views on a wide range of international matters.

'I ope posh and becks fall in luv with Spain and never cum back. *or revoy* 2 de pair o dem'. Racey's Rockett.

'A transsexual on Big Bruv? Wot next? Do C4 think this will boost the ratings? Do u hav 2 b gay, irish or "other" or all 3 2 get on TV these days?' Dengal, Devizes.

'Bush wil 1 day try 2 take Britain the same way hes tryin 2 take the rest o the world. sum 1 shld try 'n' stop him B4 its 2 late.' Foggy, Newcastle.

'Is it jus me or is that bird on the latest Sainsburys ad a pukka babe?' Dano, Minehead.

'Dyke or not Sam Fox is still the fittest girl ever.' Jumbo, Aldershot.

'Mssg 4 justin – if britney dont want u im hre 4 u 24/7.' Joss, Bishops Stortford.

'Kerry… c u nex week at da club. Drinks r on me.' Stevo, Plymouth.

See also AS EVER; MIDLANDS, SHELL-SUITED WORKING-CLASS WOMEN FROM THE; PEOPLE, REAL.

Flake, a total. Contrary to popular opinion, Dr David Starkey has never called Mary, Queen of Scots 'a total flake' in any of his illustrated television lectures.

See also ACCESSIBLE; HARASSMENT, SEXUAL; HISTORIANS, CELEBRITY; HISTORY, THE NEW; STARKEY, DR DAVID.

Flat. 'Are you following me, Simon? Are you actually *following* me? That is *so* pathetic! What do you mean, it's *your* flat? We'll see what my lawyer has to say about that!'

See WALL, THE WRITING ON THE.

Flaubert, Gustave (1821–80). He suffered throughout his life from ill-health brought on by coffee poisoning, but this in no way stinted his quest for literary perfection. He once spent three days trying to arrive at the correct word for a certain context.

See also ÉMIGRÉS.

Flirtation. Always 'brief'.

Florence. Always a disappointment. A kind of walking museum, crammed with works of art, many of which date back to the 15th century.

'Not to forget the many lively bars for young people.'

'Indeed. Nor the many agreeable boulevards where visiting English *littérateurs* can, for as little as £50, be disciplined over fire hydrants by Brazilian transsexuals.'

See also ALDEBURGH; AUSTEN, JANE.

Flutter. Always 'occasional'.

'I'm not really a betting man. I just have the occasional flutter.'

Flying Squad, the. Forever swooping on addresses in South London.

'Evening all. Nothing personal.'

See also DEALERS, DRUG.

Foix. The administrative centre of Ariège *département*. The court of Gaston Phoebus, count of Foix from 1343, was famous for its luxury. Visiting Foix is like stepping back in time.

See also ARIÈGE; AUDE; AUTOIRE; AVEYRON; BLESLE; CONQUES; COURSEGOULES; DOMME; LOCRONAN; LOT; LOZÈRE; SAINT-MÉDARD-DE-PRESQUE; SOLOGNE.

Food for thought. *See* ANIMALS.

Football. A game of two halves.

'In fairness, Barry, they stuffed us none–two in the first half. But then we changed ends and they stuffed us none–two in the second half.'

'Thank you, Kevin.'

See also FORM; GAME, THE.

For a woman, surprisingly well informed. *See* COMING SECOND; HENDRICK, MIKE.

Ford, Glenn (1916–). Canadian-born Hollywood actor. A reliable performer, but it is unlikely that anyone under the age of 60 will remember his work.

Ford, John (1895–1973). Film director. He wanted to be a tug-boat captain but God made him a poet.

Forensic. *See* BOYS; SCIENTISTS.

Forever hold thy peace, speak now or. *See* ARIÈGE.

Forewarned is forearmed. *See* ABUSE, VERBAL.

Form. 'When the whistle goes at 3 o'clock form goes out of the window. It's just eleven lads against eleven other lads.'

'Thank you, Mark.'

See also FOOTBALL; JUST ANOTHER GAME.

Former glory. *See* BUILDINGS, OLD.

Fornicating in the streets. *See* MARCUSE, HERBERT.

45 in April. 'It's hard to believe that the elfin American actress will be 45 in April. She has the skin of a 22-year-old.'

'Indeed she has. But behind the flawless complexion there is an unmistakable fragility. I can't help wondering whether the Tinseltown vamp is Tinseltown victim.'

'Sacrificed on the altar of our fantasies?'

'Precisely.'

See also MONROE, MARILYN.

49-year-olds. Forever being pronounced 'dead on arrival' after being rushed to hospital in an ambulance.

See also AMBULANCES; 47-YEAR-OLDS.

41-year-olds. Forever stepping forward to say they were date-raped twenty years ago.

47-year-olds. Always in a 'stable condition' after being rushed to hospital in an ambulance.

See also AMBULANCES; ARRIVAL, DEAD ON; 49-YEAR-OLDS.

42-year-olds. Forever claiming that they were abused as children by a close member of the family. Happily, they were able to suppress the memory until they were old enough to deal with it.

Forurzeetullbejerstanuzzèreguème. *See* JUST ANOTHER GAME.

Fosse, Bob (1927–87). American choreographer and film director. With Fosse the camera became another dancer. What this means no one can guess.

'Surely it was of Fosse that that wise man Barry Norman said, "With the impeccable timing of the true professional, Bob Fosse chose the opening night of his new Broadway musical to drop dead of a heart attack."'

'In fact, Norman was talking about Gower Champion, the former Hollywood hoofer, who, with his sister Marge, graced many a big-screen epic, including *Show Boat* (1955). Your point holds, nonetheless.'

Foster, Jodie. *See* FANS; INSIDERS, TINSELTOWN.

Foucault, Michel (1926–84). French philosopher and writer. It is surely no coincidence that this most French of intellectuals should have chosen late in life to embark on a study of sexuality as his *chef d'oeuvre*. Who but the French could have produced a Michel Foucault?

Foyle's War. *See* HORNBY, MRS.

France profonde, La. As that wise man Jonathan Meades has observed, stroll through any wood in *La France profonde* and you'll come across your bank manager and his family happily picking *chanterelles* and *cèpes*.

'Shows how much he knows. My bank manager has never heard of *La France profonde*, never mind picked *chanterelles* there.'

'He wasn't specifically referring to your bank manager, Daphne.'

'My God, he is cute, though.'

'Your bank manager?'

'No. Roberto. And my bank manager, come to that.'

See also GASTRONOMIC REVOLUTION.

Franco, Francisco, *in full* **Francisco Paul Hermenegildo Teodilo Franco Bahamondo** (1892–1975). Spanish dictator.

'I'd be the last person on earth to defend *El Caudillo* for the many excesses carried out during his regime, but at least you could enjoy your evening *paseo* down Barcelona's celebrated *Ramblas* without being offered drugs or having pornography thrust under your nose.'

'We should have been so lucky.'

'Yes, thank you for that, Susan.'

See also KEANE, ROY.

Francophiles. Always 'unashamed'.

See also ARIÈGE; AUDE; AVEYRON; CONQUES; LOT; LOZÈRE; SOLOGNE.

Frank, Bruno (1887–1945). Interestingly enough, not an erroneous way of listing the British heavyweight boxer, Frank Bruno, in a reference book, but the name of a German writer born in Stuttgart who wrote historical novels such as *Die Fürstin* (1915) in a style reminiscent of Thomas Mann.

Frankel, Susannah (1970–). Fashion editor (*see* BRIEFS, SILK FLORAL; FRUMP; KNICKERS, FRENCH).

Fraser, Lady Antonia (1932–). Popular historian (*see* MARIE ANTOINETTE).

French, Dawn (1960–). Comedienne (*see* HUMOUR, A SENSE OF).

French cooking. French cooking draws attention to the cook; Italian cooking to the food.

'An insight due to Nigella Lawson, unless I'm much mistaken.'

'And, since we're in a Spanish restaurant, what about Spanish cooking?'

'You've got me there, I must confess.'

'It certainly takes a long time coming! Miguel!'

'For goodness sake relax, Simon. They can't have eyes in the back of their heads, you know.'

'At least we're not missing anything good on telly.'

'I disagree. Ali G's on Channel 4. He's brilliant.'

'Correction, Susan. He *was* brilliant.'

'He still...'

'Alas, what was satire has become celebration. However, I've remembered to set the video for *The Disappearing Osprey* on BBC2.' (*See also* AIREY, DAWN; *BADGER, THE DISAPPEARING*; *BARN OWL, THE DISAPPEARING*; *RED SQUIRREL, THE DISAPPEARING*.)

'Isn't that Antony Worrall Thompson?'

'On the telly?'

'No. Over there.'

'So it is. Actually, Susan and I swear by Sophie Grigson.'

'Ah! *La* Grigson!'

'*La* Grigson indeed!'

'Ah! Here's Miguel! And about time too!'

'Get a move on, bro.'

'That will be four crabcakes and...'

'Actually Daphne and I were going to have the gazpacho.'

'So you were! Correction!'

'Make your mind up, John. I haven't got all night.'

'Right. As starters, two crabcakes and two gazpachos.'

'Coming up!'

See also CORRECTION.

French impressionists. *See* CAGNEY, JAMES; EASTWOOD, CLINT; MARVIN, LEE; PESCI, JOE; ROBINSON, EDWARD G.; WIDMARK, RICHARD.

Friend, in a pig's arse. *See* ABODE; CRAPS, A CROWD OF; LARKIN, PHILIP; MEET THERE SOME TIME, WE MUST; 'VERS DE SOCIÉTÉ'.

Front office, the. The suits in the front office have ruined Hollywood. They can read a balance sheet but they can't read the heart of Joe Public (*see also* ACCOUNTANTS).

'Surely it was Michael Parkinson who pointed out "the old-style studio heads were illiterate first-generation immigrants, but they knew what put bums on seats".'

'Barry Norman, in fact, but the point holds. Louis B. Mayer could never watch *Gone With The Wind* without a tear in his eye.'

'That says it all.'

'Won't be long now before the nosh arrives!'

Frostrup, Mariella (1963–). Television presenter (*see also* ESKIMOS WORKING IN THE UNITED KINGDOM; JUDGES, BOOKER PRIZE).

Frump. The line between 'formal' and 'frump' isn't always an easy one to draw.

'Thank you, Susannah. Sounds like one for "Fashion & Style".'

See also FRANKEL, SUSANNAH.

Fun. Should be 'harmless'.

Funerals. Always say of the dead man: 'Extraordinary! I dined with him only last Thursday!'

Funny. Often 'painfully'.

Game, the. No one's bigger than the game, not even the prima donnas of Manchester United.

'In fairness, Ray, United are being given a masterclass in one-touch football by the skilful little Spaniards.'

'They've got it all to do, Ron.'

See also FOOTBALL; MANCHESTER UNITED; NAMES; STUFFING.

Game of two halves, a. *See* FOOTBALL.

Games, the Olympic. Not everyone wants them in their back yard. They can turn out to be a political football.

Gap-toothed Brazilian. *See* RONALDO.

Garonne Your Bike and Down the Lot. Good name for a book about the wines of southwest France.

See also LOT.

Gastronomic revolution. 'As that wise man Jonathan Meades recently remarked, if there has been a gastronomic revolution in England, how come all our elvers are exported to Spain?'

'They're more than welcome to them, in my opinion.'

See also FRANCE PROFONDE, LA.

Gates, Gareth (1983–). Pop singer (*see* DIVAS).

Gateway drug. *See* CANNABIS; CHOCOLATE.

Gazpacho. 'Interestingly enough, Vernon, the best gazpacho Susan and I ever had wasn't in a five-star "nosherie" in Madrid, but in a little family rest...'

'Actually, Simon, I didn't think...'

'Excuse me, Susan, I'm talking to Vernon. Where was I?'

'The best gazpacho you ever had.'

'Thank you. The best gazpacho Susan and I ever had was in a little family restaurant we found well off the beaten track near Badajoz. I won't divulge...'

'I'm sorry, Simon, but I...'

'...its whereabouts. Don't want the world and his wife beating a path to its door!'

See also CRABCAKES; WALL, THE WRITING ON THE.

Generalizations. Always 'wild'.

Genet, Jean (1910–86). French homosexual and writer. His turbulent life and early years spent in prison are reflected in his dramas, in which the characters act out bizarre and violent fantasies via elements of ritual, role-play and illusion.

See also VILLON, FRANÇOIS.

Geordie, the affable. 'This is likely to be the affable Geordie's last game at the highest level.'

See also AMERICAN GIRL, THE BIG; BRAZILIAN, THE GAP-TOOTHED; BULGARIAN GIRL, THE UNFANCIED; GHANAIAN, THE LIPPY; GLASWEGIAN, THE CHIRPY; INDIAN, THE WRISTY LITTLE; IRISHMAN, THE EASY-GOING; LANCASTRIAN, THE GRITTY; SPANIARD, THE MERCURIAL; TURKEY, THE CRUDE SLUGGER FROM.

Georgian town houses. They don't come cheap.

Germans, the. They organize these things better.

See also NEEDLESS TO SAY; THINGS, THESE; TRUE, SAD BUT.

Get, what you see is what you. *See* AIREY, DAWN; BIO-HAZARDS, HUMAN; BOYCOTT, GEOFF; FERGUSON, SIR ALEX; FIRM BUT FAIR; KEANE, ROY; KNOCKS, THE UNIVERSITY OF HARD; WADE, REBEKAH; WATERHOUSE, KEITH; WATERMAN, PETE.

Ghanaian, the lippy. *See* BENCH, THE.

Gibraltar. *See* ATMOSPHERE.

Gide, André (1869–1951). Like all French immoralists he remained at bottom a theologian *manqué*. Who but the French could have produced an André Gide?

Giving the media the slip. *See* CELEBRITIES.

Glasgow. Formerly something of a black spot in terms of that most indefinable of qualities, 'style', Glasgow has in the past few years experienced a cultural renaissance. A branch of Harvey Nichols has recently opened, a new four-star hotel is being built, and top chef Gordon Ramsay...

See also BIRMINGHAM; BRADFORD; BRISTOL; GLASWEGIAN, THE CHIRPY; LEEDS; MANCHESTER; NEWCASTLE; SHEFFIELD.

Glass, Philip (1937–). Composer of 'minimalist' music. Musical wallpaper, or an innovative exploration of minute harmonic and rhythmic shifts that has rescued contemporary classical music from the aleatory aridities of Boulez and Stockhausen? The debate continues.

'A kind of Nicholson Baker of contemporary art music, would you say?'

'Not really, no.'

'I stand corrected.'

Glaswegian, the chirpy. 'He's not only respected throughout Europe for his astute reading of the game, he's one of the nicest men in football.'

'I'll second that. In an age where the cheque-book speaks louder than loyalty, he's always remained close to his footballing roots.'

See also GEORDIE, THE AFFABLE; IRISHMAN, THE EASY-GOING; LANCASTRIAN, THE GRITTY; TURKEY, THE CRUDE SLUGGER FROM.

Glubb, John Bagot (1897–1986). British military commander and founder of the Arab Legion. Known as 'Glubb Pasha', he lost an arm in a skirmish with the Turks.

See also DE VIVAR, RODRIGO DÍAZ; MALLARMÉ, STÉPHANE; MAUPASSANT, GUY DE; RICHARD I; RIMBAUD, ARTHUR; VEGA, LOPE FELIX DE.

Goats and monkeys. *See* ATKINSON, RON.

God. His finger is in every pie.

Go figure. Contrary to popular opinion, Andrew Marr has never said 'go figure' in any of his agreeably relaxed commentaries or in his chatty column in *The Daily Telegraph*.

See also MARR, ANDREW.

Gogol, Nikolai Vasilievich (1809–52). Russian writer. In a fit of religious fervour he burned all his manuscripts and then starved himself to death. Only Mother Russia could have produced such a son. On mention of his name, cry: 'Heavens, how strange! Russia without Pushkin!'

See NOSE, THE.

Goldwyn, Sam (1882–1974). Film producer. A staunch upholder of family entertainment based on the American way of life, Goldwyn knew better than most what put bums on seats. The French were the first to perceive this.

Asked by a reporter from *Life* magazine to explain what he looked for in a picture, Goldwyn replied:

'I'll tell you what pictures are all about. Cunt and horses. Pardon me, Miss Casparry, but I said cunt and horses.'

'An agreeable anecdote, but you'll forgive me if I take it with a dose of salts.'

'As Sam himself might have said!'

'Raise the *Titanic*? It would have been cheaper to lower the Atlantic. My life!'

'That was Lew Grade.'

'If you say so.'

See also ACADEMICS; BUMS ON SEATS; EDUCATION, FORMAL.

Goodrem, Delta (1983–). Aussie soap-babe (*see* FANTASIES, SEXUAL).

Good taste. Always 'innate'. Sometimes 'suffocating'.

Grannies, 79-year-old. Forever taking the government to court over their inability to get a hip replacement.

See also PENSIONERS.

Grannies on holiday. Forever having their heads bitten off by lions in zoo stunts in Alicante.

'Sounds like one for *Real Lives*, Rebekah.'

See also ELEPHANTS; *NEWS OF THE WORLD, THE*; PENSIONERS; WADE, REBEKAH.

Gr8 4 c n soccer tossers b n b10 up by bad rs dormen. *See* ALCOHOLIC; WELLINGTON, THE.

Great healer, time is the. *See* DIVORCE.

Great ironies of history. Surely it is one of the great ironies of history that Richard Coeur de Lion and Saladin – two men who were obsessed with each other – never actually met.

'That said, Saladin continues to inspire Arab leaders to this day.'

Greco, El (1541–1614). The strangely elongated figures in his paintings were the result of a tragic defect in his eyesight. This was how he saw people and objects, so this was how he painted them.

'Thats so crap that!'

'You have a point to make, Sharon?'

'Im tracey, in fact – 'n' yes i hav.'

'We're all ears! This will be good!'

'N e fool cld c his odd shapes an that cant hav had n e thing 2 do wiv his isight bein' dodgy.'

'And why not? I fear the reason escapes me.'

'Thick as shit u. Woz u called planx at scool or wot? Spose his defect had been that 2 him dogs looked like cats. Sum 1 takes his dog round 2 b painted. El thingy wld hav painted wot in the event lkd 2 him like a cat. But only if it lkd like a dog 2 everyone else. If 2 the owner o the dog it now lkd like a cat it would hav lkd like a dog to el wotsit. Got it? If it was like *ordinary* figures he saw as elongated hed have lkd at the elongated figures in his paintings and said to himself, "Hullo! Wot the fuck r these?" Pardon my French – but sum people! Talk about stupid! i mean!'

'Thank you, Tracey. For the moment I'm dumbfounded.'

Greece, the real. *See* STRUMMER, JOE.

Green, Robson (1964–). Television actor. He's only 5ft 4in, but every inch a sex symbol.

Grey area, a. *See* AUTOBIOGRAPHY; CONCEPTUAL ART; NORMAL.

Grieve. We need time to grieve.
  'And space?'
  'If you say so.'
  'Would it be fair to say that it's too soon yet for closure, but that the healing process has begun?'
  'I think it would.'
See also RELATIVES.

Grigson, Sophie. *See* NEWLY PAIRED-OFF THIRTYSOMETHINGS.

Grind to a halt. *See* COMMUTERS; PUBLIC TRANSPORT.

Grit in the oyster, the. *See* ANIMALS, WILD.

Gritty Lancastrian, the. He's been blunting the edge of the world's most feared fast-bowling attacks for nigh-on two decades.
  'Not any longer, thank God. Charmless git.'
See also TURKEY, THE CRUDE SLUGGER FROM.

Grossed out. *See* FANTASIES, SEXUAL; GOODREM, DELTA.

Gudjohnsen, Eidur. *See* ESKIMOS WORKING IN THE UNITED KINGDOM.

Gudjonsson, Joey. *See* ESKIMOS WORKING IN THE UNITED KINGDOM.

Guilty, we are all. *See* BYRON, LORD GEORGE; CASS, MAMA; HENDRIX, JIMI; HUTCHENCE, MICHAEL; JONES, BRIAN; JOPLIN, JANIS; MONROE, MARILYN; MOON, KEITH; WALES, DIANA, PRINCESS OF.

Guilty as charged. *See* AGAIN; DISTINCTION.

Guinness, Sir Alec (1914–2000). An actor born with a capacity for anonymity. The illegitimate son of a barmaid named Agnes de Cuffe – from whom he disassociated himself at the age of 18 – his birth certificate bore a blank space where the name of his father should have been. With characteristic drollery, he called his memoirs *My Name Escapes Me*.

'A particularly agreeable anecdote comes to mind.'

'The floor is yours, Vernon!'

'On one occasion, fearing he'd been recognized, Guinness was disconcerted when, on handing in his hat at a hotel cloakroom, he wasn't asked for his name.'

'For Sir Alec, an alarming moment!'

'Indeed. Imagine his relief, when he discovered at the evening's end that his ticket bore the inscription, "Bald with glasses".'

'That says it all!'

See also 'MIDST, THE STRANGER IN OUR'.

Gullibility. Is there no limit to human gullibility? *The Daily Mail* has not been deceived.

See also ASYLUM-SEEKERS; BENDING OVER BACKWARDS TO HELP SCROUNGERS; WE BRITISH.

Gymslip gangsters. Contrary to received opinion, the majority of lawyers, accountants and middle managers seen lurking in school playgrounds are there to score their weekly stash from pubescent drug-fiends. Because the gymslip gangsters lack business acumen, their more worldly customers are able to make a small profit when redistributing their supply at fortysomething dinner parties in North London and SW6. *The Daily Mail* has been deceived.

See also DAILY MAIL, THE; POTTERS BAR.

H

Haddock, mad as a. *See* BOWYER, LEE.

Hagler, Marvin (1954–). Pound for pound the finest middleweight ever to pull the gloves on.

'I don't hope to see a better in my lifetime.'

See also ALI, MUHAMMAD; DURAN, ROBERTO; HEARNS, THOMAS 'THE HITMAN'; LEONARD, SUGAR RAY; MARCIANO, ROCKY; MOORE, ARCHIE; PEP, WILLIE; ROBINSON, SUGAR RAY.

Half-time, just before. Psychologically, the best time to score a goal.

'The lads had soaked up a lot of pressure out there, John, but they were beginning to get back into the game. Then the other lads scored what I'd call a soft goal just before half-time. Psychologically that was a real sickener. I saw my lads' heads go down.'

See also LADS, THE.

Hall, Wesley Winfield (1937–). With Charlie Griffith he formed the finest opening partnership in fast-bowling history.

'I don't hope to see a better in my lifetime.'

See also AMBROSE, CURTLEY and WALSH, COURTNEY; BRIGHTWELL BALDWIN and STEEPLE BUMPSTEAD; HOLDING, MICHAEL and ROBERTS, ANDY; COMPTON PAUNCEFOOT and UPTON SNODSBURY; LINDWALL, RAY and MILLER, KEITH; MCGRATH, GLENN and LEE, BRETT; TRUEMAN, FREDDIE and STATHAM, BRIAN.

Halliwell, Geri (1972–). The rumour that Geri Halliwell is being considered for the part of Olive in a remake of *On the Buses* is untrue, but significant for all that.

See also EROTICISM IN THE CINEMA; LEZZING IT UP.

Halves, a game of two. *See* FOOTBALL.

Hangman. A job passed down from father to son.

Happiest of metaphors, not perhaps the. *See* JAMES, C.L.R; KANT, IMMANUEL.

Happily married men. *See* TRANSVESTITES.

Happiness. Refer to the transitory nature of human happiness.
   'You can't get happiness on prescription, that's what I always say.'
   'Nor from banned substances.'
   'Seen your boy lately?'
   'Just a phase.'
See also JET TO SPAIN; NATURE, DAME.

Harassment, sexual. 'Interestingly enough, Vernon, the first example of sexual harassment at work is now recognized to have been the inappropriate demands made by Mary, Queen of Scots (1542–87) of her secretary, Rizzio.'
   'Rather to the embarrassment of so-called feminists, I imagine!'
   'Very much so, Vernon. She would often keep him working late and make leading remarks in French – suggesting that they jump into the sack together.'
   'Michael Parkinson?'
   'Dr David Starkey, in fact, but I take your point. Be that as it may, Rizzio was forced to opt for early retirement when he was threatened with disembowelment with a hot iron.'
   'An interesting parallel with today, when, all too often, it is not the persecutor but the persecuted who is punished.'
   'I'll drink to that! MIGUEL!!'
See also FLAKE, A TOTAL.

Hard-luck stories galore. Forever emanating from the Anfield boot room.

Harrogate. Whether for its fancy cakes or conference facilities, this North Yorkshire spa town has always been a hit with visitors.
See also BRITAIN IN BLOOM.

Haste. Always 'indecent', or 'unseemly'.

Hatfield House. The mop-headed ilexes in the East Garden at Hatfield House are worth the entrance fee alone.
'How true! And why? Because the Marchioness of Salisbury is one the few great gardeners in Britain who understands garden design as well as she understands plants.'
'I've never cared for her myself.'
'Well, there you are.'

Haul, drugs. Always worth £5m on the street.

He. Disquietingly ubiquitous.
'He could be out there now, Sergeant. Watching us.'
See also TOUCH OF FROST, A.

Headlines. Behind the headlines there is often a more complex story.
'Joining me here to discuss the stories behind the headlines are satirist Rory Bremner, *Daily Mail* columnist Quentin...'
'Fuck off, Kirsty.'
'There's no need to be unnecessary, Susan.'

Healthy. *See* VULGARITY.

Heaps, ant. Contrary to popular belief, ant heaps are, inch for inch, extremely spacious and organically constructed and are thus not at all a suitable analogy for the overcrowded and jerry-built tower-blocks to which they were so often compared in the 1970s.

Hearns, Thomas 'The Hitman' (1958–). Pound for pound the finest boxer ever to pull the gloves on.

'I don't hope to see a better in my lifetime.'

See also ALI, MUHAMMAD; ARMSTRONG, HENRY 'HANK'; DURAN, ROBERTO; HAGLER, MARVIN; LEONARD, SUGAR RAY; MARCIANO, ROCKY; MOORE, ARCHIE; PEP, WILLIE; ROBINSON, SUGAR RAY.

Heart. So-called scientists would have us suppose that the human heart is a mere pump. But they have never been able to explain how a pump could produce so much poetry and music of enduring beauty.

'Sounds like one for *The Oldie*, Richard.'

See also DOCTORS; INTELLECT; MATERIALISM.

Heat of the moment, the. 'OK, fair play, Gary. I agree it looked bad. The big Irish lad took the little Swedish striker by the throat, spat in his face, knocked him over and stamped on his leg, breaking it in three places. I'm not defending the lad, but these things happen in the heat of the moment. There's a lot of pressure out there at this stage of the season.'

'Thank you, Mark.'

Hedge, a. Always a cause of controversy.

'It makes me so *damned* angry! That hedge was there in my grandfather's day and now some fucking faceless bureaucrat – I'm sorry, Daphne – but it makes me *boil!*'

See also BUREAUCRATS; SACRED?, IS NOTHING.

Hedonism. Hedonism takes its toll.

'Seen your boy lately?'

'Just a phase.'

Hell and back. *See* ANDERTON, SOPHIE; WESTBROOK, DANIELLA; WINDSOR, BARBARA.

Help, cries for. *See* AFFAIRS, EXTRA-MARITAL; PROMISCUITY; SHOP-LIFTING.

Hendrick, Mike (1948–). With Ken Higgs (1937–) he formed the most innocuous opening partnership in fast-bowling history.

'I hope to see many better in my lifetime. Yes, Susan?'

'What about dear old Tom Cartwright and the other one?'

'I take my hat off to you, Susan. For a woman, you're surprisingly well informed!'

Hendrix, Jimi (1942–70). Like many people with a full address book, he found there were times when no one was in.

See also BYRON, LORD GEORGE; CASS, MAMA; HUTCHENCE, MICHAEL; JONES, BRIAN; JOPLIN, JANIS; MONROE, MARILYN; MOON, KEITH; WALES, DIANA, PRINCESS OF.

Henry VII (1457–1509). King of England from 1485. Contrary to popular opinion, Professor Simon Schama has never said, 'Henry VII decided it was time to carry out a reality check on the country's finances,' in any of his innovative TV lectures.

See also HENRY VIII; HISTORIANS, CELEBRITY; HISTORY, THE NEW; STARKEY, DR DAVID.

Henry VIII (1491–1547). King of England from 1509 (*see* RUBBISH, FEELING).

Henry, Thierry (1977–). French soccer player. Forever latching on to Edu's raking through ball to fire the Gunners ahead.

Heroin. Contrary to received opinion, more US servicemen were killed in Vietnam by Vietcong bullets than died from heroin abuse.

See also CANNABIS.

Heroines, kick-arse. On any list of the hundred leading kick-arse heroines of all time, you'd expect to find Sigourney Weaver, Diana Rigg, Grace Jones …

'You've gone rather pale, Simon. Are you all right?'

'Quite all right, thank you. Do continue.'

'If you say so. Brigitte Nielsen, Pussy Galore, Serena Williams, Angelina Jolie …'

'Yes, a short walk, I think … Rather hot in here … back in a minute…'

See also EROTICISM IN THE CINEMA.

Herpes. Contrary to received opinion, more people catch herpes from frankfurters each year than take their holidays in Norfolk.

'You've gone rather pale, Dr Death.'

'De'ath. Jolyon *De'ath*.'

'I don't doubt it. However, it doesn't alter the fact that you've gone white as herring roe.'

Hesse, Hermann (1877–1962). German-born Swiss novelist and poet. His heroes have a disagreeable tendency to withdraw from their social and family responsibilities in order to concentrate on what they take to be their spiritual development.

'Small wonder that he enjoyed a cult following in California in the so-called Sixties – an era now happily behind us.'

'Laborious windbag.'

'I wouldn't go that far, Susan.'

'Not Hesse. You.'

'Spoken like a loyal wife. Tell me, Vernon: *The League of Gentlemen*? See the joke, do you?'

See also SIXTIES, THE.

Hirst, Damien. *See* AGAIN.

Historians, celebrity. *See* ACCESSIBLE; FERGUSON, PROFESSOR NIALL; GOOD TASTE; HISTORIANS, PHOTOGENIC; HISTORY, THE NEW; HUNT, DR TRISTRAM; SCHAMA, PROFESSOR SIMON; STARKEY, DR DAVID.

Historians, photogenic. *See* ACCESSIBLE; FERGUSON, PROFESSOR NIALL; HISTORY, THE NEW; HUNT, DR TRISTRAM; SCHAMA, PROFESSOR SIMON; STARKEY, DR DAVID.

History, the New. 'The Kings and Queens of England – History without the Lecture!'

'Sounds like one for Channel 5.'

'Or even BBC2 these days.'

'*O tempora, o mores…!*'

'Ah! Here comes the nosh at last!'

'All things come to he who waits!'

'On with the feed bags!'

'*Bon appétit!*'

'Pass the cruet.'

See also ACCESSIBLE; BARBARIANS, THE; FERGUSON, PROFESSOR NIALL; HARASSMENT, SEXUAL; STARKEY, DR DAVID.

Histrionics. Foreign soccer players are often guilty of histrionics in the box.

'The little Romanian should apply for membership of Equity!'

'Thank you, Barry.'

See also IONESCO, EUGÈNE.

Hitchcock, Alfred (1909–89). Film director. He gave a new meaning to the word 'suspense'.

'Part of his public image was to be unknowable, but we know him through his films.'

'Im off 2 the toilet, me. u comin, trace?'

'u bet.'

Hitchens, Christopher (1949–). Polemicist. His energetic prose can have its awkward moments, but he is a master at maintaining interest in subjects ranging from Kipling to Andy Warhol.

'I never read him.'

'Nor do I.'

'Well, there you are.'

Hoddle, Glenn (1957–). Footballer. All the skill in the world but his show-pony manoeuvres weren't appreciated in the North.

'Nor in the South, come to that.'

Mention work-rate.

Holding, Michael (1954–). With Andy Roberts he formed the finest opening partnership in fast-bowling history.

'I don't hope to see a better in my lifetime.'

See also AKRAM, WASIM and YOUNIS, WAQAR; AMBROSE, CURTLEY AND WALSH, COURTNEY; BOWES, BILL and LARWOOD, HAROLD; DONALD, ALLAN; HALL, WESLEY and GRIFFITH, CHARLIE; LILLEE, DENNIS and THOMPSON, JEFF; LINDWALL, RAY and MILLER, KEITH; MCGRATH, GLENN and LEE, BRETT; TRUEMAN, FREDDIE and STATHAM, BRIAN.

Hole, the. What you need at the top level is a player in the hole behind the striker, someone with a bit of nous. A lad like Teddy Sheringham who can put those little balls through to the big lad in the number 9 shirt who isn't afraid to stick his head in where the boots are flying about.

'Thank you, Ron.'

See also BALLS, LITTLE; SHERINGHAM, TEDDY.

Holiday, Billie (1915–59). If Bessie Smith was the singer whose example ennobled the jazz tradition, Billie Holiday was the singer who spelt out the perilous implications of that tradition.

See also JAZZ; SMITH, BESSIE.

Holiday Reps. Channel 4, 8 p.m. Jason decides whether to have his genitals pierced. Last in the series.

'Sound like one to miss, Simon.'

'I was quite looking forward to it, Susan.'

Home. It is the special privilege of womanhood to turn a mere dwelling house into a home.

'No man ever took up a sword in defence of a hostel, that's what I always say.'

'I've heard that under so-called 'New Labour' no fewer than 304 different officials can now enter an Englishman's home without a warrant.'

'On the other hand, if you've nothing to hide, why should that bother you?'

'Indeed, indeed. I read recently, and coincidentally, that men living on their own die on average six years before those living with a woman.'

'Well, there you are. Dr Death's gone rather pale again.'

'So he has.'

Homer (8th century BC). Man or woman, sighted or blind, one individual or a committee of itinerant bards? The debate continues, but the *Iliad* and the *Odyssey* remain. On mention of his name, murmur 'the wine-dark sea'.

'It has been said that a month in the thick of a tribal war in Africa would teach you more about the *Iliad* than seven years in the Bodleian Library.'

'If you came out alive from either, that is!'

'Ah! Dr Death. Still with us, I see! Thank you for that.'

'Don't mention it, Mr Biggleswade.'

'Wigglesworth.'

'I'll take your word for it.'

Homosexuality. Causes earthquakes.

'Seen your boy lately?'

'I've persuaded him to join a religious cult in California.'

Homosexuals. All wear moustaches.

Honesty. Often 'brutal'.

Hong Kong. When appearing on *Richard and Judy*, it is amusing when a matinée actor, on mention of Hong Kong, adds, 'Of all places!'

'I was appearing in this play in Hong Kong – of all places! – and...'

Hopkins, Sir Anthony (1937–). The 66-year-old Welsh actor met his third wife, Stella, 46, a businesswoman, in a furniture store.

See also CAMERA, THE.

Horizontal jogging. *See* ALCOHOLIC.

Hornby, Mrs. 'Going through a lady's belongings isn't a very gentlemanly thing to do, Inspector.'

'Murder isn't a very gentlemanly thing either, Mrs Hornby.'

'*Inspector Morse*? *A Touch of Frost*?'

'*Foyle's War*, in fact.'

'I don't think I'm familiar with that one.'

'It made no great impact.'

See also PATTERSON, MRS; PERKINS.

Horny hitmaker. *See* MADONNA.

Horse, the. The modern horse is descended from an animal no bigger than a vole. In an occasional column it might be amusing to refer to a horse as 'the domesticated perissodactylate mammal, *equus caballus* – yes, it's our old friend the horse!'

'If a horse knew its own strength!'

Hospital, a medicated out-patient from the Chelsea and Westminster. *See* SHERWOOD, JAMES.

Hostelry. A word that sits well in an occasional column.

See also ABLUTIONS; ABODE; ALFRED; AMERICAN ACADEMICS; BUSTS; DANE, HAMLET THE MOODY; DUCK, DONALD; EATERIE; EMBONPOINT; INFELICITOUS; KEATS, JOHN; LIBATION; MEADOWS, MY POULTERER, THE ESTIMABLE MR; NOSHERIE; OCCASIONS; REPORTER; THESPIAN; VARIETY, BIRDS OF THE FEATHERED.

Hot babes. As the *Telegraph* has correctly observed, 'They're forever close to tears when dumped by hunks.'

See also BEAUTIES, SHATTERED; VIPs, BUSTY.

Hot Celebs! 'On sale from 1st June! Don't miss *The Sunday Times*'s raunchy new supplement, *Hot Celebs!* – 'The Frox! The Chix! The Goss! The Pix! The Seriously Rich without a Stitch!' In this week's edition:

'Telly's top 10 celeb crack-ups! Doncha you just lurve it when they lose it!'

'"Blokes never try it on with me" – *Emmerdale* Amy's shock confession!'

'Melinda: "I don't regret my boob job!"'

'*Big Brother* Phwoooar! Why series 4 will be the steamiest yet!'

'"My New Fella – the Bombay Bonker!" Liz reveals all!'

'Lisa "I'm Kylie (!) ambitious!" Scott Lee sees herself as the female Robbie Williams – without the questionable sexuality!'

Houston, we have a problem. Good headline for an article about Whitney Houston.

'Whitney had it all. The looks, the heritage and the elemental voice. So where did it all go wrong?'

'The diva who fell to earth, would you say?'

'As it happens, I was never a fan of Whitney Houston – it wasn't necessary. Whitney was something that simply happened to you, whether you wanted her to or not – like the weather.'

'How true.'

Hugo. *See* CAROLINE AND TOBY; HUMPHREY; MELISSA; NEWLY PAIRED-OFF THIRTYSOMETHINGS.

Human mind. The human mind is a strange thing.

'And to whom do we owe this insight? John Cleese?'

'Richard Madeley, in fact, but I take your point.'

'By the same token, the memory plays tricks.'

'Indeed it does. For instance, very few people remember how many episodes John Cleese made of his matchless sitcom – horrible expression! – *Fawlty Towers*.'

'I do. Twelve.'

'Thank you, Susan. Tell me, Vernon. The unspoilt Sologne? Have you and Doris ever been there?' (*See* SOLOGNE.)

Humble. *See* ABODE.

Humour, a sense of. Often 'infectious'. Sometimes 'saving'. Point out that humour is a very personal thing.

'Dawn French makes some people roar with laughter.'

'As indeed do the off-the-wall duo, Reeves and Mortimer.'

'What about David Baddiel?'

'That's going a bit too far, perhaps.'

In a discussion on humour try to work in a reference to Sigmund Freud. At some point you will be able to say:

'Ah yes, but Freud never played the Glasgow Empire on a Monday night!'

See also BERNARD, JEFFREY; COMEDY; IRONY.

Humphrey. *See* CAROLINE AND TOBY; HUGO; MELISSA; NEWLY PAIRED-OFF THIRTYSOMETHINGS.

Hunt, Dr Tristram. Good name for a photogenic historian. Contrary to received opinion it is not the case that Dr Hunt repeatedly refused to leave his location trailer during his latest television shoot, pleading that he was having a 'bad hair day'. The story is significant nonetheless.

Hurley, Elizabeth (1965–). Actress and model. No one has ever used the language of clothes more cleverly. That said, will our fascination with the girl from Basingstoke endure? The jury's out.

Hurt, John (1940–). Actor. His weather-beaten face can portray a world of emotion with the slightest change of expression, helped by that marvellously gravelly voice. Small wonder he never made it in Hollywood. They didn't know what to do with him.

Hussar, The Gay. Restaurant in Greek Street, London, serving Hungarian cuisine.
See also BRITAIN'S NUCLEAR SECRETS; DRIBERG, TOM.

Hutchence, Michael (1960–97). Australian pop singer with INXS. Like many people with a full address book, he found there were times when no one was in.
See also BYRON, LORD GEORGE; CASS, MAMA; DEAN, JAMES; EPSTEIN, BRIAN; HENDRIX, JIMI; JONES, BRIAN; JOPLIN, JANIS; MONROE, MARILYN; MOON, KEITH; TOULOUSE-LAUTREC, HENRI; WALES, DIANA, PRINCESS OF.

Hype. *See* NOVELS, THIRD.

Hypnotists, celebrity. *See* AGUILERA, CHRISTINA.

Ibiza. 'Win a holiday for two in the sunshine island of Ibiza! Just answer this simple question. What is the capital of Iraq? (a) Barcelona? Or (b) Baghdad?'

'*The Sunday Times*?'

'*The News of the World*, in fact, but I take your point.'

See also INTIMACY.

Ice-cream vendors. Always Neapolitan.

Ideas, abstract. Thunder against them. Usually from the Continent.

'Wasn't it that wise woman Margaret Thatcher who had it that "abstract liberty, like other mere abstractions, is not to be found"?'

'Burke?'

'There's no need to be offensive, Simon. Time to leave, Daphne. Hullo! Where is the woman?'

'She's in the toilet, Mr Pratley. With the Italian stall…'

'Yes, thank you, Miguel. But that's *Plimmer*.'

'If you say so, bro. If I was you I'd get a life. Cheers!'

'Well really! That's a first! Get a life? That's never been said to me before by a Spanish waiter!'

'You surprise me.'

'Thank you, Dr Death.'

'Don't mention it, Mr Parsnip.'

See also JOHNSON, SAMUEL.

I don't care what you do as long as I don't know about it. *See* ANYTHING, IF MEN BELIEVE THAT THEY'LL BELIEVE; CHELSEA GIRL ESCORTS; IF YOU MUST DO IT, AT LEAST HAVE THE DECENCY TO DO IT WITH A PROSTITUTE.

If you must do it, at least have the decency to do it with a prostitute. 'Do you really mean that, Susan?'

'Of course I do.'

'Okay. I've got a small confession to make.'

'Go on.'

'Well, I was very drunk one night with "Tubby" Walton. It was after Salter's bachelor party. To cut a long story short, we visited Chelsea Girl Escorts in Beauchamp Place and...'

'I don't *believe* what I'm hearing! That is *so* sad. It's pathetic! What sort of man are you? Did I actually marry a man who has to *pay* for it? Uuugh! No, don't touch me! You make me feel sick. Physically sick!'

See also ANYTHING, IF MEN BELIEVE THAT THEY'LL BELIEVE; CHELSEA GIRL ESCORTS; I DON'T CARE WHAT YOU DO AS LONG AS I DON'T KNOW ABOUT IT.

I'm on the train. *See* JEREMY.

In art, as in life. *See* BRUCKNER, ANTON.

Indian, the wristy little. Cricketer.

'When the questions were asked, the wristy little Indian had the answers.'

'Over to you, Richie.'

'Thank you, Mark. Good morning, everyone.'

See also GRITTY LANCASTRIAN, THE.

Inexplicable. True wisdom resides in realizing the importance of the inexplicable.

'Sounds like one for *The Oldie*, Richard.'

In fairness. *See* AGENDA; BLING-BLING; BODY LANGUAGE; FOOTBALL; GAME, THE.

Infelicitous. A word that sits well in an occasional column.

See also ABODE; EATERIE; EMBONPOINT; HOSTELRY; LIBATION; NOSHERIE; OCCASIONS; REPORTER; THESPIAN.

Inflation. Always 'galloping'.

'This will interest you, Vernon. In the Weimar Republic, if you had been told that you needed a wheelbarrowful of notes to buy a loaf of bread, by the time you had got to the shop you'd have needed two wheelbarrowsful.'

'A lesson we forget at our peril!'

'Indeed. Paradoxically, in conditions of spiralling inflation, those with most money are hardest hit.'

'Wise words. I see Diageo are up. Care for another?'

Innocent. It's the innocent who end up on a slab in the morgue. *See also* CRIME.

Innovate. To innovate is not necessarily to reform. *The Daily Mail* has perceived this.

See also DAILY MAIL, THE; MAN, THE PERFECTABILITY OF; NATURE, HUMAN; PROGRESS, BELIEF IN THE ILLUSION OF; REAL WORLD, THE; UTOPIA, THE SEARCH FOR.

Insiders, Tinseltown. Forever disclosing that, since becoming mums, superstars like Jodie Foster are in the habit of sending their fans reeling by shopping in supermarkets in old flip-flops and baggy jumpers. *See also* FANS.

Insights. Should be 'penetrating'.

'Hold hard, Vernon. Unless I'm very much mistaken, I've just had a penetrating linguistic insight. Odd, isn't it, that in the context of a football commentary you can have a "square ball"?'

'So you can!'

'And here's another. Football commentators allot emotions to body parts, as in "Gerrard drills the ball past the despairing hands of the German keeper." It works less well, however, with other parts of the anatomy. Despairing feet? Hardly. A despairing lunge, yes, but not despairing feet. Equally, you can't imagine "an unsuspecting instep", can you?'

'Any more penetrating linguistic insights and I think I'll hang myself.'

'Thank you, Susan. This may interest you, Vernon. In sex

between pipefish, the male is the passive partner...'

'No prizes for guessing why this interests Simon!'

'Thank you, Susan, but I'm talking to Vernon. Where was I? Ah yes. The male pipefish is the passive partner, being penetrated by the female...'

'What did I tell you?'

'Yes, thank you, Susan. The female pipefish uses a protruding ovarian duct to insert...'

'That's done it! Toilet everyone?'

'After you, Sue.'

'SUSAN!!! Oh well. Here's one, Vernon. They have a saying in Russia. Women are like buses.'

'Yes?'

'That's it.'

Institutions, our. Our institutions are the envy of the world. They have served us well for nigh-on a thousand years, but that's no reason to suppose that they can be successfully transplanted onto non-Anglo-Saxon soil.

'I agree. What would your average Pueblo Indian make of Arthur Askey and Richard "Stinker" Murdoch?'

'I'm sorry?'

'Before your time.'

Instructions. Should be read carefully. If the symptoms persist after four weeks, you should consult your doctor.

Instrument. If used to commit a crime, 'blunt', unless 'sharp'.
See also MURDERERS; ORIGINAL INSTRUMENTS.

Intellect. The intellect is a poor instrument for discovering what goes on in the heart.

'Sounds like one for *The Oldie*, Richard.'
See also DOCTORS; HEART; MATERIALISM.

Intellectual, liberal. Your liberal intellectual, because of the way his mind has been trained, is cut off from the natural roots of his existence and from the instinctive understanding of life which your simple countryman possesses in such abundance.

'Or my poulterer, the estimable Mr Meadows – a true philosopher.'

'And one of nature's gentlemen?'

'Indeed.'

'A thought occurs.'

'I'm all ears.'

'Would you say it's not always easy to distinguish between one of nature's gentlemen and a gentle giant?'

'You have an example?'

'Henry Cooper – "Our 'Enery", of boxing fame.'

'He was both.'

'And Ian Botham?'

'He's neither.'

See also EDUCATION, FORMAL; KNOWLEDGE, REAL.

Intervals, theatre. Always too short.

Intimacy. Sex in the absence of intimacy and loving communion reduces the other person to the status of mere object.

'Just as it should be…'

'Ah Susan! Back at last. I think, however…'

'Fidelity might be OK for swans but it would bore the tits off anyone else. What do you like, Trace?'

'Me? I like a dark 'n' broodin stranger 2 do me upside down over a bollard in the car park at The Desert Inn, Chingford, ignorin' my sweet feminine bat-like squeaks of protest. That or dun rs up over a drystone wall in Ibiza by a local barboy. Wot about u, sue?'

'Susan! I forbid you…'

'I like to be pegged out on a croquet lawn, naked except for my stockings and stilettos and hooped at my delicate wrists and ankles, thereafter malleted heartlessly into the shrubbery where I am repeatedly enjoyed by under-gardeners and their common friends from the village. What about you, Sharon?'

'That did it 4 me 'n' all. Scuse me. Im off 2 the toilet.'

'That just leaves you, Daphne. What do you like?'

'Oh I'm very boring, I'm afraid. I suppose I'd like Roberto to dance me into a doorway, fold me into his manly chest and breathe softly in my ear, "Oh lyric love/Half angel and half bird…" Oh dear. It's back to the Ladies for me.'

'Me too!'

'Susan! I positively forbid you...'

'Too late!'

See also IBIZA; WALL, THE WRITING ON THE.

Intuition, women's. Not as strong as is generally supposed. A woman can usually tell when her husband has had garlic for lunch but not when he is sleeping with her aerobics class.

See also WOMEN'S INTUITION.

Ionesco, Eugène (1912–94). Dramatist and leading exponent of the Theatre of the Absurd. He customarily walked round Paris claiming that he had turned into a rhinoceros, but was not believed. Who but the French could have produced an Ionesco?

'In fact he was Romanian.'

'Thank you, Julian. Haven't heard from you for a while.'

'Jolyon.'

'Of course.'

'I was wondering where Roberto was. You haven't seen him, have you?'

'I think he may be in the toilet. I don't suppose he'll be long. You know what Italians are like. Well, of course you do.'

See also ITALIAN POLICE, THE.

Irishman, the easy-going. 'The easy-going Irishman charms as much in conversation as he does on the field of play.'

See also AMERICAN GIRL, THE BIG; BRAZILIAN, THE GAP-TOOTHED; BULGARIAN GIRL, THE UNFANCIED; EUROPEANS, SOUTHERN; GHANAIAN, THE LIPPY; GLASWEGIAN, THE CHIRPY; INDIAN, THE WRISTY LITTLE; LANCASTRIAN, THE GRITTY; SPANIARD, THE MERCURIAL; TURKEY, THE CRUDE SLUGGER FROM.

Ironside, Virginia (1941–). Agony aunt and journalist.

'Surely it was that wise woman Virginia Ironside who pointed out that a woman is a woman first, a wife and mother second.'

'Isn't a mother tautologically a woman, then?'

'I rather think so, yes.'

'Thank you, Virginia.'

Irony. Should be 'gentle', unless 'grim'.

'I hope your dentistry is less clumsy than your irony, Wordsworth. Come along, Susan.' (*See also* SUSAN.)

Americans have no sense of irony.

See also ADAMS, DOUGLAS; AMERICAN ACADEMICS; RAVEL, MAURICE.

Isle of Man. Famous for its Manx cats, yet no one has ever been there.

See also MAN, ISLE OF.

Italian police, the. Notoriously excitable. Armed to the teeth, they are compelled by the national characteristic of premature ejaculation to shoot first and take the bribe later.

See also JAMES, C.L.R; MEN, SPANISH.

Italian women. Exquisite for six months at the age of 18, but they all come back from their honeymoons looking like Pavarotti.

J

Jacques, Hattie. *See* COMEDY, UNSUNG HEROES OF BRITISH.

Jagger, Bianca (1945–). Political scientist. Could Bianca have maintained such a high profile if she hadn't taken Jagger's name? The debate continues.

    'If she'd married Tiny Tim she'd be known as Mrs Tim!'

    'An agreeable notion! Care for another?'

Jagger, Mick (1943–). His bottom made Kylie Minogue's bottom possible.

See also BARDOT, BRIGITTE; MINOGUE, KYLIE; VALANCE, HOLLY.

James I (1566–1625). King of England from 1603 and Scotland (as **James VI**) from 1567. Contrary to received opinion, Dr David Starkey has never said, 'James I? Wot a tosser!' in any of his popular television programmes.

James, C.L.R. (1901–89). 'Wasn't it the unlikely voice of a Trinidadian Marxist that opined, "What know they of cricket that only cricket know?"'

    'I haven't the faintest idea. That said, it's amazing, isn't it, the transmogrification in 12 months of Michael Vaughan from cricketing Cinderella to elegantly prolific belle of the international cricketing ball.'

    'Not one of your happiest metaphors, Vernon.'

    'Ah Daphne! Back from the Ladies already!'

    'There you are, Vernon. I said that Italians didn't take long!'

    'Thank you for that, Simon. On the other hand, your significant other is still nowhere to be seen.'

'Discussing Media Studies with Sharon and Tracey, I expect.'
'Of course.'

Jazz. The world divides into those for whom jazz is *the* great musical innovation of the 20th century and those who don't see the point of it at all.

'Ahem.'

'Yes, Jolyon? Feeling better, are you?'

'Indeed. I am aware that Ken Clarke – lost leader of a once great party – belongs in the first category. I for one am delighted to place myself in the second. Surely it was the German social theorist Theodor Adorno who aptly described jazz as "musical masturbation"?'

'Rather an unhappy choice of apologist for an anti-jazz stand-point, Dr Death.'

'*De'ath!*'

See also HOLIDAY, BILLIE; SMITH, BESSIE.

Jealousy. Always 'destructive'. No need to explain why.

'Those wise people, the Eskimo, have no word for it in their language.'

'I can add to that.'

'Yes, Julian?'

'Jolyon.'

'Of course. The floor is yours.'

'In some societies one is obliged to share one's wife with an honoured guest.'

'Not a problem with which you've ever been confronted, I imagine. That said, Roberto's looking strangely flushed.'

See also ESKIMOS WORKING IN THE UNITED KINGDOM.

Jen and Brad. *See* TINSELTOWN SIZZLERS.

Jenkins, the late Lord. *See* MARCUSE, HERBERT; MASSAGE PARLOURS.

Jeremy. Forever phoning Pippa from a train outside Reading (*see also* PIPPA).

Jerome, Jerome K. (1859–1927). Remembered now only for *Three Men in a Boat* (1889) and *Three Men on the Bummel* (1900), he also wrote a successful play, *The Passing of the Third Floor Back* (1907), in which the inmates of a Bloomsbury boarding house are intimidated by a strange lodger resembling Christ.

Jet to Spain. Today's young wannabes can jet to Spain at the last moment, but are they any happier?
See also HAPPINESS.

Johnson, Boris (1964–). Politician and journalist (*see* WIDDECOMBE, ANNE).

Johnson, Samuel (1709–84). In an occasional column always 'the Immortal Sam', or even merely 'Sam'.

'Jumping Jesus! Yes, Jolyon? You have a point?'

'Just this. While there is undoubtedly merit in some of his writings, Sam, like all truly civilized men (one might mention Isaiah Berlin, Maurice Bowra, Noel Annan, "Dadie" Rylands, "Binkie" Beaumont) was seen at his best in conversation.'

'If you say so. This may interest you, Vernon…'

'May I continue?

'If you must.'

'His real importance – I'm talking about the Immortal Sam – consists, surely, in his commonsensical refutation of Berkeleyan idealism – by kicking a stone and exclaiming, "I refute it thus!" – and for his defence of free will – "Sir, I know I am free and there's an end on it."'

'You've made your point, Jolyon. This may interest you, Vernon. The nine-banded armadillo…'

'If I may sum up, then? So-called academic philosophers have failed to improve on his robust – and very English – refusal to be taken in by abstract ideas.'

'Thank you, Jolyon. As I was saying, Vernon. The nine-banded armadillo. When erect, its penis is roughly one-third of its body length. What do you make of that?'

'I couldn't help noticing that Roberto's…'

'Yes, thank you, Miguel. I don't think Mr Pratley needs to know…'

'Plimmer.'

'Nor him. You're looking very pale, Vernon. Allow me to replenish your glass... MIGUEL! Damn me, he's gone again.'

See also BOWRA, MAURICE; DONS, OLD-STYLE BACHELOR; IDEAS, ABSTRACT; PENIS; PIPE-SMOKING SODOMITES; REPROOFS; SPARROW, JOHN.

Jokes, dirty. They all originate on the floor of the Stock Exchange.

Jokes, racist. In spite of the usual shrill cries of protest from the politically correct, racist jokes build bridges between cultures and defuse potentially dangerous situations.

'I agree. Here's one. Did you hear about the Irishman who won the *Tour de France* and did a lap of honour?'

'And who's leading the laughter? Paddy over there. Just as I predicted!'

'Here's another! Did you hear about the Irish footballer who missed a penalty? The goalkeeper sent him the wrong way! B!**!SLUR***RP!!***'

'What happened?'

'Paddy smacked me in the mouth.'

'Well, there you are.'

Jones, Brian (1942–69). Pop guitarist. Like many people with a full address book he found there were times when no one was in.

See also BYRON, LORD GEORGE; CASS, MAMA; COBAIN, KURT; EPSTEIN, BRIAN; GUILTY, WE ARE ALL; HENDRIX, JIMI; HUTCHENCE, MICHAEL; JOPLIN, JANIS; MONROE, MARILYN; MOON, KEITH; TOULOUSE-LAUTREC, HENRI; WALES, DIANA, PRINCESS OF.

Jones, Tom (1940–). Pop singer. In spite of great riches and all the trappings of fame, Jones remains at heart a miner's son from Wales.

'You astound me.'

Jonsson, Ulrika (1967–). Blonde bombshell. Will the raunchy Eskimo ever find Mr Right? The debate continues.

See also AUTOBIOGRAPHY; CELEBS; ESKIMOS WORKING IN THE UNITED KINGDOM.

Joplin, Janis (1943–70). An exciting talent laid to waste by the excesses of stardom. She never discovered who she really was.

See also CASS, MAMA; GUILTY, WE ARE ALL; HUTCHENCE, MICHAEL; JONES, BRIAN.

Jordan, *properly* **Katie Price** (1978–). Silicone-enhanced glamour model.

'Gareth Gates, the pint-sized diva, says he can't write songs because he has no experience with women. Of course, if he *had* shagged Jordan, the rubber-breasted disco slapper, he could have written *Climb Every Mountain*!'

'An item in *The Daily Star's* always lively "Bitches" column?'

'In fact a story in the *Telegraph's* greatly improved *Diary*, but I take your point.'

See MATT, ELECTRICIANS CALLED.

Journalists. 'Well, well, well! If it isn't the ladies and gentlemen of the fourth estate!'

'I'll deal with this, Jack.'

'But, Guv…'

'That will be all, Jack.'

Judges, Booker Prize. The facetious rumour that the Booker Prize judges for 2004 were to be Ian Hislop, Mariella Frostrup, Jerry Hall, Linford Christie, Vanessa Feltz and Alan Titchmash was quickly scotched when it was announced that they were to be Sir Trevor MacDonald, Joanna Lumley, Ben Elton, Janet Street-Porter, Trevor Brooking and Charlie Dimmock.

Judges, High Court. What a sad reflection on the times in which we live that high court judges are now in touch with the real world.

'Indeed. I gather that when interviewed recently in *The Sunday Times's Hot Celebs!* supplement, Lord Woolf, the Lord Chief Justice, admitted that his fave pop artiste was hip hop star Ol' Dirty Bastard.'

'I can add to that. He then pronounced Liberty X stunner Michelle Heaton the fittest babe on the planet, later admitting that Lisa Lashes, the mistress of hard house, was his fave DJ.'

'Truly a jaw-dropping revelation. In bygone days, judges

wore black lace body-stockings under their robes and were up for a thrashing after hours, but they knew when to put a halter round a fellow's neck ... You've gone very pale, Simon. Are you all right?'

'Yes, thank you, Vernon. Perfectly all right. You were saying...'

'Judges. They'd sentence a chap to death and then repair to their robing room, where the clerk to the assizes, armed with a Swaine Adeaney riding crop ... You're breathing rather heavily, Simon ...'

'Excuse me, a moment, Vernon. Breath of fresh air ... must have drunk too much ... back in a minute ...'

'Extraordinary.'

Juggling work and kids. *See* BALL, ZOE; TODAY'S WOMAN.

Jury-rigging. A fox should not be of a jury at a goose's trial.

Just another game. 'Games don't come much bigger than this, do they, Arsène?'

'Mebbe nurt, Gary. But 'avving sed zatt, forurzeetullbejerstanuz-zèreguème.'

'Confident words there from the *Arsène*-al manager!'

'Well done, Gary. I've not heard that one before.'

'Just doing my best, Steve.'

See also FORM.

Justly proud. *See* BUDAPEST.

Kant, Immanuel (1724–1804). German philosopher. His life was so regular that the inhabitants of Königsberg used to set their watches by the time he started his afternoon walk. Nevertheless, his critical philosophy was said to embody a Copernican revolution in the theory of knowledge. This was not perhaps the happiest of metaphors, for while Copernicus displaced man from the centre of the Universe, Kant's philosophy claims that the causes of human perception are in man himself.

'Wherever you put it, I reckon it's your round, Marty.'

'Down the hatch, Con.'

Kama Sutra, The. Contrary to popular belief, Barry Norman has never said, 'This film makes *The Kama Sutra* look like *Noddy In Toyland*', in any of his agreeably wry commentaries.

See also NORMAN, BARRY.

Kay, Jay (1971–). Rock star. He's only 4ft 8ins but every inch a Cat in a Hat.

Keane, Roy (1971–). Irish sociopath and soccer player.

'Unfair! If he didn't play like Roy Keane he wouldn't be Roy Keane, that's what I always say.'

'I concur. With Roy Keane in the side, Manchester United never know they're beaten until they're beaten.'

'Precisely. What people who criticize players like Keano, Lee Bowyer and Alan Smith fail to understand is that their passionate desire to win makes them perform at the very edge of what's acceptable.'

'As used to be said of General Franco.'

'I stand refuted. Pass the condiments.'

See also FRANCO, FRANCISCO PAUL HERMENEGILDO TEODILO FRANCO BAHAMONDO; HADDOCK, MAD AS A.

Keats, John (1795–1821). In a humorous column it might be amusing to refer to him as 'the melancholy Mr Keats'.

See also ALFRED; AMERICAN ACADEMICS; DANE, HAMLET THE MOODY; DUCK, DONALD; MEADOWS, MY POULTERER, THE ESTIMABLE MR.

Kelly, Grace (1928–82). Film actress. She led a turbulent private life, but her only real love affair was with the camera.

See also BERGMAN, INGRID; BOGARDE, DIRK; LEIGH, VIVIEN.

Kennedy, John Fitzgerald (1917–63). President of the United States of America from 1961. It is now known that he was unable to walk without calipers and had to be carried round the White House on the back of a special counsel to the President, yet his sexual appetite was so voracious that he kept a permanent love-nest in the Watergate Building.

'How deliciously ironic!'

'Indeed. He would approach this at speed on a specially constructed underground railway (wheelchair gauge), running through a complex of drainage systems and ducts. A dumb-waiter took him to the fifth floor and ejected him into his suite, where he would have sexual relations with the mistress of Mafia chieftain Sam Giancana.'

'Lucky her.'

'Thank you, Susan.'

Kepler, Johannes (1571–1630). German astronomer. He found harmony in the heavens but only discord in his private life. Perhaps there's a lesson here.

Keyhole of eternity, peeping-toms at the. *See* SCIENTISTS.

Kick-arse heroines. *See* EROTICISM IN THE CINEMA; HEROINES, KICK-ARSE; WEAVER, SIGOURNEY.

Kids, the wife and. The wife and kids come first. A mystery.

'At the end of the day, Barry, I turned down the move to Roma because of the wife and kids.'

'Thank you, Kevin. Back to you, Gary.'

'Thank you, Barry. Over to you, Mark.'

'Thank you, Gary.'

Kitchen. In the kitchen, as in life, the best things that happen are seldom the result of planning.

'Thank you, Nigella.'

Some women unwind after a hectic day by pottering in the kitchen.

See also COOKING; MELISSA; NEWLY PAIRED-OFF THIRTYSOMETHINGS.

Knickers, French. Always 'frilly'.

Knocks, the University of Hard. *See* WATERHOUSE, KEITH; WATER-MAN, PETE.

Knowledge, real. It's difficult these days to remain ignorant enough to have any real knowledge.

'Sounds like one for the *Oldie*, Richard.'

See also INTELLECTUAL, LIBERAL; MEADOWS, MY POULTERER, THE ESTIMABLE MR.

Kurosawa, Akira (1910–89). Japanese film director. On mention of his name, point out that *The Magnificent Seven* is no more than a pale reworking of Kurosawa's *Seven Samurai* (1954). In any list of the ten greatest films of all time at least two by Kurosawa would have to be included.

L

Labradors. Contrary to received opinion, more seven-year olds in rural Hertfordshire are savaged annually by labradors than by Alsatians.

See also DOGS.

Lacan, Jacques (1901–81). It was no coincidence, perhaps, that this most French of intellectuals should have chosen to abandon Cartesian clarity so completely that, shortly after finishing an article, he was unable to remember what it meant. Who but the French could have produced a Jacques Lacan?

Lads, our. *See* BODY BAGS; BRITS; COACHING.

Lads, the. All credit to the lads.

See also FINAL, THE CUP; FORM; HALF-TIME, JUST BEFORE.

Land it on a sixpence, cross a ball and. *See* BECKHAM, DAVID.

Language, lavatorial. A substitute for real talent. William Shakespeare didn't need to use four-letter words.

'Nor he did, Vernon! *Antony and Cleopatra* is recognized as the most erotic play in the language, yet there's not an indecent word in it.'

'Yes there is. Its full ov rude words, the meanin' o wich wld not hav bin lost on a contempry audience. 4 xample, frot, shag, shrive…'

'Thank you, Tracey, I don't think…'

'Sharon, actually… fart, rut, nog, jumm…'

'Sharon, please…!'

'... pizzle, take, rake, tuck, root, frig, jack, cod, codlings, hairy-pie, cum, jism, quim, spend, bawd, pipe, tupp, xxxxxxfucker...'

'Do you mind, Sharon? I haven't finished my crabcakes yet.'

'I woz jokin about xxxxxxfucker. Im in Media Studies, me.'

'So you keep telling us.'

Language of clothes. *See* HURLEY, ELIZABETH.

La Plagne. If you're looking for a budget holiday in an established resort with extensive skiing, plenty of chalets on offer and excellent last-minute deals, La Plagne is the place for you.

'Sounds like one for the Travel section, Cathy.'

Lap of luxury, living in the. *See* ASYLUM-SEEKERS.

Larkin, Philip (1922–85). Normality was his disguise.

See ABODE; CRAPS, A CROWD OF; 'FRIEND, IN A PIG'S ARSE'; MEET THERE SOME TIME, WE MUST; 'VERS DE SOCIÉTÉ'.

Lashes, Lisa (1977–). The mistress of hard house (*see* JUDGES, HIGH COURT).

Last words. *See* BELLAMY'S VEAL PIES; 'BUGGER BOGNOR!'; CHARLES I; EDWARD II; MOTHER, THE QUEEN; WILLIAM I.

Law. Ignorance of the law is no excuse.

Lawyer. 'Are you speaking to me as my lawyer, Gregory?'

'No Doris. As your friend.'

'Daphne.'

'Daphne. Of course.'

Lawrence of Arabia (David Lean, 1962). In spite of Lean's sweeping re-telling of the T.E. Lawrence myth, and a promising debut from Peter O'Toole, the real star of the picture, of course, is Freddie Young's Oscar-winning cinematography.

'But Freddie Young didn't win an Oscar for *Lawrence of Arabia*. A circumstance caused no doubt by the fact that he wasn't on this occasion the cameraman.'

'Thank you, Susan. My point precisely. How's the gazpacho, Daphne?'

'Word up! She's in the toilet, bruv. With Roberta. Shout if you need me. Top bombing.'

'Yes, thank you, Miguel. Tell me, Vernon. Leonardo. A man listening to voices unheard by other people, would you say?'

'I think you may be on to something.'

See also DOCTOR ZHIVAGO; LEAN, DAVID.

'Lead on, MacDuff.' *See* AGAIN.

Leads. It's always too early for any leads.

'Any leads, Inspector?'

'It's early days yet.'

Leads, jump. The best investment a motorist can make.

League title, the. All important.

'To be fair, Gary, winning the League title, or the Premiership – call it what you will – isn't about strolling to a six–none win at home against Bolton Wanderers in what amounts to a training-ground kickabout. The true indicator of a championship-winning side is the ability to be outplayed for 89 minutes in the mud at Southampton of a wet November evening and pick up all three points with a goal in the 90th minute.'

'Thank you, Mark.'

See also CUP, THE.

Lean, David (1908–91). As a film-maker he was years ahead of his time. The French were the first to perceive this. That said, the weather was always the real star of his films.

See also DOCTOR ZHIVAGO; LAWRENCE OF ARABIA.

Leatherhead, pensioned old folk from. Forever emptying their bank accounts to pursue a retirement dream of vineyards and tumbledown *châteaux* in France and thereafter moaning to a rodent-faced young woman on *Watchdog* that they've lost the lot to a vanishing time-share salesman.

See also PENSIONERS.

Leavis, Dr F.R. (1895–1978). 'What a shame he never learned to write English, that's what I always say!'

'A quite remarkable infelicity of expression!'

'Indeed, and unlike our finest academic brains, he never understood that the true scholar expresses himself best in conversation.'

'Who are you thinking of, Simon?'

'Well, Susan – since you ask – Maurice Bowra, Isaiah Berlin, John Sparrow, Leslie Rowse, "Dadie" Rylands, "Dickie" Bickle, Lord David Cecil…'

'Pipe-smoking sodomites the lot of them, with a book by E.M. Forster in their pockets.'

'Yes, thank you, Susan. I think you're confusing them with the Cambridge Marxists of the 1930s.'

'I'm confusing them with no-one, thank you, Simon. What do you think, Shar?'

''Bout what?'

'Dr Leavis.'

'4 me, yeah, the nuts, like defnitly the gr8est english critic since arnold. But 4 him, d.j.enright, howard jacobson, simon gray, john bird, craig brown…'

'Tell me, Vernon. The Vaucluse. Ever been there, have you? You and Daphne? Where is she, by the way?'

'Where do you think she is, John? She's back in the toilet with Roberta.'

'Yes, thank you, Miguel. We'll call you if we need you. This may interest you, Vernon. There's a species of mouse in Salt Lake City which grooms itself so thoroughly that it has no hair.'

'I confess I don't know what to say.'

See also DONS, OLD-STYLE BACHELOR; VAUCLUSE.

Le Corbusier, *properly* **Charles-Édouard Jeanneret** (1887–1965). Swiss-born French architect and architectural theorist. He transformed space with reinforced concrete. His ideas were put into practice with the *Unité d'habitation*, a block of flats in Marseilles (1947–52), but no one has ever wanted to live in it. Who but the French could have produced a Le Corbusier?

Leeds. Formerly something of a black spot in terms of that most indefinable of qualities, 'style', Leeds has in the past few years experienced a cultural renaissance. A branch of Harvey Nichols has recently opened, a new four-star hotel is being built and top chef Gordon Ramsay...

See also BIRMINGHAM; BRADFORD; BRISTOL; GLASGOW; MANCHESTER; NEWCASTLE; SHEFFIELD.

Legs. The legs are always the first to go.

Leggy lovelies. *See* BEAUTIES, BIG-SCREEN.

Le Mesurier, John, *properly* **John Charles Elton Le Mesurier De Somerys Halliley** (1912–83). Born in Bedford, he started his working life as a solicitor's articled clerk but became one of our best-loved actors. He was entangled in a love triangle when his third wife, Joan, left him for Tony Hancock.

See also BLUTHAL, JOHN; CHALLIS, JOHN; CRIBBINS, BERNARD; CRYER, BARRY; JACQUES, HATTIE; LLOYD PACK, ROGER; LODGE, DAVID; MAGEE, HENRY; SMITH, LIZ; STARK, GRAHAM; TODD, BOB; WHITFIELD, JUNE.

Leigh, Vivien. *See* BEAUTY, GREAT; BOGARDE, DIRK; KELLY, GRACE.

Lennon, John (1940–80). We all experience pain, but John Lennon shared his with the world.

'That's done it. I've given up the will to live.'

'Here, su. U like ever tried Ketamine?'

'Don't think so. What is it?'

'A horse tranquillizer. Mor fav with yung clubbers now than ecstasy. Makes u feel ur dead.'

'Yeah, wow! – *That's* what I need.'

'Join Daph n Roberto in the toilet?'

'After u, shar.'

Leonard, Jason (1968–). English loose-head prop.
See also BEN, DAN, JEREMY, JOSH, WILL, CHARLIE, JULIAN, MARTIN, DANNY, JAMES AND JONNY; EASY MISTAKE TO MAKE; QUIRKE, PAULINE.

Leonard, Sugar Ray (1956–). Pound for pound the finest boxer ever to pull the gloves on.

'I don't hope to see a better in my lifetime.'

See also ALI, MUHAMMAD; ARMSTRONG, HENRY 'HANK'; HAGLER, MARVIN; HEARNS, THOMAS 'THE HITMAN'; LOUIS, JOE; MARCIANO, ROCKY; MOORE, ARCHIE; PEP, WILLIE; ROBINSON, SUGAR RAY.

Leopard seal, the. At the top of the Arctic food chain, the leopard seal regulates the penguin population.

Lesbo Love Romps. See AIREY, DAWN; BEDWORTHY, BARBARA.

Letters. In an 'up for it' magazine edited by a middle-class thirty-something woman, always 'missives', unless 'epistles'.

Level, the highest. At the highest level it's all about shot selection.

'And body shape?'

'Of course'

'Not forgetting stride pattern.'

'Precisely.'

'Argue me this, however. At this level, can you legislate against skill on the ball?'

'You've got me there!'

Lewis, Lennox Claudius (1966–). His left jab has intensive care written all over it.

See also ARMSTRONG, HENRY 'HANK'.

Lévi-Strauss, Claude (1908–). Social anthropologist. It is no coincidence, perhaps, that this most French of intellectuals should have spent so much of his life writing about food. He held the view that one should never judge, condemn or try to change people, but was firm to a fault with his own children.

'Who but the French could have produced a Lévi-Strauss?'

'The Belgians, in fact. He was born in Brussels and lectured at São Paolo University, Brazil, from 1934 to 1939. He subsequently worked in New York before becoming director of studies at the *École Pratique des Hautes Études* in Paris (1950–74).'

'Thank you, Dr Death. My point holds nonetheless.'

Lezzing it up. Easily explained as long as you only did it once and didn't enjoy it.

'And I *was* drunk.'

'Thank you, Geri.'

See HALLIWELL, GERI.

Liam, rock stars called. Forever telling their fans to 'fuck off'.

Libation. A word that sits well in a humorous column.

See also ABLUTIONS; ABODE; EATERIE; EMBONPOINT; HOSTELRY; INFELICITOUS; NOSHERIE; OCCASIONS; REPORTER; THESPIAN.

Liberties. Always 'diabolical'; unless 'cherished'.

See also INSTITUTIONS, OUR.

Life. Do you have a life – or just a menu?

'Try our quiz to discover whether you're a diet obsessive or simply sensible.'

'Sounds like one for "Monica's Health Club", Rebekah.'

See also NEWS OF THE WORLD, THE; WADE, REBEKAH.

Life, loss of. If British, 'tragic'; if not British, 'collateral damage'.

Life, Real. You can't top Real Life. Michael Parkinson has perceived this.

Life, the meaning of. The only significant question, though it admits of many significant answers.

'*Unica est quaestio, sed multifarae sunt responsiones.*'

'As the man said!'

Life-styles. Should be 'hectic'.

See also CELEBRITIES; JUGGLING WORK AND KIDS; SCHEDULES.

Light at the end of the tunnel, the. *See* BERNARD, JEFFREY.

Like. As that wise woman Virginia Ironside has pointed out, you can love someone without actually liking them.

'Or *vice versa*, would you say?'

'Indeed.'

'Or neither.'

'Ah Susan! Back from the Ladies! Thank you for that. This may interest you, Vernon. The European freshwater mussel...'

'*Margaritifera margaritifera*...'

'Thank you, Jolyon. May I continue?'

'Pray do.'

'The European freshwater mussel can reach the age of 90. What do you say to that?'

Like stepping back in time. *See* FOIX; ORANGE; PORVOO; SALA-MANCA; SIDI BOU SAID.

Lindwall, Ray (1921–96). With Keith Miller he formed the the finest opening attack in fast-bowling history.

'I don't hope to see a better in my lifetime.'

'Yet he was only 5ft 8in, you know.'

'Ah yes. But every inch a cricketer.'

See also BRIGHTWELL BALDWIN; COMPTON PAUNCEFOOT; NEMPNETT THRUBWELL; PAPWORTH EVERARD; STEEPLE BUMPSTEAD; STRATTON STRAWLESS; TURTON BOTTOMS; UPTON SNODSBURY.

Litter. It is not generally known that there was no word for litter in the Spanish language until the influx of British tourists in the early 1960s.

Little Romanian, the. *See* HISTRIONICS.

Liver. 'Well, it's your liver I suppose! Cheers!'

Lloyd Pack, Roger (1944–). An unsung hero of British comedy.

See also BLUTHAL, JOHN; CHALLIS, JOHN; CRIBBINS, BERNARD; CRYER, BARRY; JACQUES, HATTIE; LE MESURIER, JOHN; LODGE, DAVID; MAGEE, HENRY; SMITH, LIZ; STARK, GRAHAM; TODD, BOB; WHITFIELD, JUNE.

Lloyd Webber, Andrew (1948–). Composer of musical comedies.

See also NOSEBAGS, ON WITH THE; NOSHERIE.

Lobsters. *See* COOK, PETER; MANSFIELD, JAYNE.

Lodge, David (1923–). An unsung hero of British comedy.

See also BLUTHAL, JOHN; CHALLIS, JOHN; CRIBBINS, BERNARD; CRYER, BARRY; JACQUES, HATTIE; LE MESURIER, JOHN; MAGEE, HENRY; SMITH, LIZ; STARK, GRAHAM; TODD, BOB; WHITFIELD, JUNE.

Logic, divine. Always 'unfathomable'.
  'And none the worse for that.'
  'As *The Daily Mail* has correctly perceived.'

London. Not so much a city as a series of villages.

Look, a good. 'That is *so* not a good look!'
  'David Starkey on Anne of Cleves?'
  'Susannah and Trinny on a fat girl shopping in Joseph, but I take your point.'

See also SUSANNAH AND TRINNY.

Lopez, Jennifer (1970–). Singer and actress. Is she the total totty package? The debate continues.

Lordship. 'Is his lordship in?' An amusing remark to somebody's secretary.

Lose the will to live. *See* AUGUSTINE, ST; LENNON, JOHN; SEX.

Lot. One of France's best-kept secrets. Cahors, the *département*'s administrative centre, was the birthplace of Pope John XXII (1316–34).

See also ARIÈGE; AUDE; AVEYRON; CONQUES; FOIX; GARONNE YOUR BIKE AND DOWN THE LOT; LOZÈRE; SOLOGNE.

Loussier, Jacques (1934–). A man who defies categorization. He has accompanied Charles Aznavour and played with Romanian gypsy orchestras in Paris. He has recorded with the English counter-tenor, James Bowman, and written his own interpretations of the music of Bach, Vivaldi, Handel, Debussy, Satie and Ravel.
  'I've never heard of him.'

'He recently accused Eminem of sampling his music without permission.'

'Thank you, Susan. I'm none the wiser. Miguel!'

Love. Paradoxically, you can love someone without actually liking them.

'And *vice versa*?'

'Indeed.'

'And, after a while, neither.'

'Your point is, Susan?'

'No particular point, Simon. Just trying to keep the conversation going.'

See WALL, THE WRITING ON THE.

Love, falling in. A man falls in love through his eyes, a woman through her ears.

'So they say, Vernon. Roberto's lilting English is certainly very attractive. One can quite see why Daph...'

'Yes, thank you, Simon.'

Love, romantic. Without being too owlish, we should define what we mean by romantic love.

Love Bug, The (Peyton Reed, 1997). Remake of the slapstick Disney comedy chronicling the adventures of the irrepressible Volkswagen Beetle. John Hannah stars.

'Sounds like one to miss, Vernon.'

'I was quite looking forward to it, Daphne.'

Love-lives. Celebs are often obliged to put their love-lives on hold while they concentrate on career options.

'Do they continue to burst out laughing?'

'I rather think they do.'

See also CELEBS.

Love-split chart-toppers. Forever jetting off to luxury destinations in the Indian Ocean in a desperate bid to sort out their troubled lives.

'We're all guilty?'

'Not necessarily. I wouldn't wish to take personal responsibility in the case of troubled Zoe and Mr Fatboy Slim.'

See also BEAUTIES ON THE BRINK; MEETINGS, CRISIS; POP HOTTIES, HIP-SHAKING.

Low, Sir David (1891–1963). His draughtsmanship was so perfect that his subjects grew to look like his cartoons.

Lowest form of wit. *See* KEANE, ROY; SARCASM.

Lozère. One of France's best-kept secrets.

'That said, this may interest you, Vernon. Lozère is the smallest of France's *départements* in terms of population.'

See also ARIÈGE; AUDE; AVEYRON; CONQUES; FOIX; LOT; SOLOGNE.

Luftwaffe. *See* TOWN PLANNERS, POSTWAR.

Luggage. Customs officials have estimated that 98% of the suspicious objects detected in luggage by electronic scans are women's personal vibrators. There may be a lesson here.

Luxuries, life's little. In the hectic world of today, a career woman must learn to pamper herself with life's little luxuries. After rushing around all day, she should take the phone off the hook, relax in a long hot bath, and empty her head of all negative thoughts.

See also VOGUE.

McCall, Davina (1967–). Pointlessly common television presenter. That said, she's looking more relaxed now that she's discovered who she really is.

McEnroe, John. *See* BORG, BJÖRN.

MacNeice, Louis (1907–63). Irish poet who was noted for the wry irony of his comments on 20th-century society. Though associated with Auden and Spender in the 1930s, his verse was less political than theirs. In his published volumes the most memorable poems are about the sadness of life. That said, he was so overcome at the funeral of the Welsh poet, Dylan Thomas, that he threw his sandwiches into Thomas's grave rather than the floral tribute which he'd brought with him. There may be a lesson here.

Madonna (1961–). Horny hitmaker. According to the *Telegraph* 'Her Madgesty wrote the book!'

Mafia, the. *See* SCRUM, THE FRONT ROW OF THE.

Magdalene College, Cambridge. The dunces' college. They throw you a rugger ball and if you catch it they let you in. If you throw it back they give you a scholarship.
See also BUZZER, THE; DUNCAN SMITH, IAIN; PERUGIA, UNIVERSITY OF.

Magee, Henry (1925–). One of the unsung heroes of British comedy.
See also BLUTHAL, JOHN; CHALLIS, JOHN; CRIBBINS, BERNARD; CRYER, BARRY; JACQUES, HATTIE; LE MESURIER, JOHN; LLOYD PACK,

ROGER; LODGE, DAVID; SMITH, LIZ; STARK, GRAHAM; TODD, BOB; WHITFIELD, JUNE.

Magnusson, Magnus and **Magnusson, Sally.** *See* ESKIMOS WORKING IN THE UNITED KINGDOM.

Mahler, Gustav (1860–1911). Composer and conductor. Though he was a bridge between 19th- and 20th-century music, it is not generally known that he was only 5ft 2in.

Major league, in the. *See* ALBATROSS.

Mallarmé, Stéphane (1842–98). French Symbolist poet. An artist who strove to write 'pure' poetry, but the harder he laboured the less he wrote. Sadly, he lost an arm in a skirmish with the Turks. His work is all but inaccessible to the non-Gallic mind.
See also RIMBAUD, ARTHUR; TURKS, A SKIRMISH WITH THE.

Mallorca, the *real*. *See* NEWLY PAIRED-OFF THIRTYSOMETHINGS.

Man, Isle of. If a postage stamp bears the Queen's head, it is still a capital offence in the Isle of Man to stick it on to an envelope upside down.
See also ISLE OF MAN.

Man, the new. He may be in touch with the woman inside himself, but is he any happier?
'Well, Tony Parsons is for one. *Man and Boy* sold two-and-a-half million copies.'
'Indeed. But before submitting it to his publishers, Parsons took the sensible precaution of showing the manuscript to eleven women of his acquaintance. As he has himself admitted, "I wanted to be sure that I'd touched those tender female buttons."'
'Im off 2 the toilet, me.'
'Very sensible.'
'Ta.'
'I wasn't referring to your decision to visit the – er – toilet, Sharon, but to Tony Parsons's wise decision not to trust the woman inside himself.'

'He was married to Julie Burchill, of course.'

'What's that got to do with it?'

'Nothing at all, as far as I know. A thought occurs, however.'

'Yes, Vernon?'

'Are women now encouraged to search for the man inside themselves?'

'Indeed they are. One only has to think of such celebrated ladettes as Denise, Zoe and Coxy getting – excuse me – well trolleyed down the Met Bar and Chinawhite…'

'Coxy? I don't think I'm familiar with her work.'

'*Coxy* and *Zoe*! i mean … *purleeze!* There *so* September/October 2002! + the *Met* Bar! Thats *so* May 2003. i mean, *wot?*'

'Thank you, Tracey.'

'Im off 2 join Sharon in the toilet.'

'I'll come with you.'

'Susan! You'll do nothing of the sort. I positively… Damn! Too late again!'

See also WELL TROLLEYED.

Man, the perfectability of. To believe in the perfectability of man is one of the endemic follies of our age. *The Daily Mail* has not been deceived.

See also DAILY MAIL THE; EVIL; MAN, THE PERFECTABILITY OF; NATURE, HUMAN; PENDULUM; PROGRESS, BELIEF IN THE ILLUSION OF; REAL WORLD, THE; UTOPIA, THE SEARCH FOR.

Manchester. Formerly something of a black spot in terms of that most indefinable of qualities, 'style', Manchester has in the past few years experienced a cultural renaissance. A branch of Harvey Nichols has recently opened, a new four-star hotel is being built and top chef Gordon Ramsay…

See also BIRMINGHAM; BRADFORD; BRISTOL; GLASGOW; LEEDS; NEWCASTLE; SHEFFIELD.

Manchester United. Forever having the stuffing knocked out of them by Del Piero's second half hat-trick.

See also GAME, THE; OLD TRAFFORD; *PROPERTY LADDER, THE.*

Manet, Édouard (1832–83). French painter. Manet was unknown when his painting *Le Déjeuner sur l'herbe* was first shown in Paris in 1863. However, this groundbreaking picture turned him into a famous figure overnight and caused a storm of protest. Many critics believed that his unorthodox style was too sketchy and they were scandalized by his frank depiction of naked women. The work has since been recognized as a masterpiece which changed the way artists thought.

Mansfield, Jayne (1932–67). American actress (*see* COOK, PETER).

Manuscripts. Forever landing on publishers' desks. Unsolicited manuscripts are never welcome.

'Thank you for your proposal for *A Pervert's Guide To English Literature*. In spite of the undoubted interest of the material, I'm afraid we must regretfully pass on this one. I'm sure you'll have no difficulty in placing it with a more adventurous house. I was sorry to hear about the result of the sigmoidoscopy.' (Dictated by Gail Rebuck and signed in her absence.)

See also NARRATIVE, THE ART OF.

Marbella, elderly bank robbers living in blameless luxury in. Forever being discourteously ambushed in the street by cocky English journalists and being asked on camera why they don't return to the United Kingdom to face trial.

See also LEATHERHEAD, PENSIONED OLD FOLK FROM.

Marciano, Rocky (1923–69). Pound for pound the finest boxer ever to pull the gloves on.

'I don't hope to see a better in my lifetime.'

See also ALI, MUHAMMAD; ARMSTRONG, HENRY 'HANK'; DURAN, ROBERTO; HAGLER, MARVIN; HEARNS, THOMAS 'THE HITMAN'; LEONARD, SUGAR RAY; LOUIS, JOE; MOORE, ARCHIE; PEP, WILLIE; ROBINSON, SUGAR RAY.

Marcuse, Herbert (1898–1979). Philosopher. Opinion is divided as to whether Marcuse caused the student riots of the late 1960s or was caused by them. Either way, his seminal contribution – the concept of repressive tolerance – meant that students were free to read his works and to fornicate in the streets. *The Daily Mail* was not deceived.

'With the late Lord Jenkins, he must carry much of the blame for the Nude Encounter Parlours that sprang up in London's West End in the 1960s.'

'And for Miss Whiplash, of Walker's Court, Soho, where in the early afternoon one could be suspended in surgical stirrups from the ceiling...'

'Miss Whiplash? I don't remember her, Simon.'

'Nor do I, nor do I. Don't know why I mentioned her.'

'You're all right, are you, Simon? You've gone rather white again ... oh dear ...'

See also MASSAGE PARLOURS.

Margaret, Princess (1930–2002). It is too easily forgotten, perhaps, that in her day she was as glamorous a figure as Princess Diana was in hers.

'Pass the cruet, Con.'

'Here you are, then.'

'Cheers.'

'What was that you were saying, Vernon?'

'About what?'

'Princess Margaret.'

'I can't remember.'

See also WALES, DIANA, PRINCESS OF.

Marie Antoinette (1755–93). Austrian-born queen of France, married to the impotent (and possibly homosexual) Louis XVI. It is not generally known that in a BBC documentary about the doomed but spoilt queen, Lady Antonia Fraser (the daughter of the late Lord Longford, let it not be forgotten) really did say:

'If she couldn't have the fucking she could at least have the shopping.'

'*O tempora, o mores!*'

'Frank would have been turning in his grave.'

'I'm not so sure.'

Marine biologists. It has been reliably calculated that marine biologists spend 93% of their time tagging sharks with colour-coded discs. Nobody knows why.

'Excuse me. I know why.'

'Why, then?'

'So that they can identify them in the future.'

'Why would they want to do that?'

'I can't imagine.'

'Well, there you are.'

See also PLASTIC RUBBISH; SHARKS, GREAT WHITE; SHARK, THE SIX-GILLED.

Marjoribanks, Major. Pronounced 'Marchbanks'.

'You may well be the Secretary of the Midsomer Florey Cricket Club, Major, but a young boy's been murdered and someone's been tampering with the evidence. Come along, Sergeant.'

See also EVIDENCE, THE; THINKING.

Markets. Often 'volatile'.

'A volatile jobs market has made people see mortgage insurance in a new light.'

'Sounds like one for the Money section, Andreas.'

Marr, Andrew (1959–). Political journalism's answer to Barry Norman.

'Nye Bevan he ain't! Enjoy!'

'Thank you, Andrew.'

'Olivier he ain't! Meanwhile, back at the ranch...'

'Thank you, Barry.'

See also DREAM ON, PAL; GO FIGURE; SEX SYMBOLS.

Marsh, Jodie. *See* SOCCER BAD BOYS.

Marshmallow, a touch of arsenic in the. *See* MOTHER, THE QUEEN.

Marshy's Mindbender. 'Every week you will have the chance to test your knowledge with "Marshy's Mindbender", the top teaser for football trivia fanatics.

'But beware! You will work up quite a thirst as you try to pinpoint the answer!

'So there's a cool case of Carling lager for the first correct answer out of the bag!

'This week's mindbender is: "With Sgt Wilko in charge, how many points did Sunderland pick up out of a possible 60?"

'Now ring 0906 36 36 960, leaving your answer, name and day-time telephone number. Calls cost just 60p a minute and last no longer than 90 seconds.

'Winners will be selected from all correct entries received by the closing date of noon next Thursday.

'Last week's answer was Trevor Brooking.'

'*The Times?*'

'*The Daily Star*, in fact, but I take your point.'

Marvellous spirit. *See* DOUBLES, MIXED.

Marvin, Lee (1924–87). Actor. There's an engaging irony in the fact that this legendary hard man of so many classic gangster films and westerns should in real life have been a cultured and sensitive man who wrote agreeably unpretentious verses and assembled the finest private collection of French impressionists outside France.

See also CAGNEY, JAMES; EASTWOOD, CLINT; PESCI, JOE; ROBINSON, EDWARD G.; WIDMARK, RICHARD.

Marx, Groucho. *See* OPPOSITES.

Mary, Queen of Scots. *See* HARASSMENT, SEXUAL.

Massage parlours. Always 'mushrooming'.

'They'll be in Taunton next.'

'And Diss.'

'Surely not!'

'I'd not be too sanguine. Diss already has a Tesco's.'

'I can scarcely believe my ears.'

See MARCUSE, HERBERT; SEX SHOPS.

Material, explicit. Always 'from abroad'.

Materialism. Always 'crass'. A philosophical theory that leads inevitably, via colour-supplement values, to pornography and violence. We can't seriously be asked to believe that *Hamlet* and *The Marriage of Figaro* and Chartres Cathedral are the results of random movements of atoms.

'Sounds like one for *The Oldie*, Richard.'

See also HEART; SCIENCE.

Matisse, Henri Émile Benoît (1869–1954). French painter. Famous for masterpieces such as *The Joy of Life* (1905) and *The Blue Nude* (1907), Matisse celebrated colour – and, by extension, life – in his art, but was criticized by some experts for the seeming ease of his paintings and for their air of self-indulgent pleasure. It has been suggested that the exuberance of his work was a reaction to the pain in his private life.

Matt, electricians called. Forever being unceremoniously dumped by bosomy Page 3 crackers.

See also JORDAN.

Maupassant, Guy de (1850–93). The unrivalled master of the short *conte*. Like so many French intellectuals, he lost his left arm in a skirmish with the Turks. Died of syphilis.

See also TURKS, A SKIRMISH WITH THE.

Meadows, my poulterer, the estimable Mr. A phrase that sits well in an occasional column.

See also ALFRED; DANE, HAMLET THE MOODY; DUCK, DONALD; EDUCATION, FORMAL; INTELLECTUAL, LIBERAL; KEATS, JOHN; NOSHERIE.

Measuring things. *See* MEN.

Media, the. Forever having 'a field day', if not 'a feeding frenzy'.

Media Studies. *See* AVEDON, RICHARD.

Meeting, the. Pertinent and reasonable objections to corporate strategies are never discussed at meetings.

'Jeremy, I wonder if we could discuss that outside the meeting? Next?'

See also JEREMY; NEWLY PAIRED-OFF THIRTYSOMETHINGS.

Meet there some time, we must. *See* ABODE; CRAPS, A CROWD OF; 'FRIEND, IN A PIG'S ARSE'; LARKIN, PHILIP; 'VERS DE SOCIÉTÉ'.

Mel B (1975–). Former member of the Spice Girls pop group. She's been looking more relaxed since she decided to put her singing career on hold and direct her energies into acting.

Meldrew, TV's Victor. Everybody's favourite Mr Grouch!
'I don't *believe* it.'
'Pray cease! I'll choke on my gazpacho!'

Melissa. 'You bastard, Simon! You've been shagging Melissa! Don't deny it, I know you have. In my flat! What do you mean, it's *your* flat? We'll see what my lawyer has to say about *that!*'

See also CAROLINE AND TOBY; HUGO; HUMPHREY; MOOD; NEWLY PAIRED-OFF THIRTYSOMETHINGS; WALL, THE WRITING ON THE.

Memory for faces, terrible. *See* AGAIN.

Men. Forever measuring things.

Men, single. Debauched egotists who sleep with their maids.

Ménages-à-trois. Forever sending shock-waves through the Establishment.
'They've never appealed to me, I don't know why.'
'At the rate your bird and Roberta are going, Mr Pratley, you may have to acquire a taste for them. Just a thought.'
'Yes, thank you, Miguel. Perhaps while we have your attention, you could oblige us with another bottle of … Well I never! He's gone again.'

Men, Spanish. Fiery local patriots who fight cocks and eat dogs. So belligerent are they that in the absence of a third party, they will attempt to beat themselves up and lay bets on the outcome. Be careful not to enliven their indignation by asking to sleep with their sisters.

See also ITALIAN POLICE, THE; TRAWLERMEN, CORNISH.

Men, Swedish. Unable to perform oral sex because their eyes are too close together.

See also BORG, BJÖRN.

Mentally ill. It is surely no coincidence that the number of offenders claiming to be mentally ill has risen in the same proportion as the number of medical practitioners prepared to claim that such a condition exists.

'Thomas Szasz has not been deceived.'

'Nor has *The Daily Mail*.'

'That, perhaps, is less surprising.'

See also SZASZ, THOMAS.

Mercury, Freddie, *originally* **Frederick Bulsara** (1946–91). British pop singer, born in Zanzibar. Always held in greater esteem by the fans than by the critics, Mercury developed an increasingly 'camp' stage presence which sometimes obscured the forcefulness of his vocal delivery.

Michelangelo painting the Sistine Chapel during an air-raid. *See* BEST, GEORGE.

Middle managers. *See* POTTERS BAR.

Midlands, shell-suited working-class women from the. Forever being invited by Kirsty Young to message their views on international affairs to Channel 5 News. Nobody knows why.

See also LEATHERHEAD, PENSIONED OLD FOLK FROM; OPINIONS; PEOPLE, REAL.

'Midst, The Stranger In Our.' Good title for an article about Sir Alec Guinness.

See also GUINNESS, SIR ALEC.

Miller, Jonathan (1934–). Doctor, writer, director of plays and operas.

'At the end of the day, would you say that the most interesting

thing about this remarkable polymath is that he knew Peter Cook?'
    'No I wouldn't. The opposite, if anything.'
    'Thank you, Miguel. But I was talking to Mr Plimmer.'
    'If you say so, John. You're the man.'

Milligan, Spike (1918–2000). The 'godfather of modern comedy', yet his ability to make millions laugh brought him only a partial solace. There may be a lesson here.

See also COOK, PETER.

Milverton. A small village not six miles from Taunton, yet one of Somerset's best-kept secrets.
    'Not anymore!'
    'Nor it is! Well, there you are!'

See also ASH PRIORS; BISHOPS LYDEARD; CORFE; SECRETS, SOMERSET'S BEST-KEPT; TAUNTON.

Minogue, Kylie (1968–). She's only 5 ft tall, but every inch the total totty package. Her bottom made Holly Valance's bottom possible.

See also DIVAS; JAGGER, MICK; VALANCE, HOLLY.

Minority. Small but vocal. Always wrong. Usually 'politically motivated', unlike the silent majority. *The Daily Mail* has not been deceived.

Mirabile dictu. *See* VAUGHAN, MICHAEL.

Misfortune. Tragedy or mere misfortune? There's a place for both but it's better not to confuse them.

See also ARISTOTLE; TRAGEDY.

Mish-mash. Always 'disappointing'.

MI6. Contrary to popular belief, the following exchange really did take place in an episode of the TV series *Spooks,* written on this occasion by National Theatre playwright, Howard Brenton:
    'Thank you, Bleasdale. You've just ensured that this is the worst night of my life.'

'But Sir Hugo…'

'First I discover that one of my best agents has been assassinated and now you interrupt the finest production of Wagner's *Parsifal* I have ever seen to tell me something I already knew.'

See also BLEASDALE.

Mistaken, unless I'm very much. *See* INSIGHTS.

Modest. *See* ABODE.

Molière, *pen name of* **Jean-Baptiste Poquelin** (1622–73). French dramatist. Best known for *Le Misanthrope* (1666), he offended the sensibilities of the devout with his *Tartuffe* (1664) and then fell down dead while playing Argan in a production of *Le Malade imaginaire*.

'What exquisite irony! Truly God is not mocked!'

On mention of his name, murmur, '*Que diable allait-il faire dans cette galère?*' No need to explain why.

See also GOD.

Molly. 'When I saw what you were doing to Hugo, I hated you, Molly. But now I don't hate you any more. I pity you.'

See also NEWLY PAIRED-OFF THIRTYSOMETHINGS.

Monday, pop totties with a single out on. Forever telling the world about their secret pain.

See also POP BABES, TROUBLED.

Monet, Claude (1840–1926). Self-taught, but, as Émile Zola famously put it, '*Voilà un homme dans la foule des eunuques.*'

Monkey bites. Responsible for more deaths than you might think.

Monkeys. If the proverbial monkey ever did type out the complete works of William Shakespeare, he wouldn't understand a word he'd written.

'And unlike Bill Shakespeare – and, in our own day, Keith Waterhouse – he might have an imperfect grasp of what puts bums on seats!'

'A delicious insight, Vernon! And this may interest you: scientists working with monkeys have discovered that if you intoxicate them with vodka and tonic the percentage that becomes alcoholic is exactly the same as obtains in the human population. The percentage which remains teetotal is also the same.'

'There may be a lesson here.'

'I rather doubt it. Paradoxically, monkeys, unlike humans, respect the alcoholics among their number and elect the one which is permanently intoxicated as their leader. The more he staggers about and falls flat on his face, the more they revere him.'

'Extraordinary!'

'Extraordinary indeed. On the other hand, monkeys who become addicted to so-called crack cocaine receive no such leniency from the group. An addicted monkey is chased up a tree, where he hides in shame with his pipe and stash of rocks.'

'Amazing. That said, I can't help noticing that your better half and Sharon have been in the Ladies for twenty minutes.'

'Thank you for pointing that out, Vernon. Girls' talk, I imagine.'

'Without a doubt.'

Monroe, Marilyn (1926–62). Like many people with a full address book she found there were times when no one was in.

'Her life lacked a third act, would you say?'

'Indeed. She was sacrificed on the altar of our fantasies.'

'I couldn't have put it better myself.'

See also BYRON, LORD GEORGE; CASS, MAMA; DEAN, JAMES; EPSTEIN, BRIAN; HENDRIX, JIMI; JONES, BRIAN; JOPLIN, JANIS; MOON, KEITH; TOULOUSE-LAUTREC, HENRI; WALES, DIANA, PRINCESS OF.

Mood. Women have to be in the mood. 'You awake, Melissa?'
See also MELISSA.

Moon, Keith (1946–78). An exciting talent laid to waste by the excesses of stardom. Did he confuse the myth with the reality? Certainly, he fell into the trap of believing his own publicity.
See also BYRON, LORD GEORGE.

Moore, Archie (1913–98). Pound for pound the finest boxer ever to pull the gloves on.

'I don't hope to see a better in my lifetime.'

See also ALI, MUHAMMAD; ARMSTRONG, HENRY; DURAN, ROBERTO; HAGLER, MARVIN; HEARNS, THOMAS 'THE HITMAN; LEONARD, SUGAR RAY; LOUIS, JOE; MARCIANO, ROCKY; PEP, WILLIE; ROBINSON, SUGAR RAY.

Moore, Charles (1956–). Reservations were expressed in some quarters of *The Daily Telegraph* when its Old Etonian editor, Charles Moore, decided to take his paper into the 21st century by making it interactive. In the event, the results have been encouraging. Among early messages and texts received were:

'I chngd 2 the Tel 3 weeks ago and am wel pleezed. Plenty 2 read, loadsa fit chix + ur backin the lads in Iraq. Keep it up.' T. Blacker, Diss.

'Westlife r total wusses 4 bottling a chart fite wiv Blue. Theyd nok there sox off.' H. Massingberd, West Kensington.

'that tosser abu hamza should b locked up in the man u dssing rm thn fergie cld kik fings at him.' Lady A. Pinter, East Sussex.

'Ur janet daley mus b 1 of the hottest chix around. N e chance of a d8, jan?' C. Brown, Aldeburgh.

'luv the paper, u guys, but wen r us gals gonna get a fella on page 3? Thierry Henry is well fit.' G. Greer, Suffolk.

'carmen electra shud nva av bin chukt off jury 4 bein 2 sexy with her flirty pranx. Werz the justice? 4 real.' I. Hislop, Sissinghurst.

Moore, Dudley (1935–2002). His Faustian pact with Hollywood did scant justice to his many gifts.

Moore, G.E. (1873–1958). His character, unusually for a philosopher, had as much force as his ideas. He held that friendship was the highest good, despite professing himself unable to define 'good'. He demonstrated the existence of the external world to the British Academy by holding up his hand in front of his face.

Moore, Patrick Alfred Caldwell (1923–). Astronomer. What an agreeable irony that when the young Patrick Moore went into Cleethorpes Public Library and asked for a book on the stars, they gave him, instead of Peter Noble's *The Great Years of Hollywood*, which he had wanted, a copy of *The Young Observer's Guide to the Heavens*. Truly, the cinema's loss was astronomy's gain.

See also NORMAN, BARRY.

Morse, Inspector. *See* ABUSE, VERBAL; BLACKMAIL; HORNBY, MRS;
MURDERERS; PATTERSON, MRS; PERKINS; PHILOSOPHER; POLITICIAN;
TOUCH OF FROST, A.

Mortgaged. Always 'to the hilt'. That said, you can't go wrong with
bricks and mortar.
See also PROPERTY LADDER, THE.

Mortimer, John (1923–). Creator of the immortal Horace Rumpole.
   'Who better understands the old truth that great trials are the stuff
of drama and great drama the stuff of the Old Bailey?'
See also COMEDY.

Moss, Kate (1974–). Supermodel. On one occasion she was,
famously, four days late for a booking with top photographer David
Bailey.
   'I gather she's looking more relaxed now that she's discovered a
new purpose in life.'
   'And what might that be?'
   'I haven't the faintest idea.'
   'Perhaps she's writing some songs with the intention of bringing
out a début album.'
   'Stranger things have happened. Er – yes, Marty?'
   't.A.T.u.? Blow your skirt up, do they, Vernon?'
   'I'm not sure if I'm familiar with their work. Tell me, Simon. Busby
Berkeley. As a film-maker, years ahead of his time, would you say?'
   'Without a doubt. The French were the first to perceive this, of
course.'

Mother, the Queen (1900–2002). A vindictive woman by all
accounts, but it has to be admitted that she redesigned the royal
publicity machine. Nor did fate always deal her the best of hands.
When her husband, George VI, died, she not only lost four of her
seventeen homes, she lost her power base, too.
   Many anecdotes attach to her name. Meeting Winston Churchill
once in the corridors of Clarence House, she said: 'You're drunk!'
Quick as a flash, the great man replied, 'Maybe so, but you're
fucking ugly!'

The story that attributes to her the comment 'It makes me feel I can look the East End in the face' following the German bombing of Buckingham Palace in the Second World War may well be apocryphal. As she stepped through the ruins of Stratford-atte-Bow, she is believed to have said, 'If we don't get the hell out of here we'll miss the 2.40 at Haydock Park.'

'Yes, Vernon?'

'What the cynics failed to understand, was that to simple, ordinary people she was as real as Dot Cotton or Bet Lynch.' (*See* PEOPLE, ORDINARY.)

'How true. She was the nation's favourite gran.'

See also 'BUGGER BOGNOR!'

Mother, the victim's. It's the victim's mother who has the life sentence. Rebekah Wade has perceived this.

See also NEWS OF THE WORLD, THE; WADE, REBEKAH.

Mothers. Mothers can't go on strike.

Motson, John (1945–). Camel-coated football commentator. Contrary to received opinion, John Motson really did say of England's 1–0 victory over Argentina in the 2002 World Cup finals: 'It's bangers with Batistuta and cornflakes with Crespo.' Equally, when Michael Owen scored the opening goal during England's quarter-final against Brazil, Motson really did say: 'England are sizzling in Shizouka and after this the sausages will be sizzling back home.'

See also FANTASY, BRAZILIAN; RONALDO.

Mousetrap, The. Nobody's seen it. A mystery.

See also DOOR-TO-DOOR ENCYCLOPEDIA SALESMEN.

Mums-of-two, single. Forever being leap-frogged in the housing queue by North African asylum-seekers.

See also AS EVER; ASYLUM-SEEKERS; BENDING OVER BACKWARDS TO HELP SCROUNGERS; BRITAIN; OLD FOLK, OUR AILING.

Munro, Hector Hugh (1870–1916). No one could recline more wantonly outside Dr Leavis's so-called Great Tradition than Hector Hugh Monro (better known as Saki to countless lovers of his agreeably light-hearted but admirably crafted fictions), yet few admitted to that stern élite have given so many hours of harmless pleasure.

'What about "Plum" Wodehouse?'

'He too was excluded by the good Doctor.'

'You amaze me.'

See also LEAVIS, F.R.

Murderers. Forever killing people with 'a powerful blow to the back of the head'. That said, they are seldom very clever.

'If you don't mind my saying so, Sergeant, it would be rather stupid to kill someone with a powerful blow to the back of the head and be seen moments later carrying a blunt instrument.'

'With respect, Inspector, there's no reason why murderers should be members of Mensa.'

'Well, there's a sort of surreal logic in that, I suppose. Come along, then.'

See also INSTRUMENT.

Mushrooms. 'This will interest you, Vernon. Did you know that there are 187 different varieties of mushroom to be found in Britain, all but two of which induce states of ecstasy, often religious?'

'Really? Seen your boy lately?'

'Just a phase.'

'Still not back from the toilet, then – your bird and my Sharon.'

'Thank you Marty. My bird – as you refer to her – happens to be my partner of eleven years.'

'Never mind. She'll be back.'

Music industry, the. Forever holding its breath waiting to discover whether Mariah Carey's magic still exists.

Mussorgsky, Modest Petrovich (1839–81). Member of the group of five St Petersburg-based composers known as 'The Five'. He died after drinking a bottle of vodka smuggled to him in hospital, but his music bears witness to the same Russia that produced Gogol and Dostoievski.

Mystic Meg. 'Really, Vernon! I'm not Mystic Meg, you know!'
'Nor are you, Daphne.'

Myth, the beauty. It has been reliably calculated that when shopping for clothes 67% of women buy into the beauty myth. They shop not for themselves but for the person they'd like to be. It is not unusual for a woman who is a size 14 to buy a dress that is size 8. She is subconsciously making the statement:
'I will love myself more when I'm a size 8.'
'We're talking body image here.'
'Sounds like one for the Fashion pages, Susannah.'
See also FRANKEL, SUSANNAH.

Myths. Often 'about to explode'.
'For Whitney Houston the myth was about to explode.'
See also HOUSTON, WE HAVE A PROBLEM.

Nabokov, Vladimir (1899–1977). His eyes glinted with mockery in an otherwise solemn face. Was he teasing us when he said he was prouder of having named a butterfly than of having writen *Ada* or *Lolita*? We shall never know, and that's how he would have wanted it.

Names. English soccer players merely 'have' names. Foreign players 'rejoice' in theirs.

'The nippy little South Korean, who rejoices in the name of Han Qi Pan Ki, is giving the big English defender a lesson in one-touch football.'

'Thank you, Barry.'

See also GAME, THE.

Namibia, the Bushmen of. Trackers of legendary skill.

'Here's one, Vernon. Did you know that a leopard goes about its predatory business so stealthily that none has ever been filmed, or even been seen, when making a kill?'

'I confess I didn't.'

'Well, there you are. That said, the Bushman of Namibia are such skilful trackers that from the examination of a single footprint or displaced leaf they can precisely infer that the kill took place at 8.16 a.m. on the previous Tuesday, what species of animal the victim was, the sex and age of the leopard, whether it had cubs, the number, sex and ages of the cubs and whether they were allowed to share the meal.'

'You amaze me.'

'Even more extraordinarily, if the Bushman happens to have

attended Winchester College, which many now have, of course, he can do quadratic equations in his head, is comfortable in Latin and Greek and will certainly be able to argue persuasively why the poems of Lord Byron sit outside the Augustan mode.'

'I'll take your word for it.'

Napoleon. Good name for a pig.

Narrative, the art of. In all good stories the ending is in the beginning, but the reader must on no account see it coming. That said, the ending always has to be changed.

'Thank you for giving us the opportunity to read your latest novel, Terence. It's a fascinating book, but we don't think the ending's quite right and, regretfully, have come to the conclusion that we'll pass on this one. However, do please send us anything else you write.'

See also MANUSCRIPTS.

Nature, Dame. 'You can't *aim* at happiness. It can never be an end in itself. It has to be a by-product of something else. The look of wonder on a child's face, a day out with Dame Nature, curling up with a good book and a glass of claret in front of a log fire...'

'That's done it. Coming to the toilet, Con?'

'After you, Marty.'

See also HAPPINESS.

Nature, human. You can't legislate against human nature. *The Daily Mail* has perceived this.

'Nor against skill on the ball.'

'How true.'

Nature, the rhythms of. Working with the rhythms of nature reaps its own reward. What this means no one can guess.

Nature's gentlemen, one of. *See* MEADOWS, MY POULTERER, THE ESTIMABLE MR.

Neck of the woods, your. *See* ABODE.

Needless to say. Needless to say, the Germans organize these things better.

'Sad but true.'

See also GERMANS, THE; THINGS, THESE.

Nempnett Thrubwell. Either a picturesque village in Somerset, or a West Indian fast bowler. The debate continues.

See also TURTON BOTTOMS.

New. New doesn't necessarily mean better. *The Daily Mail* has not been deceived.

See also PROGRESS, BELIEF IN THE ILLUSION OF.

Newcastle. Formerly something of a black spot in terms of that most indefinable of qualities, 'style', Newcastle in the past few years has experienced something of a cultural renaissance. A branch of Harvey Nichols has recently opened, a new four-star hotel is being built and top chef Gordon Ramsay...

See also BIRMINGHAM; BRADFORD; BRISTOL; CARDIFF; GEORDIE, THE AFFABLE; GLASGOW; LEEDS; MANCHESTER; SHEFFIELD.

Newly paired-off thirtysomethings. Forever being invited to supper parties by other newly paired-off thirtysomethings and being force-fed green salads from bottomless wooden bowls.

'... it's a Sony Ericsson P800 ... flip-down keypad ...'

'... £1.5m ... Shoreditch ... done and dusted ...'

'... between a rock and a hard place ... I said, "look, Humphrey..."...'

'... daylight robbery ...!'

'... the powers that be ...!'

'... the usual suspects ...!'

'... you're looking fantastically sexy tonight, Caroline ...'

'... well, thank you, kind sir! ... more salad ...?'

'... not at the moment, thanks Caroline ... might have got more ...'

'... easily converted ... '

'... quite frankly, it's quicker to go by ...'

'... Melissa? What about you? More salad?'

'... Peter Jones? Can you believe it? £85! Gillian thought it was a Julien McDonald! What was that, Caroline?'

'... I said help yourself to salad ...'

'... not for me, thanks ... the boots ...?'

'... I said, "change your accountant, Nigel!" ... well, you know me! ...'

' ... would you believe it? ... Manolo Blahnik ...?'

'... still at Hodder Headline, Melissa ...?'

'... *voilà* ...!'

'... no ... Random House now ... head of publicity! ... frightfully grand! ...'

'... an arm and a leg ...'

'... Julian Barnes? ... I don't know if we publish him ... I could find out, I suppose ...'

'... I said "get thee behind me, Satan!"... well, you know me! ...'

'... Adrian Gill ... *so* cruel ... but frightfully funny ... don't you think ...?'

'... what's your news? ... do tell ...!'

'... yes, it's an NEC e606 ... video calls ... video and picture messaging ...'

'... not forgetting our Arab friends ...!'

'... a country mile ...'

'... proactive ...!'

'... what a muppet ...!'

'... the latest Arabella Weir ... *so* accurate ... I keep thinking "that's *me*! ...'

'... Melissa! You're still not eating any salad ... where is she, by the way? ... has anyone seen Melissa ...?'

'... *pour encourager les autres* ...'

'... and that's pounds, not dollars ...'

'... I said, "Methinks the lady doth protest too much!" ... well, you know me! ...'

'... and you can download video clips and local street maps ...'

'... no, no, no ... you should turn off at junction 7 ... take the B209 to Hook ...'

'... Humphrey and I swear by Sophie Grigson ... she's *such* a star ... isn't that right, Humphrey? ... where's Humphrey? ... that's odd ... has anyone seen Humphrey ...?'

'... the handset has two built-in cameras ...'

'... shedloads of it ... don't begrudge him it for a minute ...

deserves every penny.'

'... hopefully, Roger ...'

'... £399 ... talk about value! ...'

'... you know me! ...'

'... the new PowerBook ... blazing G4 processor, super-crisp display (1024 x 768mm) ... here, have a look ...'

'Salad ...'

'... Scott Henshall ...'

'... £285 ...'

'... tell me, Hugo ... are you and Melissa going to be in London this weekend, by any chance ...?'

'... I'd better check with Melissa ... this weekend ... are we going to the cottage ... that's odd ... where's Melissa ...?'

'... as you were ... junction 9 and take the B210 to ...'

'... I said, "if it was such rubbish how come 3 million people read it?" Well, you know me! ...'

'... 50K a week. Wouldn't get out of bed for less ...'

'... I said, "Charles, you're preaching to the converted" ...'

'... yes, it's an easy-going red ... Sainsbury's, would you believe? ...'

'... Caroline and I are thinking of taking ashtanga yoga classes ...'

'... MELISSA! Well, well, well! What's a nice girl like you doing in Caroline's kitchen ...?'

'... now don't be naughty, Humphrey! ... *no!* ...'

'... slot-load CD-burning/DVD-playing Combo drive ...'

'... oh come on, Melissa ... a snatched moment of dark, shallow, meaningless sex, who'd say no to that?'

'... with an underlying note of peach ...'

'... and integrated Bluetooth ...'

'... you were up for it in the vestry at Pippa's wedding ...'

'... I said *no*, Humphrey! ... absolutely *not* ...!'

'... and with Jeremy, when Pippa was in labour with the twins ...'

'... a 1.9 litre diesel-powered Peugeot 307 LX hatchback at the moment ... hell of a lot of grunt ... 0 to 70 in six seconds ... can't complain ...'

'... plus a battery that lasts for up to 5 hours ... all engineered into a package that's just 1.2cm thick ... '

'... more salad ...'

'... £75,999 ...'

'... oh come on, Melissa! ... here, against the aga ... wearing just your boots ... Damn, it's my mobile ... "Hullo? Yes? Jeremy! You're *where* ...?"'

'... *no* Humphrey! ... take your hand *out* of my ... *no no NO*...!'

'... "sorry about that, Jeremy. You're on a *train*? Stuck outside *Reading*? Look, can't really talk. I'm at a supper party. Caroline and Toby. I'll crunch some numbers and get back to you tomorrow ... love to Pippa..." ... Sorry about that, Melissa ... now, I'll just slip your dress off ... Christ, you're not wearing any ...'

'... correction! ... got it right first time ... you turn off at junction 7 and ...'

'... converting a barn in Diss, I hear. Great for the kids ... yes, two ... Camilla's sweet ...'

'... no, Purves and Purves, I think ...'

'... behave yourself, Humphrey ...!'

'... *Sex and the City* ... *so* real ... Humphrey and I are positively *addicted* ... where is he, by the way? ... has anyone seen Humphrey ...?'

'... Miu Miu ... £500, I think ... no, £600 ... that was it ...'

'... to Turkey this year. And you ...?'

'... who's for more salad, then ...?

'... Mallorca ...'

'... I've got the receipt somewhere ...'

'... the *real* Mallorca, of course. Up in the northwest of the island ...'

'... salad ...?'

'... it has retained its true *ambienza campesina,* as it were ...'

'... twelve bottles and you get a jolly generous discount ...'

'... come on, Melissa! ... here, in just your boots ... on the kitchen table ...'

'... no, I tell a lie ... you turn off at junction 11 and ...'

'... Humphrey ... for the *last* time ... *NO!* ... I *mean* it ... ooooooooh ...!'

'... so what's your news, Davina ...?'

'... oooooohhhhhhh ...!'

'... well off the beaten track ...'

'... my broker told me I was long in *Hachette* ...'

'... junction 9 ... that's it ...'

'... so when they said "sell", I did, jolly pronto ...'

'... ooooooohhhhhhhhhhh ...!'

'... poor old Bunty caught a bit of a cold ... should have listened to me ... now the cottage may have to go ...'

'... you know me ...'

'... and the Merc ...'

'... get thee behind me, Satan ...!'

'... aaaaaaahhhhh ... lower ... *lower,* Humphrey! ... no, not *that* low ... you're not concentrating ... you've got to *concentrate* ...'

'... so I said "methinks the lady doth protest too much!"... well ... you know me ...!'

'... higher ... and slower ...'

'... or do I mean junction 12 ...?'

'... and don't forget my breasts ... don't *grab* them! ... *stir* them ... that's better ... now ... bear down on me ... softly at first ... not *that* softly ... harder ... and now *faster* ... *yes* ... aaaaaaaaaahhhhh-hhhhhhh ...!'

'... more salad, Jocasta ...?'

'... aaaaaahhhhhhhhhh ...'

'... damn ... hang on, Melissa ... it's my mobile again. "Hullo? Daphne! Well I never! Where *are* you? The *what? ...*"'

'... aaaaaaahhhhhhhhhhhhhhhhhhhh ...!'

'"... sorry about that, Daphne. You're where? The *Goya!* Yes, I know it. In Islington, yah? With *who*? Good God! Rather you than me! Fearful bore. Where? In the *Ladies*? Well, good for you! ..."'

'... yyyyyeeeeeeeeeeeeeeeeee ...!'

'"... I'm still here, Daphne. No of *course* I won't! Not a soul. My lips are sealed. Your secret's safe with me! Look, can't really talk now ... I'm at this supper party ... bye!" ... fearfully sorry about that, Melissa ...'

'... eeeeEEEEEEEEEE ...!'

'... guess who that was? Daphne! And where do you think she is? The Goya in Islington. In the Ladies with an Italian ...!'

'... eeeeeeeeeEEEEESSSSSSSSSSSSSSSSSSS ...!!!!!!!'

'... I'll just leave the salad here, then ...'

See also MELISSA.

Newscasters. Off screen they are constantly being mistaken for one another by little old ladies in supermarkets.

'Or so they claim when interviewed by Michael Parkinson on his agreeably lighthearted "chat" show!'

'Sometimes, and even more amusingly, a little old lady will say, "Usen't you to be Sandy Gall?" On such occasions, Parky has to wipe away the tears of laughter!'

'A true professional!'

See also PARKINSON, MICHAEL.

News of the World, The. *See* OLD FOLK, OUR AILING; PAROS; SENTENCE, THE REAL LIFE; TURNING ANGUISH INTO MONEY; TURNING TEARS TO GOOD USE; WADE, REBEKAH.

Newspaper, a rolled-up. As good as a swordstick in the right hands.

Newton, Isaac (1642–1727). There may be a lesson in the fact that, at the age of 54, Newton turned his back on the cloistered groves of academe to achieve worldly success in the City of London.

'Many people may conclude that his work at the Royal Mint was of more lasting relevance than the equations he composed in his Cambridgeshire orchard!'

'My feelings precisely, Vernon.'

See also PENIS.

Nijinsky, Vaslav Fomich (1890–1950). Russian ballet dancer with the Diaghilev company.

'This will interest you, Vernon. His legendary powers of elevation were explained by the fact that, like a bird, he had an extra bone in each foot.'

'How fascinating! I'd not heard that before.'

'Excuse me.'

'Oh dear. Yes, Con?'

'Birds don't fly with their feet.'

'Nor they do. Tell me, Vernon. Robert Helpmann. Remember her, do you?'

19th-century missionaries. Forever being eaten or crucified.

No. Only a small word, but the one that some hard-pressed mums find the most difficult to say.

See also PARENTING, INCONSISTENT; TODDLERS.

Non-Gallic mind, all but inaccessible to the. *See* MALLARMÉ, STÉPHANE.

Noose, the. *See DAILY MAIL, THE*; EVIL; PENDULUM; PROGRESS, BELIEF IN THE ILLUSION OF; REAL WORLD, THE.

No reasonable man could expect. *See* ACT OF GOD.

Norfolk, people who live in. Forever measuring their dining-rooms before driving into Diss with a view to bidding for a refectory table at a Saturday morning furniture auction.

'Excuse me, but I think Diss may be in Suffolk.'

'I don't doubt it for a moment.'

See also SUFFOLK, PEOPLE WHO LIVE IN.

Normal. There's no such thing as normal. After using the word always add, 'whatever that means'. A very grey area.

'Not for Posh and Becks it isn't.'

'Would you care to elaborate?'

'Indeed. In a recent press release from Beckingham Palace, the lovebirds' £2.5m home in Hertfordshire, Posh said: "We are both very normal."'

'Yet the rumour persists that Posh prefers to take it...'

'Right! That's it, Susan! You're going home!'

'Oh fuck off, Simon. Toilet, shar?'

'U bet.'

Norman, Barry (1933–). What an agreeable irony that when the young Barry Norman went into Cleethorpes Public Library and asked for a book on the stars, they gave him, instead of *The Young Observer's Guide to the Heavens*, which he had wanted, Peter Noble's *The Great Years of Hollywood*.

'Truly, astronomy's loss was the cinema's gain!'

'They say he's turned the baggy eyelid into an erogenous zone!'

'What would you know about erogenous zones?'

'U herd o mary normal, trace?'

'Cant say i hav, shar.'

See also MOORE, PATRICK ALFRED CALDWELL.

Nose, the. In human beings and other primates, the prominent structure between the eyes. The name of a short story by Gogol.

See also CHRISTMAS, GETTING A NEW NOSE FOR; GOGOL, NIKOLAI VASILIEVICH; WESTBROOK, DANIELLA.

Nosebags, on with the. A construction that sits well in a restaurant column by Andrew Lloyd Webber.

See also EATERIE; NOSHERIE.

Nosherie. A word that sits well in a humorous column (or in a restaurant column by Andrew Lloyd Webber).

See also ABLUTIONS; ABODE; CELEBS; CRABCAKES; DUCK, DONALD; EATERIE; EMBONPOINT; GAZPACHO; HOSTELRY; INFELICITOUS; LIBATION; MEADOWS, MY POULTERER, THE ESTIMABLE MR; OCCASIONS; REPORTER; THESPIAN.

Nous. *See* BRAIN, A GOOD FOOTBALLING; HOLE, THE; SHERINGHAM, TEDDY.

Novels, first. Always 'an assured debut' (*see* PIPPA'S FIRST NOVEL).

Novels, second. Always 'a disappointment' (*see* PIPPA'S SECOND NOVEL).

Novels, third. Always fail to live up to the hype.

Nude Encounter Parlours. *See* MARCUSE, HERBERT.

Nuts, Brazil. In Brazil they are referred to merely as nuts, of course (*see* PUB, ENGLISH; UNCLE, DUTCH).

'Here. Hang about.'

'Oh dear. Yes, Sharon?'

'Tracey, actually.'

'Of course.'

'I've seen 'Full English Breakfast' advertised in many of London's top hotels.'

'I'm not at all surprised to hear it.'

Nuts, looked the. Contrary to popular opinion Professor Simon Schama has never said 'In her new ball gown, Mary, Queen of Scots must have looked the nuts' in any of his illustrated television lectures.

See also FERGUSON, PROFESSOR NIALL; HISTORIANS, CELEBRITY; HISTORY, THE NEW; HUNT, DR TRISTRAM; STARKEY, DR DAVID.

O

Objection. 'Objection! You're rushing the witness, counsel!' An amusing way to turn down a marriage proposal from a fellow lawyer.

Obvious, the. Ironically, it's always the obvious that's the least susceptible to proof.
   'Dame Mystery perceives more than Squire Doubt, that's what I always say.'
   'Sounds like one for *The Oldie*, Richard.'

Occasions. In a humorous column, always 'lawful'.
   'After a long run of bad luck, might it not be amusing to murmur, "How all occasions do inform against me!"?'
   'A delightful suggestion, Vernon! Allow me to replenish your glass!'

Old folk, our ailing. Forever being leap-frogged by North African asylum-seekers in the queue for life-saving surgery. Rebekah Wade has not been deceived.
See also ASYLUM-SEEKERS; *NEWS OF THE WORLD, THE*.

Ol' Dirty Bastard. American rap artiste (*see* JUDGES, HIGH COURT; PROFESSORS OF ENGLISH LITERATURE).

Olds, ninety-six-year-. Always 'sprightly'.

Old Trafford. 'Wherever you look in the Theatre of Dreams there's a headline waiting to be written. Over to you, Trevor.'
   'Thank you, Gary. Over to you, John.'
   'Thank you, Trevor. Oh I say! Ronaldo has fired *Real* into the lead! After only 30 seconds! That's a headline we weren't expecting! Trevor?'
See also SPANIARDS, SKILFUL LITTLE.

Olivier (of Brighton), Laurence Kerr, Baron (1907–89). For several decades, our finest player. Burgundy to Gielgud's claret, he gave every word of a part the rasp of danger. Too good an actor to play real people, his Othello had more essential *negritude* than ever Paul Robeson's did.

'Ahem. Ahem.'

'Lord help us. It's Dr Death again! You have something to say?'

'Just this. Will anyone who saw Olivier's Oedipus at the New Theatre in 1942 ever forget his terrible cry of anguish in Act III? It was based, a theatrical colleague told me, on the low moaning of a North American female moose in season.'

'Well there you are. Tell me, Vernon ...'

'According to green room gossip, Olivier – ever the perfectionist – spent nine months practising it in a forest 30 miles from Quebec. With such success, in fact, that he got shot four times. A theatrical jest, current at the time, had it that an even worse fate might have befallen our first player!'

'I'm tempted to go to the toilet, Vernon.'

On the Buses. *See* HALLIWELL, GERI.

Once Upon a Time In The West (Sergio Leone, 1968). In spite of Leone's operatic direction and Henry Fonda's 'against type' icy-eyed gunslinger, the real star of the picture, of course, is Ennio Morricone's unforgettable score.

See also DOCTOR ZHIVAGO; LAWRENCE OF ARABIA.

£1m. A lot of money in anybody's language.

Opinion. Should be 'unfashionable'.

'Here's one, Vernon. I hold the unfashionable opinion that to place Badly Drawn Boy, Coldplay and Radiohead in the musical pantheon alongside Bach, Beethoven and Brahms is to debase the currency of our cultural discourse.'

'Ha! That's rich! Tell you what, Shar. I once found *Abba Gold* in the glove compartment of Simon's Audi!'

'U *never*! Wot woz his x scuse?'

'He claimed that the opening bars of "Gimme! Gimme! Gimme! (A Man After Midnight)" reminded him of a Janáček string quartet!'

'u cud nok me down wiv a dingo's donger!'
See WALL, THE WRITING ON THE.

Opinions. Ordinary people have a right to their opinions.
'Further, to message them to Kirsty Young.'
'And, even more extraordinarily, to Peter Snow at Channel 4.'
'Ah, Susan. Ever the elitist!'
'I should certainly hope so.'
See also MIDLANDS, SHELL-SUITED WORKING-CLASS WOMEN FROM
THE; PEOPLE, ORDINARY.

Opposites. Opposites attract. Mention Tom Eliot and Groucho Marx.

Optimism. Always 'premature'.

Options. Should be 'weighed up'. *Brookie* babe Jennifer Ellison is
weighing up the options.
See also BABES, *BROOKIE*; ELLISON, JENNIFER.

Orange. Historic French town in the *département* of Vaucluse.
A synod held here in AD 529 was of importance in the Pelagian
controversy. It has been said that visiting Orange is like stepping
back in time.
See also BUILDINGS, OLD; FOIX; PORVOO; SALAMANCA; SIDI BOU
SAID.

Orchestra. Of an orchestra of only thirty, cry: 'It was good enough
for Mozart!'
See also ORIGINAL INSTRUMENTS.

Order, the old. Often 'threatened'.
'For Albert, the old order seemed to be threatened. His son, the
Prince of Wales, was getting his leg over Lillie Langtry and three
other...'
'Niall Ferguson?'
'David Baddiel, in fact, but I take your point.'

Ordinary people. Not to be confused with 'real' people (*see*
OPINIONS; PEOPLE, REAL).

Orgy. It's important for a female columnist on a liberal broadsheet to have been to an orgy, but by her own account she should have left after a matter of minutes.

'Not yours truly's scene at all!'

Original instruments. What was good enough for Bach should be good enough for us.

'I enjoy small orchestral forces in pre-Classical music as much as the next man, Vernon. That said, however, one would be surprised if one's consultant at the Middlesex removed one's appendix using an 18th-century oyster fork.'

'A bombshell indeed, Simon.'

See also INSTRUMENT.

Oscar night. It's no expense spared on Oscar night!

Osprey. Nothing daunts the hunting osprey. That said, the stormy petrel can appear from nowhere.

Ostrich. Its stomach can digest a stone the size of a cannon ball.

O'Sullivan, Ronnie (1975–). Snooker player. When Ronnie O'Sullivan comes to the table, fans have learned to expect the unexpected.

'If that's true, it follows that the fans should expect the expected, since that would be the last thing they'd expect.'

'I don't know what you're talking about, Susan, but I'm obliged to you nonetheless. This may interest you, Vernon. Did you know that only 3% of all species of mammal are monogamous?'

'I confess I didn't.'

'Seems unlikely that Daphne falls into…'

'Yes, thank you, Simon…'

Ouche. *See* PILGRIMS, MEDIEVAL.

Out, chilling. Contrary to received opinion, Dr Tristram Hunt, the photogenic historian, has never said, 'Before the Battle of Naseby, Oliver Cromwell spent the night chilling out with his senior commanders.'

Out, going. Women are delightfully contrary creatures. They enjoy dressing up to go out more than actually going out.

'All the odder in that case that their constant complaint is "You never take me out any more!"'

Out and about. One should get out and about as much as possible. One should walk the streets of London, look upwards and ask oneself, 'How fares the classic skyline in the modern world?'

Outsiders. Always 'rank' (*see also* BULGARIAN, THE UNFANCIED).

Oval, the. Cricket ground in Kennington, London. Notorious for its slow wicket. 21 against Shane Warne on a sticky dog in Brisbane is worth 274 not out against Donald and Pollock at the Oval. Despite its name, its shape only approximates to an oval.

Over-55s, the. Forever being advised to take up pottery classes. *See also* DEMENTIA; SOCIALIZING, WEEKLY.

Over-90s, the. *See* PICNIC.

Owen, Michael (1979–). Like all *natural* strikers, Owen always knows exactly where the goal is.

'Except when he clearly doesn't.'

'Point taken.'

See also CRICKETER, THE NATURAL; MOTSON, JOHN.

Owlish. *See* LOVE, ROMANTIC.

Paderewski, Ignacy Jan (1860–1941). Polish concert pianist and composer. That said, in 1914 Polish politics became his keyboard.

Paint. It's amazing what a coat of paint will do.

Pals, showbiz. Forever fearing that stressed-out celebs are cracking up as they battle to save their marriages.
See also BALL, ZOE; LOVE-SPLIT CHART-TOPPERS; PREVIOUSLY LOVED-UP SUPERBABES; VIPs, BOSOMY.

Pan-fried. *See* SEA BASS.

Pants, how totally. Contrary to popular opinion, Dr David Starkey has never used the expression, 'How totally pants!' in any of his illustrated television lectures.
See also STARKEY, DR DAVID.

Papworth Everard. Either a picturesque village in Cambridgeshire, or a West Indian fast bowler. The debate continues.
See also STRATTON STRAWLESS.

Parenting, inconsistent. Child-rearing practices should be consistent. If, as parents, we avoid saying 'no', it can make children feel unsafe. Whether it's dealing with a tired toddler who is throwing a wobbly in a supermarket queue (don't they all!), or a testing teenager demanding the latest designer goods, we must as parents learn to say 'no'. Teenagers as much as toddlers want clear boundaries, and inconsistent parenting causes them to become confused.

'Sounds like one for "Parentscope", Corinne.'

See also NO; TODDLERS.

Paris. Has more English-language bookshops than there are in the whole of Suffolk.

Parkinson, Michael (1935–). Contrary to received opinion, it is not the case that the chat-show legend appeals only to daft old trouts.

'How true! My wife's a daft old trout and she can't stand him.'

'Well there you are.'

See also ASTAIRE, FRED; AS THE MAN SAID; AVEDON, RICHARD; BARNSLEY; BEATLES, THE; BEST, GEORGE; ECONOMISTS; PROFESSIONAL, A TRUE.

Parmenides (*c*.510–*c*.450 BC). Greek philosopher. His belief that there is no such thing as change has surely been overtaken by events.

'So much for philosophy!'

See also PHILOSOPHY; PLATO.

Paros. Greek holiday island forever being invaded by lardy English girls with bubbly personalities.

'Residents on the holiday isle of Paros may not like it when fat girls from South London demonstrate their bubbly personalities by mooning in the street...'

'I imagine not. Still less, I should think, when their lager-swilling boyfriends wade knee-high into the sea where they urinate like horses.'

'Indeed. Here's my point, however: they'd be the first to complain if English tourists took their money elsewhere.'

'Good point! Sounds like one for us, Rebekah!' (*See* NEWS OF THE WORLD, THE; WADE, REBEKAH.)

'Hang about.'

'Oh dear. Yes, Tracey?'

'Sharon, actually.'

'Of course.'

'r u goin 2 continu 2 refer 2 rebekah wade as editor o' *The News of The World* now that shes editor o' *The Sun*?'

'Yes.'

'Well there u r i spose.'

See also BUBBLY PERSONALITIES.

Parsons, Tony (1955–). Author and journalist (*see* BUTTONS, TOUCHING THOSE TENDER FEMALE; MAN, THE NEW).

Past. What are we, after all, but tomorrow's past? A sobering thought.

Patterson, Mrs. 'We're not here to judge you, Mrs Patterson. We're here to find your brother's killer and we'll do that quicker if you cooperate.'

See also HORNBY, MRS; PERKINS; THINKING.

Peasants. Notable for their enormous hands, natural dignity and great wisdom. Usually French. They see things unperceived by other men. That said, they are extremely cunning in business: it is always a mistake to buy land from a peasant.

Pedantry. Should be avoided. 'Surely too agreeable an idea to sacrifice on the altar of pedantry.'

Pendulum. The pendulum has swung too far. *The Daily Mail* has perceived this.

See also PROGRESS, BELIEF IN THE ILLUSION OF.

Penguin. *See* LEOPARD SEAL, THE.

Penis. As that wise agony uncle Phillip Hodson has pointed out, penis size is unimportant. A shared sense of humour is what counts.

'If u believe that, u'll believe anything!'

'I agree with Tracey.'

'I'm sure you do, Susan. Tell me, Vernon. Did you know that among Sir Isaac Newton's many achievements was the invention of the cat-flap?'

'I confess I didn't.'

See also JOHNSON, SAMUEL; NEWTON, SIR ISAAC; WALL, THE WRITING ON THE.

Pensioners. Forever playing carpet bowls in a day room, with the exception of Mrs Huggins of Leatherhead who is waiting for someone to come and put ointment on her leg.

See also DEMENTIA; ELEPHANTS; GRANNIES ON HOLIDAY; LEATHER-HEAD, PENSIONED OLD FOLK FROM; SOCIALIZING, WEEKLY.

People, ordinary. Ordinary people 'fly', celebrities 'jet'.

'How true! I read in my copy of the *Telegraph* on Thursday that 79-year-old Emily Foster had flown to Perth, Australia, to visit her grandchildren whom she hasn't seen for eleven years. On another page they reported that Ulrika Jonsson had jetted to the Bahamas for a well-earned break.'

'Did she look relaxed?'

'She certainly did. She was dead on arrival.'

'The saucy Swede dead?! I can scarcely…'

'No no no! I thought you were enquiring about 79-year-old Emily Foster. She died mid-flight.'

'Thank God! For a terrible moment there I thought the bosomy beauty had fallen off the perch!'

People, real. Forever being plucked from obscurity and catapulted to pop stardom. When not being catapulted, they leave floral tributes outside the homes of dead celebrities whom they've never met, sign books of condolence and text their opinions to Kirsty Young at Channel 5 News.

'Join me, Kirsty, after the break, for more Real News, Real Stories about Real People.'

'I've often wondered what would happen if you asked Kirsty what counts as Unreal News, Unreal Stories about Unreal People.'

'She wouldn't understand the question.'

'I dare say you're right.'

'That said, she would recognize that Real People are not to be confused with Ordinary People. "Join me, Kirsty, after the break for more Ordinary News, Ordinary Stories about Ordinary People" has entirely the wrong ring to it.'

'I agree. She does a professional job.'

See also FIVE NEWS; MIDLANDS, SHELL-SUITED WORKING-CLASS WOMEN FROM THE.

People, young. Forever being sent the wrong signals.
See also SIGNALS, QUITE THE WRONG.

Pep, Willie (1922–). Pound for pound the finest boxer ever to pull the gloves on.
'I gather that he once won a round without throwing a punch!'
'I don't hope to see a better in my lifetime.'
See also ALI, MUHAMMAD; ARMSTRONG, HENRY 'HANK'; DURAN, ROBERTO; HAGLER, MARVIN; HEARNS, THOMAS 'THE HITMAN'; LEONARD, SUGAR RAY; LOUIS, JOE; MARCIANO, ROCKY; MOORE, ARCHIE; ROBINSON, SUGAR RAY.

Perfectly weighted pass. 'Little run into space from Scholes to deceive the defender; perfectly weighted pass from Beckham; little lay-on from Butt to Van Nistelroy, and it's thank you very much.'
'The prolific Dutchman doesn't miss those, does he, Alan?'
'You have to ask, where was the Liverpool defence?'
See also VAN NISTELROY, RUUD.

Performance (1970). Psychedelic rock, gang violence and avant-garde film-making collide in this notorious cult film. Co-director Donald Cammell made three more movies and then blew his brains out. There may be a lesson here.

Peril, we forget this at our. *See* BABY, HAVING A; INFLATION.

Perkins. 'When I want advice from a convicted gamekeeper with a criminal record, I'll ask for it, Perkins. Come along, Sergeant.'

Personalities. Should be 'bubbly'.
'I agree with Pete. U cant really sing, luv, but yuv gotta bubbly personality wich cud take u a long way in this bizness. Back to u, Davina.'
'Thank you, Geri.'
See also BUBBLY PERSONALITIES; HALLIWELL, GERI; PAROS; WANT IT.

Personal medical records, our. Often found in a skip in Stevenage.
See also BRITAIN'S NUCLEAR SECRETS.

Perugia, University of. *See* MAGDALENE COLLEGE, CAMBRIDGE; DUNCAN SMITH, IAIN.

Pesci, Joe (1943–). Actor. There's an engaging irony in the fact that this legendary hard man of so many classic gangster films should in real life be a cultured and sensitive man who writes agreeably unpretentious verses and owns the finest collection of French impressionists outside France.

See also CAGNEY, JAMES; EASTWOOD, CLINT; MARVIN, LEE; ROBINSON, EDWARD G.; WIDMARK, RICHARD.

Petrel, the stormy. *See* OSPREY, THE.

Philosopher. 'I never thought of it in that way. You're quite a philosopher, Inspector.'

'No, Sergeant. Just a working copper.'

See also COPPERS; PLUMBER; PSYCHOLOGY.

Philosophy. Time was when philosophers saw it as their duty to teach men how they ought to live their lives. Since Wittgenstein, Austin, Ryle and Strawson they have, like wasps trapped in a jam-jar, concerned themselves with increasingly trivial linguistic problems.

'But, Guv...'

'Cut the philosophy, Jack. If you've got something to say, say it.'

See also PLATO.

Piaf, Edith, *stage name of* **Edith Giovanna Gassion** (1915–63). French *chanteuse*, known as the Little Sparrow. Such was her concentration that she would become absent-minded when preparing for a concert, sometimes defecating into a shoebox and throwing the contents out of the window on to the heads of sophisticates dining on the *Champs Élysées*. The story may be aprocryphal, but is no less telling for that.

'The Little Sparrow did it her way!'

'Delightful! Apropos, I recall hearing that Gary Player was concentrating on one occasion on the 18th green when...'

'Surely the dapper little South African didn't...'

'No, no. The story goes that he was about to putt to win the Open at Carnoustie when Concorde flew directly overhead. Later he was congratulated by his opponent, Arnold Palmer.

'"I'm amazed that the aeroplane didn't put you off," said Palmer.'

'"What aeroplane?" said Player.'

'That says it all.'

Picnic. Life's no picnic for the over-90s.

See also STARVING.

Pigeon, the lesser Paraguayan. *See* PROFESSIONAL, A TRUE.

Pigeon-holing, an artist who defies. *See* AGAIN; HIRST, DAMIEN.

Pilgrims, medieval. Forever emerging from the wooded slopes of the River Ouche and being informed that they were nearing Conques.

See also AVEYRON; CONQUES.

Pint after the game, a. *See* SCRUM, THE FRONT ROW OF THE.

Pipe-smoking sodomites. *See* DONS, OLD-STYLE BACHELOR.

Pippa. Forever being phoned by Jeremy from a train outside Reading. 'Hullo! It's Jeremy. I'm on the train! We're stuck outside Reading! Someone on the line at Goring and Streatley. Sorry? Can't hear you. Damn. The line's breaking up. Pippa? Pippa? Oh well.'

See also JEREMY; NEWLY PAIRED-OFF THIRTYSOMETHINGS.

Pippa's first novel. An assured début.

Pippa's second novel. A disappointment.

See also NOVELS, THIRD.

Pity, and more's the. *See* ACCESSORY.

Plants. Contrary to popular belief, the line, 'Don't tell me how to look after my plants, Kenneth, and I won't tell you how to run your diamond business,' really did occur in an episode of *A Touch Of Frost*.

Plastic rubbish. It has been reliably estimated that plastic rubbish thrown into the sea kills a million birds and 100,000 marine creatures per annum.

Plato (*c.*427–347 BC). It has been said that the history of philosophy is no more than footnotes to Plato.

'Indeed, and academics...'

'Oh God. Yes, Jolyon?'

'Academics in their ivory towers would do well to remember that the author of the *Symposium* saw nothing incongruous in allowing laughter, gaiety and good fellowship their place in intellectual discussions, in which, significantly, men of affairs played a prominent part.'

'Really? Tell me, Vernon...'

'But then, of course, Plato believed in strong government by the great and the good, and was fortunate to live at a time when it was not regarded as improper to say such things.'

'Is that it?'

'Indeed.'

'Good. MIGUEL! Where is the blighter?'

'Need you ask?'

See also PHILOSOPHY.

Players, French rugby. Knock them over and their heads go down.

'They didn't go down last weekend in Paris, squire.'

See also CALYPSO CAVALIERS; VOLATILE.

Plonk. It's a shame to waste a good bottle of plonk.

Ploppies, The. Channel 4 insiders have recently announced a new light entertainment programme, devised by Chris Evans and to be named *The Ploppies*.

'Pray cease! Already tears of laughter...'

'Wait for it! Celebs such as Jono "The Mouth From Down Under" Coleman, Neil and Christine Hamilton and lesbian funnygirl Rhona Cameron will be given a low-calorie lunch, after which...'

'I think I can see what's coming!'

'...they will be made to sit on a revolving machine placed over a giant chamber pot, while space-age characters dance around shouting "Plop! Plop! Plop!"'

'Enough! A pause, for pity's sake, while I get my breath back!'

'The celeb who holds on to his lunch for longest will win a prize for the charity of their choice!'

'I think I've cracked a rib!'

See also BEST TELEVISION IN THE WORLD, THE.

Plumber. A society that values a plumber less than a philosopher will produce neither pipes that work nor a philosophy which holds water.

Poitiers, Raymond of (1097–1149). 'Answer me this. Did Raymond of Poitiers ever get Eleanor of Aquitaine into the sack?'

'David Starkey?'

'Lily Savage, but I take your point.'

Polanski, Roman (1933–). Polish film director. He may be in the business of telling stories but his own narrative is out of bounds.

'I cannot allow myself to go too deeply into the past,' he has said. 'My art is fiction.'

'That says it all.'

'Thank you, Barry.'

'Meanwhile, back at the ranch...'

Police, the. Forever asking people where they were last Thursday between 9 and 11 p.m.

Political football. *See* GAMES, THE OLYMPIC.

Politically correct, usual shrill cries of protest from the. *See* JOKES, RACIST.

Politician. 'Answering a question with a question, Inspector? You should have been a politician! Come along, Daphne.'

Politicians. Their first thoughts are always with the loved ones of the British serviceman tragically killed in action (*see also* LADS, OUR).

'And whether they'll vote New Labour at the next election...'

'There's no need to be cynical, Susan.'
'Why not.'
'You've got me there.'

Pop babes, troubled. Forever reassuring worried fans by opening their hearts to *The News of the World*.
See also DIVAS; MONDAY, POP TOTTIES WITH A SINGLE OUT ON.

Pop hotties, hip-shaking. Forever in crisis meetings trying to save their rocky marriages.
See also BALL, ZOE; BEAUTIES, SHATTERED; DIVAS; POP BABES, TROUBLED.

Pop Idol. During the winter of 2001–2002, *Pop Idol* fever gripped the nation to such an extent that more people voted on the outcome than had gone to the polls in the 2001 general election. There may be a lesson here.

Popper, Sir Karl (1902–94). Philosopher of science (*see* FALSE; SHOPPING).

Pop stars. Forever releasing solo albums after four years away from the studios.

Popular song, the American. Surely we are mature enough as a society to acknowledge that the American popular song – as exemplified by Sinatra's Capitol recordings (now seen as having captured the *real* Sinatra) – says as much about what it is to be human as a Mahler symphony or Sibelius tone-poem?
'Want another Ketamine, Susan?'
'You bet I do.'

Populists. Always 'unashamed' (*see* AIREY, DAWN).

Pornography. Always 'boring'. Paradoxically, a generator of vast wealth. The only sites that make money on the Internet.
See also DETECTIVES, SEASONED.

Portals. In an occasional column, always 'hallowed'.
'Positioned directly above the hallowed portals of London's

Victoria & Albert Museum is a larger than life-size portrait of Linda Evangelista, shot by Irving Penn!'

'Whatever next!'

'Guests to the gallery, which houses one of the most respected collections of applied arts in the world, will suffer the indignity of walking between the supermodel's legs to get through the door! But who would expect anything less from the sex-charged, glamour-fuelled world of Gianni Versace, a major retrospective of whose work opens at the Museum next week?'

'Thank you, Susannah.'

See also BRIEFS, SILK FLORAL; FRANKEL, SUSANNAH; FRUMP; KNICKERS, FRENCH.

Port Bou. *See CASABLANCA; CHIX WITH DIX.*

Porvoo. Finland's second-oldest town, founded in 1346, is on the Porvoo river. It has retained much of its charm as a wooden medieval town and boasts a delightful selection of sights, including a cathedral, the Town Hall Square and the home of Finland's national poet, J.L. Runeberg. Don't miss the Doll and Toy Museum and the crafts-men's workshops by the river. It has been said that visiting Porvoo is like stepping back in time.

Potters Bar. It has been calculated that 97% of middle managers commuting by train between Potters Bar and the City of London have at some stage of the journey announced: '*A Brief History of Time?* Please! I gave up on page 29!'

See also BIMBO; WATERHOUSE, KEITH.

Pound for pound the greatest boxer ever to pull the gloves on. *See* ALI, MUHAMMAD; ARMSTRONG, HENRY 'HANK'; DURAN, ROBERTO; HAGLER, MARVIN; HEARNS, THOMAS 'THE HITMAN'; LEONARD, SUGAR RAY; LOUIS, JOE; MARCIANO, ROCKY; MOORE, ARCHIE; PEP, WILLIE; ROBINSON, SUGAR RAY.

Powell, Anthony Dymoke (1905–2000). Pronounced 'Pole', as in 'Before we get to Pavia, the Po'll've overflowed its banks.' The urbane tone of his writing is agreeably spiced with scenes of magic and sensuality, decorously etched.

Practising what one preaches. *See* ROUSSEAU, JEAN-JACQUES.

Prawn malai. *See* RESONANT.

Prejudice, refreshingly free of. While there is still a certain ingrained 'won't-touch-it-if-it's not-French' conservatism in the traditional wine drinker, the more demotic palate of the younger drinker is refreshingly free of such received prejudice.

'Nor are they afraid to talk of the latest album by the Red Hot Chili Peppers in the same breath as Schubert's *Winterreise*.'

'Thank you, Susan. But I was talking about wine.'

'Well I wasn't.'

Presenters, TV. Always 'troubled', often 'shamed'.

Presley, Elvis (1935–77). American singer. For the last five years of his life, Presley lived in virtual isolation in his mansion, Graceland, guarded by a private army of South Korean karate experts. He ate only hamburgers, brought to his bedroom by under-age cheerleaders, who would oil his fantastically bloated body while he ate. When he died, he weighed 27 stone and his body had to be craned from his bedroom window to the waiting hearse by a system of weights and pulleys.

'Yet in death, as in life, he has kept the cash registers ringing.'

'How true! That said, he'd be 68 now, had he lived.'

'And your point is?'

'Rather long in the tooth for a rock 'n' roll singer!'

'But he isn't still alive.'

'Nor he is. I withdraw the allegation!'

Pressures. The pressures of stardom can sometimes take their toll.

Previous. It's always a mistake to have previous.

'You're a million to go in the frame, son. You've got previous. Nick him, Sergeant.'

Previously loved-up superbabes. Forever sending their fans reeling by admitting through a spokesman that their marriages have hit the rocks.

See also BALL, ZOE.

Principles, liberal. Always 'lofty'.

Prison officers. The cons get out eventually but the screws are in for life.

See also SENTENCE, THE REAL LIFE.

Private Lives. A light comedy (1930) thought by many to be Noël Coward's masterpiece.

'Interestingly enough, he wrote it when his personal life was at sixes and sevens.'

'Is that so?'

'Indeed. Its inspiration was the 5th Earl of Amherst, an old Etonian and former officer in the Coldstream Guards, with whom Coward was in love and with whom he departed in 1929 on an extended tour of the Far East…'

'With 27 pieces of luggage and a gramophone.'

'Thank you, Susan. But I'll complete the anecdote, if you don't mind.'

'If you must.'

'Alas, Coward's feelings for Amherst were not returned. The latter preferred a boxer called Gerry MacCarthy whom he had met in Jersey City. The resulting tension was reflected in the play Coward sat down to write in the Cathay Hotel, Shanghai – *Private Lives*.'

'So it's a play, really, about four men.'

'I think you're confusing it with Edward Albee's *Who's Afraid of Virginia Woolf.*'

'I know what I'm confusing it with, thank you, Susan.'

See also AGAIN; COWARD, NOËL; WALL, THE WRITING ON THE.

Problem, a. You don't solve a problem by throwing money at it.

Professional, a true. 'Here! I've got one!'

'Oh dear. Yes, Sharon?'

'Tracey, in fac.'

'Of course.'

'2 b a tru profeshnal do u hav 2 b like over 70?'

'Good point. Let's see. David Attenborough, Michael Parkinson, Barry Norman, Judith Chalmers, Esther Rantzen, Michael Aspel…

Yes, it rather looks as if you do.'

'Wot about Simon Schama, then?'

'A *natural* professional, perhaps.'

'Wot? Like Ant and Dec?'

'If you wish. This may interest you, Vernon. The lesser Paraguayan pigeon. I read recently that before intercourse the male indulges in an elaborate hour-long mating ceremony and then expires from exhaustion. What do you say to that?'

'Hardly a true professional, then!'

'Delightful. That said, Roberto's looking a little fatigued. I wonder why that is?'

'Probably because he keeps copping off to the toilet with…'

'Yes, thank you, Miguel. That will be all for the moment.'

Professionals. Should be 'consummate' (*see* ATTENBOROUGH, SIR DAVID).

Professors of English Literature. Forever declaring the lyrics of hip-hop star Ol' Dirty Bastard to be comparable with the Anglo-Saxon epic poem *Beowulf*.

See also OL' DIRTY BASTARD; OPINION; PREJUDICE, REFRESHINGLY FREE OF.

Progress, belief in the illusion of. One of the endemic follies of our age. *The Daily Mail* has not been deceived.

See also DAILY MAIL, THE; EVIL; MAN, THE PERFECTABILITY OF; NATURE, HUMAN; NOOSE, THE; PENDULUM; REAL WORLD, THE; UTOPIA, THE SEARCH FOR.

Prohibition. We all know where that leads.

'We do indeed. Addiction. Misery. Squalor…'

'Thank you, Susan…'

'Old folk mugged for their pension books. Senseless deaths. Turf wars. Innocent bystanders gunned down in the cross-fire…'

'Yes, thank you, Daphne…'

'Celebs obliged to appear in *Crossroads* so they can afford a new nose for Christmas. Young people getting gangrene by injecting themselves with brick dust…'

'Thank you, Susan. I think you've made your point. I was refer-ring to the prohibition of alcohol, of course.'

'Really? You astound me.'

See also LIVER.

Promiscuity. *See* AFFAIRS, EXTRA-MARITAL.

Property Ladder, The. Channel 4, 8.30 p.m. 'Sarah Beeny meets a couple who have bought a house near Scunthorpe. Last in the series.'

'I'm not surprised.'

'Here's one!'

'Oh dear. Yes, Tracey? A received idea, is it?'

'No. A joke acsherly. Wot r 3 football clubs wiv a rude word in there names?'

'I confess I'm defeated.'

'Arsenal, Scunthorpe and fucking Manchester United!'

'I'm totally baffled. Tell me, Daphne... Oh, she doesn't seem to be here.'

'Nor does Roberto. Nothing to worry about, I don't suppose, Vernon.'

Prostitutes. Always 'common' (*see also* CALL GIRLS).

Prostitutes, French. The rudest and most expensive in Europe. They sneer at their customers' techniques and raucously call out their deficiencies to their colleagues working in adjacent rooms. They have breasts like fried eggs and enormous pubic bushes reeking of garlic. Upper-class French girls combine sulkiness with notor-ious French *chic*, and are even ruder than the prostitutes. They are famed for their prudishness and will only accept dinner dates if accompanied by the *concierge* who will see that they are home by midnight and whom you are expected to tip heavily.

Prostitutes, German. They are all civil servants who expect you to do everything in triplicate.

Proust, Marcel (1871–1922). French novelist. He slept by day in a cork-lined room, emerging at night to wander the streets of Paris.

He dunked madeleines in absinthe and picked up destitutes, whom he would take to the Ritz for breakfast. Who but the French could have produced a Marcel Proust?

Proverbial match against Mars, the. 'Here's one, Vernon. Given a choice between the big American girl, the unfancied Bulgarian, the gap-toothed Brazilian, the affable Geordie, the chirpy Glaswegian, the easy-going Irishman, the gritty Lancastrian, the mercurial Spaniard, the volatile Pakistani and the crude Turk, who would you go for as your main striker in the proverbial match against Mars to determine the future of the universe?'

'I'd go for the full-breasted Swede every time.'

'Oh grow up, the pair of you.'

'Thank you, Susan.'

Prunes. *See* REGULARITY.

Psychology. Never well regarded.

'We're enjoying a quiet drive in the country, Sergeant, and you have to spoil it all by bringing psychology into it.'

'Sorry, Guv.'

See also COPPERS; PHILOSOPHER; SNOOKER.

Public, the general. All too often fobbed off with a fairy-tale version of events.

Publicity, believing your own. Always a mistake.

See also HALLIWELL, GERI; HOUSTON, WE HAVE A PROBLEM; MOON, KEITH.

Public transport. Always 'grinding to a halt'.

See also COMMUTERS; JEREMY; PIPPA; ROCKET SCIENCE.

Publishing. No longer an occupation for gentlemen (*see* ACCOUNTANTS; MANUSCRIPTS). These days it would be unusual for an author to have met his publisher.

'He's tied up. Can I help?'

When Elias Canetti was awarded the Nobel Prize for Literature in 1981 he rang up his publisher, Jonathan Cape, and asked to speak to his editor. The receptionist refused to put him through since he was unable to say what company he represented.

See also BRUSH, BASIL; DESIGN; EDITING.

Pubs, English. In England, they are known merely as pubs, of course (*see also* NUTS, BRAZIL).

'Yes, Sharon?'

'Sum pubs wont open after hours even 4 a chart-topper. I read it in *The Daily Telegraph*.'

'You astound me.'

Puncher, a. Always in with a chance.

'One clean shot and it's "goodnight Vienna".'

'Thank you, Reg.'

Punishment, capital. 'Interestingly enough, Vernon, I'm an unashamed non-hanger.'

'As was that admirable man, Sir Robert Mark.'

'Indeed. And for the same reason. Not because capital punishment is morally objectionable, but because on balance it doesn't work.'

'I agree. Since mistakes can occur, why hand liberals a stick to beat us with?'

'Absolutely right! Keeping a man locked up for the rest of his life for something he didn't do is one thing. Dangling him on the end of a piece of rope quite another.'

'Thank you, Susan. I was half-expecting a facetious contribution from your quarter.'

'At least she isn't in the toilet like Mr Pratley's bird.'

'Yes, thank you, Miguel. I'll call you if I need you.'

'Stay gold, John.'

Q's, P's and. On meeting a famous logician at a publishing party it might be amusing to say, 'I must watch my p's and q's'. This should make him roar with laughter if it's not been said to him before.

Quality. Often 'indefinable.'
   'I can't put my finger on it, Kevin, but this girl's got a quality which could really work for us.'
See also AIREY, DAWN; GOLDWYN, SAM; TITS.

Queen Elizabeth II (1926–). Forever having to cancel her engagements because of a slight chill.

Questions. Should be 'good'.
   'Why was £1.5m spent on the trial of the royal butler?'
   'Good question!'
   'Why did the Queen wait so long to come forward?'
   'Good question!'
   'Why didn't the police seek to interview the Queen?'
   'Good question!'
   'Why were the Princes misled by the police at Highgrove?'
   'Good question!'
   'Why did the prosecution try to keep evidence secret?'
   'Good question!'
   'Where does Welsh rugby go from here, Jonathan?'
   'Pardon?'

Questions, hypothetical. Needn't be answered. No one knows why.
   'Really, Jeremy! Do I want to be Prime Minister? You should know better than to ask hypothetical questions!'

Questions, leading. Needn't be answered. No one knows why.

'Really, Jeremy! Do I want to be Prime Minister? You should know better than to ask leading questions!'

Quine, Willard van Orman (1908–2000). American logician. Quine held that all statements are false, though some (historical ones) are more obviously false than others (mathematical ones).

'Surely it was Dr David Starkey who said, "Quine? I never read him."'

'A.J.P. Taylor, in fact, but the point holds.'

Quirke, Pauline. *See* LEONARD, JASON.

Quite frankly. 'Quite frankly, Susan and I are totally bored by the whole drugs issue. Isn't that right, Susan? Susan! SUSAN! Where is the woman?'

'Powdering her nose, John. Need you ask?'

'Of course. Yes, thank you, Miguel. The *postres* menu, if you'd be so good.'

'Coming up, John.'

Rabelais, François (1494–1553). Only an ex-monk could have been as Rabelaisian as Rabelais. Died of dropsy. Who but the French could have produced a François Rabelais?

See also RABELAISIAN.

Rabelaisian. A word that sits well in a theatrical review.

Racing. Always 'in the blood'. No one knows why.

'My father was a bookmaker, so naturally racing's in my blood.'

Rainwear. Whether it's classic trench or mini-mac, rainwear has never been so sexy.

'A medicated out-patient from the Chelsea and Westminster Hospital?'

'James Sherwood, *The Independent's* cutting-edge fashion guru, in fact, but I take your point.'

See also DIETRICH, MARLENE.

Rantzen, Esther (1940–). Yet on screen you couldn't meet a nicer person.

'All part of the job, I dare say.'

See also PROFESSIONAL, A TRUE.

Rat. In most cities in the Western world one is seldom more than six feet away from a rat.

See also SHOREDITCH.

Rattigan, Terence (1911–77). A first-class dramatist of the third rank, or a third-class dramatist of the first rank? The debate continues.

'It's fashionable these days to deride him as a mere exponent of the "well-made" play, but many playwrights of the new school – including Howard Brenton and David Hare – have admitted that everything they know of solid craftsmanship they learned from the plays of Rattigan.'

'The Galsworthy of drama.'

'Indeed. But so was Galsworthy.'

Ravel, Maurice (1875–1937). There is an engaging irony in the fact that this most fastidious of musical colourists is chiefly remembered for his vulgar *Bolero*.

Ray, Satyajit (1921–92). A film-maker who evokes an almost Chekhovian poetry in his images of village life in India. In any list of the ten greatest films of all time at least two by Satyajit Ray would have to be included.

Reader, gentle. A construction that sits well in an occasional column.

Reader, the true. The true reader will read anything rather than nothing. It's an addiction. In the absence of a book, he will peruse train timetables, the back of a cornflakes packet, *The Daily Mail,* the advertisements on the side of a bus.

'Alain de Botton's *The Consolations of Philosophy*?'

'Well, that might be stretching it a bit.'

Real **Sinatra, the.** *See* POPULAR SONG, THE AMERICAN.

Real world, the. We live in the real world. *The Daily Mail* has perceived this (*see DAILY MAIL, THE*).

See also STATUE.

Rear Window (Alfred Hitchcock, 1954). A masterclass in film-making.

'I've never cared for it myself.'

'Nor I.'

'And yet received opinion has it as Hitchcock's most unforgiving examination of the director as *voyeur*.'

'Well there you are. What do we know?'

'Precisely.'

Red Squirrel, The Disappearing. *See* FRENCH COOKING.

Referee. The good referee is the one you don't see.

Regularity. Always 'alarming'. On the other hand, a sign of good health (*see* PRUNES).

Relatives. Always grieving. What they want is justice. Rebekah Wade has perceived this.
See also GRIEVE; *NEWS OF THE WORLD, THE*; WADE, REBEKAH.

Renoir, Jean (1894–1979). His father was Pierre-Auguste Renoir, yet his mother tongue was film (*see also* VAN NISTELROY, RUUD). *Nana* (1926), *La Grande Illusion* (1937) and *Le Déjeuner sur l'herbe* (1959) are considered to be among the masterpieces of the cinema.
   'Would it be fair to say, then, that in any list of the ten greatest films of all time at least two by Jean Renoir would have to be included?'
   'You've taken the words out of my mouth.'

Reporter. In a humorous column always 'your intrepid'; sometimes 'Fleet Street's finest'; in an episode of *Inspector Morse* or *A Touch of Frost* always 'the ladies and gentlemen of the fourth estate'.

Reproofs. Should be 'Johnsonian'.

Rescue services, the. Forever rescuing pot-holers trapped in Derbyshire caves over the Easter bank holiday.

Resistance. If British, 'heroic'; if enemy, 'fanatical'.

Resonant. Contrary to received opinion, Fay Maschler really did refer to 'the sparky prawn malai and the resonant roghan josh' in one of her refreshingly unselfconscious restaurant columns.

Reviews, book. Always 'rave', unless 'mixed'.
See also PIPPA'S SECOND NOVEL.

Rhetoric. Should be used sparingly. 'Spare me the rhetoric, Inspector.'

Rhino, the black. The black rhino faces an uncertain future.
See also VETS, WILDLIFE.

Rhodes, Harold (1936–   ). Fast bowler, of whom it could be said that one hoped to see many better in one's lifetime. It was his misfortune to be no-balled by his father, A.E.G.('Dusty') Rhodes, of whom John Arlott ('the Voice of Summer') wrote:

'One of the most humorous and companionable of cricketers; a man of jokes, none richer than his umpiring.'

Richard I (1157–99). King of England from 1189.

'This may interest you, Vernon. Did you know that in order to pay the ransom demanded to free Richard I – generally known as Richard Coeur de Lion (the Lion Heart) – from incarceration in the dungeons of Leopold of Austria, every man jack in England was taxed one quarter of his income?'

'Is that a fact? You astonish me. It's hard to imagine a grateful nation stumping up the air fare to bring Tony Blair home from Paris if he was locked up by Jacques Chirac!'

'Did he lose an arm in a skirmish with the Turks?'

'Who?'

'Richard I.'

'I think not.'

'You surprise me.'

See also GREAT IRONIES OF HISTORY; TURKS, A SKIRMISH WITH THE.

Rigg, Diana. *See* HEROINES, KICK-ARSE.

Rights, human. Once we start talking about human rights we're on a slippery slope.

See also SLOPES, SLIPPERY.

Rimbaud, Arthur (1845–91). After an unhappy childhood, Rimbaud lived for a time with Paul Verlaine, but following an argument he left for Africa. From Cairo he wrote to his mother: 'Life here is boring and costs too much.' He returned to France, where he died of coffee poisoning. Who but the French could have produced an Arthur Rimbaud?

See also PROUST, MARCEL; VERLAINE, PAUL.

Rimsky-Korsakov, Nikolai (1844–1908). A member of 'The Five'. Famous for his opulent and exotic scores, he is now chiefly remembered for *The Flight of the Bumble Bee*.

Ring, the boxing. The loneliest place in the world. You can run but you can't hide.

Rizzio, David. *See* HARASSMENT, SEXUAL.

Robbie's ANTics DEC'em. Good headline for a story in *The Sunday Times's* supplement, *Hot Celebs!*

'Pop god Robbie Williams had celeb pals in stitches when he clowned it up at London's posh Nobu restaurant! Telly duo Ant and Dec were among showbiz insiders who burst out laughing as Robbie rolled around on the floor!

'If this is the kind of wacky fun to be had on a night out with Robbie, us Goss girls are up for any shenanigans you might have in mind, Mr Williams...'

See also HOT CELEBS!; WILLIAMS, ROBBIE.

Robespierre, Maximilien (1758–94). Like all terrorists he was a puritan at heart; and, like all terrorists, he fell victim to the terror which he himself created.

Robinson, Edward G. (1893–1973). Actor. What an engaging irony that this legendary hard man of so many classic *films noirs* should in real life have been a cultured and sensitive man who wrote agreeably unpretentious verses and owned the finest collection of French impressionists outside France.

See also CAGNEY, JAMES; EASTWOOD, CLINT; MARVIN, LEE; PESCI, JOE; WIDMARK, RICHARD.

Robinson, Sugar Ray (1920–89). Pound for pound the finest boxer ever to pull the gloves on.

'I don't hope to see a better in my lifetime.'

See also ALI, MUHAMMAD; ARMSTRONG, HENRY 'HANK'; DURAN, ROBERTO; HAGLER, MARVIN; HEARNS, THOMAS 'THE HITMAN'; LEONARD, SUGAR RAY; MARCIANO, ROCKY; MOORE, ARCHIE; PEP, WILLIE.

Rocket science. Always 'not exactly', or 'hardly'.

'Your opinion on this, Vernon: a properly functioning transport system? Hardly rocket science, would you say?'

'Certainly the French don't seem to find it so. Take Eurostar. It wheezes its way through Kent at the speed of a pre-Beeching branch line suffering from emphysema, but as soon as you're in France it's off and away quicker than – excuse me – shit through a goose!'

'Or the knickers off a Montmartre *danseuse!*'

'Down the hatch!'

'Up yours Delors!'

'O 4 fucks sake! U2! Ur really common! Toilet, trace?'

'After u, shar.'

Rogers, Roy (1912–98). American actor. With his horse Trigger he made more than 600 Westerns. As a mark of respect, he was stuffed when he died and now stands with Trigger outside the main gates of Universal Studios in Hollywood.

Roghan josh. *See* RESONANT.

Rogues. Always 'lovable'. Women find it hard to resist a lovable rogue.

'This may interest you, Vernon. No actress appearing in a TV drama has ever been obliged to say: "Better a lovable rogue than a boring Sir Galahad!"'

'Not even Honor Blackman?'

'Not even Honor Blackman.'

'You surprise me.'

Ronaldo (1976–). Contrary to received opinion, when commentating on the the gap-toothed Brazilian striker's World Cup-winning performance in 2002, the veteran BBC commentator John Motson really did say: 'In 1998 he suffered a seizure; in 2002 he seized the moment.'

See also MOTSON, JOHN; OLD TRAFFORD.

Rooms. They tell us a lot about their occupants. Some rooms cry out for a feminine touch. Paradoxically, it's harder to keep a small room tidy than a large one. Women know this (*see also* THINGS WOMEN KNOW).

Rossini, Gioacchino Antonio (1792–1868). His father was a trumpeter and his mother an opera singer. Upon discovering the fact that, at the age of 37, Rossini gave up composition and devoted himself to writing cookery books, cry 'How delightfully Italian!' Contrary to poular belief, the sentence 'Rossini could no more be solemn than he could stop breathing,' really does occur in Bernard Levin's *Conducted Tour* (1980).

Rousseau, Jean-Jacques (1712–78). Like many so-called intellectuals, he didn't always practise what he preached. A 'progressive' educational theorist, he himself cocked up on the parenting front.

Rubbish, feeling. When lecturing on Henry VIII, and contrary to popular belief, Dr David Starkey has never said, 'OK, after going on a diet prescribed by his doctors, Henry managed to lose weight, but he felt rubbish.'
See also STARKEY, DR DAVID.

Rubinstein, Artur (1887–1982). Polish-born pianist. In his 95 years, he played as many melodies on the heartstrings as on the keyboard.
See also PADEREWSKI, IGNACY JAN.

Rumours. Forever 'flying thick and fast'.

Rural post offices. Always 'under threat'.

Russian gangsters, unscrupulous. Forever forcing asylum-seekers to work in sordid Soho brothels (*see* BRITAIN; SOHO BROTHELS).
    'They'll be in Somerset next, mark my words.'
    'And Aldeburgh.'

Ryle, Gilbert (1900–1976). Philosopher (*see* FATALISM).

Sackings. Always 'unceremonious'.

Sacred?, is nothing. *See* HEDGE, A.

Safeguards. Ordinary people have a right to know that safeguards are in place.

Salamanca. Capital of Salamanca province in west-central Spain. Any tour of the city must start at the historic Plaza Mayor. That said, the richly decorated façade of its university (1529) epitomises the flamboyant Plateresque style. The visitor to Salamanca will find culture on his doorstep.

'That must be a bit of a shock first thing in the morning.'

See also ARIÈGE; AUDE; AVEYRON; CONQUES; CULTURE; HARROGATE; LOT; LOZÈRE; ORANGE; PORVOO; SIDI BOU SAID.

Sale, playwrights who spent their early years in. Forever claiming in later years that hiding under the counter in dry-cleaning shops run by their mothers gave them their ear for dialogue.

Salisbury, people who live near. Forever driving 75 miles on a Saturday morning for a drinks party with Jeremy and Pippa Dalrymple.

See also WILTSHIRE, PEOPLE WHO LIVE IN.

Saloon-bar Socrates. *See* BERNARD, JEFFREY; WATERHOUSE, KEITH.

Sanctum, inner. Always 'penetrated'. 'So! At last I've penetrated your *sanctum sanctorum*! I'm privileged indeed!' An amusing remark to make on being admitted to someone's office.

Sang-froid. Always 'imperturbable'.

Sarcasm. Contrary to popular belief, the line 'Do I detect a note of sarcasm from the blushing bride?' really did occur in an episode of *Inspector Morse* written by the late Malcolm Bradbury, once Professor of Modern Literature at the University of East Anglia.

See also FACETIOUSNESS.

Sarcastic. There's no need to be sarcastic.

See also UNNECESSARY.

Sartre, Jean-Paul (1905–80). French philosopher. He famously wrote that hell was other people, yet was to be found each day outside *Les Deux Magots* in Paris surrounded by students and bereted *poètes-chansonniers*. He proved that nothingness *is* by saying that if you went into *Les Deux Magots* expecting to see Pierre, and Pierre wasn't there, Pierre was not not there in the sense that the Pope or the Prime Minister of England was not there. Rather, Pierre's not being there was reflected back at you from *Les Deux Magots'* every particular. Pierre's absence was palpable. A.J. Ayer, the English philosopher, argued that the whole of Existentialism failed by its inability to deploy the verb '*être*' correctly, to which Sartre replied, with unusual brevity, '*Ayer est un con.*'

'Did someone mention my name, Marty?'

'No, I think they were talking French, Con.'

Satire. Should be 'affectionate'. The best satire is, after all, a kind of tribute to its target. 'Small wonder that Rory Bremner and Tony Blair have become friends.'

See also BREMNER, RORY.

Sausage, the English. An institution.

See also INSTITUTIONS, OUR; MOTHER, THE QUEEN; RUNNER BEANS.

Scepticism. Always 'healthy'. But we must guard against cynicism.

Schedules. Should always be 'hectic'.

See also JUGGLING WORK AND KIDS; LIFE-STYLES; TODAY'S WOMAN.

Schmeichel, Peter. *See* ESKIMOS WORKING IN THE UNITED KINGDOM.

Schoenberg, Arnold Franz Walter (1874–1951). Austro-Hungarian composer who became a United States citizen in 1941. He developed the 12-tone system of musical composition which was not to everybody's taste. However, Schoenberg himself believed that the music which grated on the ears of his contemporaries would in the future be whistled in the streets by cheery errand boys as they went about their business.

'I gather that *BBC Music Magazine* recently carried out an experiment to see if two trained choirboys could be taught to whistle a few bars of his music.'

'And the outcome?'

'I don't recall.'

Science. What is science, after all, but another belief system. It works because we think it's going to work.

'Sounds like one for *The Oldie*, Richard.'

See also MATERIALISM.

Scientists. Peeping-toms at the keyhole of eternity. Always 'so-called', often 'boffins', sometimes 'the boys in forensic'.

'I think we'll leave this to the boys in forensic, Jack.'

'But, Guv...'

'That will be all, Jack.'

See also BOYS.

Scotsmen, strawberry-nosed. *See* FERGUSON, SIR ALEX.

Scrum, the front row of the. It guards its secrets as closely as the Mafia.

'There was plenty going on out there, Jeremy, but it was all forgotten over a pint after the game.'

Sea bass. Always pan-fried.

Sea cow. Oddly enough, the sea cow is more closely related to the elephant than to the farmyard animal from which it gets its name.

Secrets, Somerset's best-kept. *See* AGAIN; ASH PRIORS; BISHOPS LYDEARD; CORFE; MILVERTON; TAUNTON.

Sellers, Peter (1925–80). British film actor. Refer to 'the mask behind the mask'.

Semantics. Always 'mere'.
  'A man's been killed, Inspector! This is no time for mere semantics! Come along, Susan.'
See also CHARACTER, THE ITALIAN; SUSAN.

Seneca (4 BC–AD 65). Tutor to Nero. His eventual suicide and Nero's subsequent career are as pertinent a comment on the dangers of higher education as they were at the time.
  '*Scientiam non dedit natura, semina scientiae nobis dedit.*'
  'I give you best! One for the road?'

Sense, common. Always 'robust'.
See also AQUINAS, ST THOMAS; EXTERIOR; JOHNSON, SAMUEL.

Sensuality. Always 'unbridled', except when 'latent'.

Sentence, the real life. Paradoxically – although not in any formal sense – it's the mother of the victim who has the real life sentence. Rebekah Wade has perceived this.
See also NEWS OF THE WORLD, THE; PRISON OFFICERS; WADE, REBEKAH.

Sentiment. Sometimes a luxury you can't afford.
  'There's no room for sentiment when the whistle goes at 3 o'clock.'
  'Thank you, Ron.'

Serious. The truly serious person can always laugh at himself.
See also BERNARD, JEFFREY.

Set, the seventh game in each. The all-important game to win in a tennis match. Why this is, nobody knows.
See also DOUBLES, MIXED.

77-year-olds. Forever passing away peacefully at home.

Sex. To the question 'how much sex is too much sex?' there appears to be no sensible answer.

'We each have to decide for ourselves.'

'Thank you, Virginia.'

'Excuse me.'

'Yes, Julian?'

'Jolyon.'

'Of course. Your point?'

'Just this. Surely it was that wise man John Mortimer who had it that, "Children, who know about most things, have grasped the fact that sex is funny. When they double up with laughter on saying 'bum' or 'knickers', they are merely echoing the best writers on the subject from Chaucer to Kingsley Amis."'

'A fascinating insight. We're indebted to you, Dr Death.'

'Don't mention it, Mr Waterworks.'

Sex shops. Springing up everywhere; except when they're being closed down.

'The trouble is, as soon as we close one down, another one springs up.'

See also MARCUSE, HERBERT; MASSAGE PARLOURS.

Sex symbols. Often 'unlikely' (*see* MARR, ANDREW; TITCHMARSH, ALAN).

Shaft (1973). Isaac Hayes's classic funk rock soundtrack drenches the movie in 'cool'.

Shagging. *See* MELISSA.

Shakespeare, William. *See* BUMS ON SEATS; GOLDWYN, SAM; KNOCKS, THE UNIVERSITY OF HARD; TITS; WATERHOUSE, KEITH.

Sharks, great white. How unquestionably they know their own marine business! That said, every time a great white shark is caught off Australia's Great Barrier Reef, a clock, still ticking, is discovered in its stomach, along with a pair of false teeth.

See also CROCODILES.

Shark, the six-gilled. So called because, unlike other sharks, it has six gills. Its dorsal fin is unusually small and situated near its tail.

Shaw, Tracey (1972–). In June 2003, and contrary to received opinion, the following passage really did appear in *The Sunday Times*'s popular 'Arts and Farces' column, edited by Carmen Duval, The Celebrity's Pal:

'There are Bard (!) times ahead for troubled former Corrie cracker Tracey Shaw!

'Her next big role, after stripping off on stage in *The Blue Room*, is taking the leading female role in Shakespeare's classic revenge play *Hamlet*. Tracey will be wowing highbrow fans in London, Birmingham and Manchester!

'The blonde babe should have no trouble getting into the role of Ophelia. The tragic Shakespearian heroine had something of a tangled love-life, just like troubled Tracey!

'Ophelia went to hell and back because she had the hots for the Prince of Denmark, while Tracey is in turmoil over the collapse of her 23-month marriage to TV producer Robert Ashworth (31).'

See also BARD, TV TRACEY'S SHAW (!) TO BE; CARMEN DUVAL, THE CELEBRITY'S PAL.

Sheffield. Formerly something of a black spot in terms of that most indefinable of qualities, 'style', Sheffield has in the past few years experienced a cultural renaissance. A branch of Harvey Nichols has recently opened, a new four-star hotel is being built and top chef Gordon Ramsay...

See also BIRMINGHAM; BRADFORD; BRISTOL; CARDIFF; GLASGOW; LEEDS; MANCHESTER; NEWCASTLE.

Sheringham, Teddy (1966–). Footballer. Not the quickest lad on the park, but he's got that all-too-rare quality, nous.

'The first yard's in his mind.'

'That says it all.'

See also BRAIN, A GOOD FOOTBALLING.

Sherwood, James. *See* DIETRICH, MARLENE; HOSPITAL, A MEDICATED OUT-PATIENT FROM THE CHELSEA AND WESTMINSTER.

Shirt, the big lad in the number 9. *See* BRAIN, A GOOD FOOT-BALLING; HOLE, THE.

Shoes. It is not generally known that their shoes are the first thing 73% of women would rescue from a fire.

Shop. It's bad manners to talk shop. No need to explain why.

'A man may well have been murdered, Inspector, but this restaurant happens to serve the best *paupiette de turbot aux jeunes légumes* in Oxford and I have no intention of insulting the chef by talking shop.'

Shop-lifting. A cry for help. Not an occasion for the full rigour of the courts.

'*De minimus non curat lex.*'

'I beg your pardon?'

'The law does not concern itself with trifles.'

'Confound the fellow, Vernon. One more interruption from Dr Death and I'll be off to the toilet myself.'

'And I'll come with you, Simon!'

'Really?'

See WALL, THE WRITING ON THE.

Shopping. When one of today's bubbly wannabes is foolish enough to take her fella with her on a shopping expedition, it has been reliably calculated that after ten minutes 97% of the fellas will look at their watch and say: 'Do you realize that it will be dark in two hours?'

'What? Even David Beckham?'

'The exception that proves the rule.'

'Popper?'

'Well, since our better halves are still in the Ladies, perhaps I will.'

Shopping mall slappers. *See* ALCOHOLIC; *BIMBO*.

Shoreditch. In super-cool Shoreditch one is never more than six feet away from a DJ (*see also* RAT).

'I gather there's a bar where jobs are available to "part-time stylists" and "installation artists" only.'

'And candidates are quizzed, I'm told, as to whether they have any Japanese friends!'

'Next you'll be telling me that there's an escort agency, one of whose girls advertises herself as having "Old skool Didas, pink tights and a Parka"!'

Showbiz world, the. Forever being shattered when a pint-sized diva ditches her lover of six months because of his controlling attitude. *See also* BEAUTIES, SHATTERED; DIVAS; POP BABES, TROUBLED.

Showgirls, French. Always English.

Show-pony manoeuvres. *See* HODDLE, GLENN.

Shulman, Alexandra (1960–). Magazine editor. The nicest thing about Alexandra Shulman is that she's not *Vogue* in that Diana Vreeland, Anna Wintour kind of way.

'I confess you've lost me, Doris. Another bottle of Sauvignon blanc, do you think, Vernon?'

Sick. Always 'violently'. Paradoxically, a sign of good health.

Sidi Bou Said. Paul Klee, August Macke and André Gide were just three of the European artists and writers to be seduced by the charm of its cobbled alleyways. Everything stops for tea in Sidi Bou Said. *See also* ARIÈGE; AUDE; AVEYRON; CAMELS; CONQUES; HARROGATE; LOT; LOZÈRE; ORANGE; PORVOO; SALAMANCA.

Sidney, Sir Philip (1554–86). English poet and soldier. Considered by many to be the *nonpareil* of the Renaissance gentleman. Severely wounded fighting the Spanish in the Netherlands, rather than slake his own thirst he gave his water bottle to a dying soldier.

Signals, quite the wrong. Forever being sent out by the government. *See also* PEOPLE, YOUNG.

Significant other. *See* AGAIN; JAMES, C.L.R.

Silence. Always 'deafening'.
'It's very quiet out there, Inspector.'
'Too quiet, Sergeant. I don't like it.'

Silent majority. *See* MINORITY.

Simenon, Georges (1903–89). The author of more than a thousand thrillers featuring the pipe-smoking Inspector Maigret. When writing a book (which took him a week) he locked himself in a cork-lined room, receiving his meals through a small hatch. In his free moments he made love to at least 5,000 local women. He was at his best when writing of provincial life.

Simple. Always 'deceptively'.
    'I recall that wise man Michael Parkinson saying, "If you appear to be working hard, you're not working hard enough. Fred Astaire taught me that."'

Sixpence. *See also* BECKHAM, DAVID; BRUNEL, ISAMBARD KINGDOM; LAND IT ON A SIXPENCE, CROSS A BALL AND.

Sixties, the. Paradoxically, the Sixties took place in the Seventies.
    'The decade that taste forgot!'
    'The Sixties?'
    'No, the Seventies.'
    'But that was the Sixties.'
    'I'm getting confused. Care for another?'

Sixties, top models in the. Once they were photographed by Donovan and Bailey, now they make their own underwear from used teabags and run donkey sanctuaries in Wales.

Size. Size is unimportant. What counts is a shared sense of humour.
    'You awake, Susan?'
See also PENIS; WALL, THE WRITING ON THE.

Skill on the ball. 'At this level, you can't legislate against skill on the ball like that.'
    'Thank you, Ron.'

Skills, problem-solving. Greatly improved by weekly socializing. Research on 3,000 people aged 65 and over found that social sessions not only improved cognitive abilities, but that improvement persisted for two years. The improvements roughly counteracted the degree of cognitive decline that would be expected over a 7- to 14-year period among older adults without dementia.

'Sounds like one for the Dementia pages, Corinne.'

Slip, giving the media the. *See* CELEBRITIES.

Slippery slopes. The ordinary person doesn't want a slippery slope in his own back yard.

'Nor weapons of mass destruction.'

'I agree.'

Sluts with Nuts. See CASABLANCA.

Smith, Bessie (1894–1937). US jazz and blues singer, known as the 'Empress of the Blues'.

See also HOLIDAY, BILLIE.

Smith, Liz. *See* COMEDY, UNSUNG HEROES OF BRITISH.

Smith, Maggie (1934–). Even as a young actress she wasn't beautiful, but she became beautiful as soon as she stepped onto a stage.

See also DENCH, JUDI; EVANS, EDITH.

Smith, Sydney (1771–1845). The ordained jester to high society.

'Sydney…'

'Any chance of cutting you off at this point, Jolyon?'

'None at all. Sydney – and how naturally one slips into Christian name terms with him – was, like all truly civilized men, essentially a diner-out, a man of gregarious temperament, whose flow of anecdotes and fantasy could set any table on a roar. Truly, like Bill Shakespeare, Sam Johnson and 'Plum' Wodehouse, one feels one knew him.'

'Thank you, Jolyon.'

Snooker. Chess in motion. At the end of the day it's all about psychology.

'It's not just about frames; it's about frames of mind.'

'Thank you, Clive.'

Sobering thought. *See* ARISTOPHANES.

Soccer bad boys. Forever trying to keep the two busty babes in their lives apart.
See also JORDAN; MARSH, JODIE.

Socializing, weekly. *See* OVER-55s, THE; SKILLS, PROBLEM-SOLVING.

Soft goal. *See* HALF-TIME, JUST BEFORE.

Soho brothels. Always 'sordid' (*see* BRITAIN).

Sologne. A region to the south of Orléans, immortalized by Alain-Fournier in his haunting autobiographical fantasy of lost innocence, *Le Grand Meaulnes* (1913). To visit the Sologne is to step back in time.
See also ARIÈGE; AUDE; AVEYRON; CONQUES; CULTURE; HARROGATE; LOT; LOZÈRE; ORANGE; PORVOO; SALAMANCA; SIDI BOU SAID.

Solskjaer, Ole Gunnar. *See* ESKIMOS WORKING IN THE UNITED KINGDOM.

Space. Women now have the space to discover who they really are, but after they've kicked off their shoes at the end of a hectic day, are they any happier?
  'Well, speaking for myself...'
  'Thank you, Susan. This will interest you, Vernon. Apropos our earlier conversation about David and Victoria Beckham, I gather that in America soccer is considered – for obvious reasons, in my opinion – a game suitable only for girls. When the Beckhams recently attempted to raise their profile in that market it was naturally assumed that Victoria was the soccer player and David some sort of fashion accessory.'
  'Indeed. I read the stories myself. Even more humiliatingly for the young couple, they were introduced at the MTV awards as "Victoria and Deirdre".'
  'Excuse me.'
  'Yes, Susan?'
  'If they thought David was a Deirdre why didn't they take him to be a soccer player too?'

'You've got me there, I must confess.'

See also BECKHAM, VICTORIA; BLING-BLING.

Spain, the real. Relocating to the real Spain means you buy a piece of history.

See also SALAMANCA.

Spaniards, skilful little. *See* BALL, BODIES BEHIND THE.

Sparrow, John (1904–86). Former Warden of All Souls, Oxford. Never wrote a book or gave a lecture, but was famous for plucking his eyebrows. Contrary to popular belief, the Oxford historian Eric Christiansen really did write:

'There is nothing wrong with plucking eyebrows. Both Darwin and Marx would have benefited by following this practice. But to broadcast the fact is to court the scepticism of the unsubtle majority. It is a sad commentary on the expectations of the public, but I dare say that if Warden Sparrow had hoped to be taken seriously as a thinker, he would have done better to have written some unreadable treatise on structuralism or to have joined a student demonstration against police violence than to have plucked his eyebrows.'

'You coming to the toilet, Trace?'

'After u.'

See also DONS, OLD-STYLE BACHELOR; JOHNSON, SAMUEL; PIPE-SMOKING SODOMITES; SPECIALIZATION.

Specialization. Always 'arid'. Time was when a don's subject was civilization itself.

See also DONS, OLD-STYLE BACHELOR; SPARROW, JOHN.

Spelling, Aaron (1928–). Television producer, based in Los Angeles. So prolific is his output that in an Aaron Spelling production actors never know in which episode or even in which series they are appearing when they shoot a scene. The story that Peter Falk, playing the crumpled detective, Lt Columbo, appeared in two episodes of *The Streets of San Francisco* without anyone noticing may be apocryphal, but is nonetheless significant for that.

Spengler, Oswald (1880–1936). Spengler claimed that no culture could understand another.

'Scarcely a promising position from which to develop a theory of world history!'

'Nevertheless, and logic-chopping apart, "Spenglerian" remains a good word to use when reflecting on the historical process.'

'I'll grant you that. The little ladies are spending an age in the toilet.'

'So they are.'

Spinoza, Baruch (1632–77). Philosopher. Never held an academic post.

'The old lens-grinder had a point, however, when he said that self-preservation is what it's all about.'

'*Conatus in suo esse perseverandi!*'

'Still in the toilet, then, your birds?'

'Yes, thank you, Miguel.'

Spiritually. Spiritually, we've lost our way.

'Sounds like one for the *Oldie*, Richard.'

See also DOUBT; FAITH.

Sports, good. Today's celebrity historians have to be good sports, ready to wear chain mail in the medieval mode and joust on a horse, and happy to dress up as if to participate in the Battle of Marston Moor.

See also HUNT, DR TRISTRAM; STARKEY, DR DAVID.

Stardom. *See* PRESSURES.

Stark, Graham. *See* COMEDY, UNSUNG HEROES OF BRITISH.

Starkey, Dr David (1945–). Celebrity historian. It says much for this most unstuffy of academics that he may be remembered less for his books, his appearances on radio quiz programmes and his many illustrated television lectures than for the fact that, along with funnymen Stephen Fry and Billy Connolly, he makes the ideal guest on *The Michael Parkinson Show*.

See HOW SAD IS *THAT!*; PANTS, HOW TOTALLY; THAT IS *SO* NOT A GOOD LOOK; TOILET, TOTALLY.

Starving. Life's no picnic for the starving.

  'Nor it is. Care for a *postre*?'

  'I'm sorry?'

  'A dessert. A pudding. A sweet.'

  'Oh dear. Decisions, decisions!'

Statue. Every block of stone contains a statue. An agreeable notion – but we live in the real world.

Steeple Bumpstead. Either a picturesque village in Suffolk, or a West Indian fast bowler. The debate continues.

See also BRIGHTWELL BALDWIN.

Stock Exchange. *See* JOKES, DIRTY.

Stoke-on-Trent. An amusing thing to say to a policeman in Stoke-on-Trent: 'Could you direct me to the best of your opera houses?'

Stonehenge. All the more impressive for the fact that no one knows what it is.

Straight between the uprights! *See* ALCOHOLIC.

Stratton Strawless. Either a picturesque village in Norfolk, or a West Indian fast bowler. The debate continues.

See also PAPWORTH EVERARD.

Strawberries, the. Always disappointing this year.

Streisand, Barbra (1942–). American singer and actress. The story that she looked in the mirror as a child and realized that she would have to be a superstar or nothing may be apocryphal, but is none the less significant for that.

  'Thank you, Barry.'

Strength. Always 'Herculean'.

Stressed-out supermodels. Forever sending their fans reeling by dumping their hunks and announcing that they intend to take six months out of the spotlight after the most emotionally draining year of their lives.

'Their heavy workload will have taken its toll.'

'Indeed.'

See also BEAUTIES ON THE BRINK.

Strikers, international. Forever recovering from groin injuries.

Struggle. Always 'titanic'.

Strummer, Joe (1951–2002). Frontman for the pop group The Clash (*see also* DIE).

'The best man at the wedding of punk and reggae, would you say?'

'I'm afraid you've lost me, Con. Tell me, Vernon. The Mani. You and Doris. You've been there, I take it?'

'I confess we haven't.'

'In that case you have a treat in store! The Mani is the *real* Greece. A bandit country of blood feuds and sublime seafood beneath the lowering mass of Mount Taigetos. Manolo and I … I mean Susan and I … spent a blissful month there once. We scrambled through rocky gorges; swam naked in blue-green waters; drank the rough local wine and feasted off pungent, lemon-drizzled *kalamares*; explored one another's bodies in simple, Spartan rooms washed by watery moonlight … What days those were! Just thinking about it makes me yearn for him … I mean her. Ah, Vernon … old chap … old friend … how strange to have met up with you again after all these years … Come with me to Stoupa! … We'll leave at once … just you and me … Vernon? VERNON? Where the hell's Vernon?'

'He went to the toilet, John. Five minutes ago.'

Students. All studying to be Marketing executives.

Stuffing. *See* GAME, THE; MANCHESTER UNITED.

Stunners, grumpy. *See* AGUILERA, CHRISTINA.

Style. Contrary to popular opinion, Joanna Lumley really did say on the *Michael Parkinson Show* that, 'Style isn't only about clothes.

Style is manners and behaviour and attitude. When St Lawrence was being burned at the stake he said: "I'm done that side, turn me round." *That's* style. To be an acceptable person these days you have to be deep and profound and rather scruffy and semi-turgid. If you appear looking like a million dollars, people think you're a silly tart who thinks of nothing and can't read a book.'

'That says it all.'

'Thank you, Michael. See you later at the Ivy.'

Success, chart. As that wise woman Gail Rebuck has said, publishing a celebrity's confessional memoirs and steering it to international chart success isn't as easy as you'd think.

'Why on earth not?'

'I can't imagine.'

See also AUTOBIOGRAPHY; JONSSON, ULRIKA.

Such things. There's a time and a place for such things. We forget this at our peril. *The Daily Mail* has not been deceived (*see DAILY MAIL, THE*).

Suffolk, people who live in. Forever driving into Diss on Saturday morning and bidding for lot 9 in a furniture auction. Nobody knows why.

'Excuse me, but isn't Diss in Norfolk?'

'It may well be, but my point holds.'

See also NORFOLK, PEOPLE WHO LIVE IN.

Sun, a beach bar in the. 'I've always had a fantasy about running a beach bar in the sun.'

'You never told me that, Simon.'

'You never asked me, Susan.'

See also SUSAN.

Sun, our inscrutable friends from the Land of the Rising. They'll be in Somerset next.

See also AGE, THE VICTORIAN; THEY.

Surveys. Always 'recent'.

Susan. 'But Susan, listen…'

'*No* Simon. This time I want to handle it *my* way.'

'But…'

'No buts. I mean it.'

'Right, right… I'll… I'll help Daphne with the dishes.'

Swede, the full-breasted. *See* PROVERBIAL MATCH AGAINST MARS.

Swedish, the. Their attitude to free love may seem very enlightened, but it is surely no coincidence that they have the highest suicide rate in the world.

'Not that they do, but the point is well made.'

Symptoms. If the symptoms persist for more than four weeks, consult your doctor.

See also INSTRUCTIONS.

Szasz, Thomas (1920–). American psychiatrist who, unusually for someone practising this profession, believes that there is no such thing as mental illness. An unwavering libertarian, he holds, for instance, that it would be none of a psychiatrist's business to try to dissuade a patient from committing suicide.

'How true. He was once seen arguing with a man standing on a tenth-floor window-ledge, but it transpired that he was merely insisting that the man pay his bill before he jumped!'

'Delightful! Would that all trick-cyclists had their feet so firmly planted in the real world.'

'Which is more than the man on the window-ledge did!'

See also MENTALLY ILL.

T

Tanned and relaxed, return from a sunshine break in the Seychelles looking. *See* BALL, ZOE.

Tapping, telephone. The police can't tap our telephones without written permission from the Home Secretary. Nobody believes this.

'They can tap my phone any time they like. All they'd hear is my better half talking to her mother! That said, she's still not back from the toilet.'

See WALL, THE WRITING ON THE.

Taste, good. Always 'suffocating'.

Taunton. It feels like a village, but under its placid exterior Taunton is a town rapidly going up in the desirability stakes. The Brewhouse Theatre and the Tacchi-Morris Arts Centre have plays, concerts and dance recitals. The Odeon has five screens, and there is also tenpin bowling. The area has riding facilities and the Wellington Sports Centre has a swimming pool. There are many antique shops and the usual high-street stores.

See also ASH PRIORS; BISHOPS LYDEARD; CORFE; MILVERTON; SECRETS, SOMERSET'S BEST-KEPT.

Tawny Pipit, The. BBC 2, 9 p.m. 'Let me see. *The Tawny Pipit* (1951). Barry Norman writes: "Agreeably unpretentious World War II movie, written and directed by Bernard Miles, about a pair of tawny pipits who foiled the Allies' plans on D-Day by nesting in a Bofors gun. Gently amusing. The French were the first to perceive this."'

'I think we'll give that one a miss.'

Tax-payers. 'That's you and me.' Always 'long-suffering'.
See also COMMUTERS.

Television. 'No, Susan and I don't watch much television. Just wildlife programmes, really, and the News, of course. Isn't that right, Susan? Susan? Damn me, she's gone again. Daphne, your glass is empty. Where's Daphne?'
   'Need you ask?'
   'Oh well. I think I'll go and have a word with Mickey Skinner.'

Ten greatest films of all time. *See* ANTONIONI, MICHELANGELO; AUTHORS; *CASABLANCA*; CIMINO, MICHAEL; EISENSTEIN, SERGEI; EYES; KUROSAWA, AKIRA; RAY, SATYAJIT; RENOIR, JEAN.

Tench, Rod and Perch. Those most agreeably English of fish. In a humorous column, a good name for a firm of solicitors.
See also TROUT.

Tendulkar, Sachin (1973–). Indian cricketer. His is the wicket that everyone wants most.
   'Shane Warne's got him with his wrong 'un! That was the wicket the Australians wanted.'
   'Thank you, Richie.'

Termites. When the queen dies, they go mad, destroying everything in their path for miles around. There may be a lesson here.

Tests, intelligence. Thunder against them. Intelligence is culturally relative.
   'If a cheery Hottentot set an intelligence test, how many Oxbridge professors would pass? That's what I ask myself.'

Thales (*c*.624 BC–*c*.546 BC). Hardly a convivial man. He held that the essence of all matter was water.
   'Now pull the other one! What's yours?'

Thatcher, Margaret Hilda (1925–). British Conservative politician. 'Say what you like about Mar...'

'Toilet evry 1?'

'U bet!'

'Well, well, well. Seems to leave just you and me, Simon. Simon? SIMON? Where's Simon?'

'He's gone to have a quick word with Mickey Skinner, I rather think.'

'So he has. Thank you, Dr Death.'

'Don't mention it, Mr Pratley.'

Then. 'That was then, Simon. Now is now. Things change. I need space to discover who I really am.'

See WALL, THE WRITING ON THE WALL.

Thespian. A word that sits well in a humorous column.

See also ABLUTIONS; ABODE; ALFRED; AMERICAN ACADEMICS; BUSTS; DANE, HAMLET THE MOODY; DUCK, DONALD; EATERIE; EMBONPOINT; HOSTELRY; INFELICITOUS; KEATS, JOHN; LIBATION; MEADOWS, MY POULTERER, THE ESTIMABLE MR; NOSHERIE; OCCASIONS; READER, GENTLE; REPORTER; THESPIAN; VARIETY, BIRDS OF THE FEATHERED.

They. They'll be in Somerset next.

'And Suffolk' (*see also* ALDEBURGH).

Things. Things change. Women know this.

See also THEN; THINGS WOMEN KNOW.

Things, these. Better organized by the Germans.

See also GERMANS, THE; NEEDLESS TO SAY; TRUE, SAD BUT.

Things women know. How to wrap up parcels.

Thinking. 'But if Major Marjoribanks isn't the murderer, then who...?'

'Sir, are you thinking what I'm thinking?'

'Yes, Sergeant, I think I am. And I think it's high time we paid another call on Mrs Patterson, don't you? Come along, Sergeant.'

See also PATTERSON, MRS.

Thought. The first thought is often the best. No need to explain why.

Time bombs, ticking. *See* RIGHTS, HUMAN; SLOPES, SLIPPERY.

Tinseltown sizzlers. Forever causing a commotion by appearing in public in a new hair-do.
See also FANS.

Titchmarsh, Alan (1950–). Gardener (*see also* JUDGES, BOOKER PRIZE; SEX SYMBOLS, UNLIKELY).

Titian, *properly* **Tiziano Veccellio** (1487–1576). The most celebrated painter of the Venetian school, famous for his use of colour and ability to capture convincing, yet flattering, likenesses. In paintings such as *Diana and Actaeon* his pioneering use of oil captured the full range of heroic action and human emotion.

Tits. If you get your tits out they don't take you seriously. On the other hand, *see* BUMS ON SEATS; GOLDWYN, SAM; QUALITY.

Today's woman. Forever juggling work and kids (*see* BALL, ZOE).

Todd, Bob. *See* COMEDY, UNSUNG HEROES OF BRITISH.

Toddlers. Forever throwing wobblies in supermarket queues.
See also NO; PARENTING, INCONSISTENT.

Toilet, how totally. Contrary to received opinion, Dr David Starkey has never used the expression 'how totally toilet' in any of his popular television shows.
See also STARKEY, DR DAVID.

Toksvig, Sandi. *See* ESKIMOS WORKING IN THE UNITED KINGDOM.

Top totty. *See* ALCOHOLIC.

Totty package, total. *See* LOPEZ, JENNIFER; MINOGUE, KYLIE.

Touch. Sometimes women don't like to be touched.
   'Don't touch me, Simon!'
See WALL, THE WRITING ON THE.

Touch, a soft. *See* ASYLUM-SEEKERS.

Touch of Frost, A. A popular television series.
See also ABUSE, VERBAL; BLACKMAIL; BRANCH, SPECIAL; BRASS, THE TOP; *MORSE, INSPECTOR*; PHILOSOPHY; PLANTS; PSYCHOLOGY.

Toulouse-Lautrec, Henri (1864–1901). Like many people with a full address book, Toulouse-Lautrec found there were times when no one was in. Died of syphilis.
See also BYRON, LORD GEORGE; CASS, MAMA; DEAN, JAMES; EPSTEIN, BRIAN; HENDRIX, JIMI; HUTCHENCE, MICHAEL; JONES, BRIAN; JOPLIN, JANIS; MONROE, MARILYN; MOON, KEITH.

Town planners, postwar. Have done more damage to the fabric of our inner cities than the Luftwaffe did.

Traffic. Always 'at a standstill'.
See also COMMUTERS; JEREMY.

Tragedy. Always 'human'.
    'Indeed, indeed. But could there be another kind?'
    'An "animal tragedy", perhaps? The death of Bambi?'
    'Would it be too owlish to say that Aristotle wouldn't have agreed?'
See also ARISTOTLE; MISFORTUNE.

Tragic irony. *See* ADAMS, DOUGLAS.

Transvestites. Always happily married men.

Trash or flash. *See* ALCOHOLIC.

Trawlermen, Cornish. Forever standing around in surly groups complaining that the Spanish are catching all their fish.
See also MEN, SPANISH.

Trifles. Always 'amusing'.

Trinny and Susannah. Fashion police. They may look like Abbott and Costello, but they do a professional job.

'And what's that exactly?'
'I haven't the faintest idea.'
'They used to make me roar with laughter.'
'Trinny and Susannah?'
'No. Abbott and Costello.'
'Well, there you are.'

Trivial. Sometimes we learn more from the ostensibly trivial than from the would-be profound.
'Sounds like one for *The Oldie*, Richard.'

Trout. One should never underestimate the intelligence of a trout.
See also PARKINSON, MICHAEL; TENCH, ROD AND PERCH.

True, sad but. *See* GERMANS, THE; NEEDLESS TO SAY; THINGS, THESE.

Trust. 'The word is trust, Susan. You'll find it in the dictionary next to "trollop".'
See WALL, THE WRITING ON THE.

Truth, the. Often 'harsh'.

Tufnell, Phil (1966–). In many ways, his own worst enemy, yet a man of jokes.
'None richer than his fielding!'
'Delightful!'

Turkish boxers. All 'crude sluggers'.
'The brave British lad has no chance against the crude slugger from Istanbul.'
'Thank you, Harry.'

Turks, a skirmish with the. *See* CALDERON DE LA BARCA, PEDRO; DE VIVAR, RODERIGO DÍAZ; GLUBB, JOHN BAGOT; MALLARMÉ, STÉPHANE; MAUPASSANT, GUY DE; RICHARD I; RIMBAUD, ARTHUR; VEGA, LOPE FELIX DE.

Turner, Joseph Mallord William (1775–1851). It has been truly said that he painted Britain. On the other hand, how strange that a

Professor of Perspective should, late in life, have chosen to paint with such total disregard for it. Or perhaps it's not so strange.

Turning anguish into money. *See NEWS OF THE WORLD, THE;* WADE, REBEKAH.

Turning tears to good use. *See NEWS OF THE WORLD, THE;* TURNING ANGUISH INTO MONEY; WADE, REBEKAH.

Turton Bottoms. Either a picturesque village in Lancashire, or a West Indian fast bowler. The debate continues.

See also NEMPNETT THRUBWELL.

24/7, the full. *See* WALSINGHAM, SIR FRANCIS.

Two-edged sword. *See* AQUINAS, ST THOMAS.

Two sides of the same coin, love and hate are but. *See* CATULLUS.

U V

Uncles, Dutch. *See* NUTS, BRAZIL.

Undisclosed destination, speeding to an. *See* BALL, ZOE.

Unless I'm much mistaken. *See* BOWES, BILL; FRENCH COOKING; INSIGHTS.

Unnecessary. There's no need to be unnecessary. *The Daily Mail* has perceived this.

See also DAILY MAIL, THE; MAN, THE PERFECTABILITY OF; NATURE, HUMAN; PROGRESS, BELIEF IN THE ILLUSION OF; REAL WORLD, THE; SARCASTIC; UTOPIA, THE SEARCH FOR.

Unpretentious verses. *See* CAGNEY, JAMES; EASTWOOD, CLINT; MARVIN, LEE; PESCI, JOE; ROBINSON, EDWARD G.; WIDMARK, RICHARD.

Ups and Downs of a Handyman, The (1975). Channel 4, 9 p.m. 'Hilarious 1970s sex romp starring Robin Askwith!'
  'Sounds like one to miss, Vernon.'
  'I was rather looking forward to it, Daphne.'

See also ACTORS, ENGLISH; BEST TELEVISION IN THE WORLD, THE.

Upton Snodsbury. Either a picturesque village in Worcestershire, or a West Indian fast bowler. The debate continues.

See also COMPTON PAUNCEFOOT.

Utopia, the search for. One of the endemic follies of our age. *The Daily Mail* has perceived this.

See also DAILY MAIL, THE; EVIL; MAN, THE PERFECTABILITY OF;

NATURE, HUMAN; NOOSE, THE; PENDULUM; PROGRESS, BELIEF IN THE ILLUSION OF; REAL WORLD, THE; UNNECESSARY; UTOPIA, THE SEARCH FOR.

Valance, Holly (1983–). Australian pop babe.

See also MINOGUE, KYLIE.

van Gogh, Vincent Willem (1853–1890). Dutch Post-Impressionist painter. Though a pioneer of Expressionism, he never sold a picture in his lifetime.

van Nistelroy, Ruud (1978–). Footballer.

'His mother tongue is Dutch, but he can make the ball talk in any language.'

'Thank you, Barry.'

Variety, birds of the feathered. A phrase that sits well in an occasional column.

See also ABLUTIONS; ABODE; ALFRED; AMERICAN ACADEMICS; BUSTS; DANE, HAMLET THE MOODY; DUCK, DONALD; EATERIE; EMBONPOINT; HOSTELRY; INFELICITOUS; KEATS, JOHN; LIBATION; MEADOWS, MY POULTERER, THE ESTIMABLE MR; NOSHERIE; OCCASIONS; READER, GENTLE; REPORTER; THESPIAN.

Vaucluse. *See* LEAVIS, DR F.R.; ORANGE.

Vaughan, Michael (1974–). Cricketer. In Michael Vaughan England seem at last – *mirabile dictu* – to have discovered a batsman of genuine world class.

'Yes, Jolyon? You have an observation to make?'

'Just this, Mr Pratley. If Australia's Matt Hayden is a robust Shiraz, England's Michael Vaughan is a more subtle varietal – a Cabernet Franc or Pinot Noir. His flavours are more muted, perhaps, than the muscular Queenslander's, but no less resonant for that.'

'Thatz dun it! I don't want 2 b rude nor nothing but cld sum 1 call this r sole a taxi?'

'Well, I must say! I've never been so insulted.'

'U must hav been.'

'Come along Roberto. We're leaving. Roberto! ROBERTO! Where's Roberto?'

Vega, Lope Felix de (1562–1635). Dramatist. The father of Spanish drama, he is reputed to have written more than 1500 plays. Like so many writers of Spain's 'golden age', he lost an arm in a skirmish with the Turks.

See also GLUBB, JOHN BAGOT; MALLARMÉ, STÉPHANE; MAUPASSANT, GUY DE; RICHARD I; TURKS, A SKIRMISH WITH THE.

Verlaine, Paul (1844–96). An intense relationship with Arthur Rimbaud broke up his marriage and he was imprisoned for shooting his fellow-poet in 1873. For a time he taught in a prep school near Hastings. His later poetry reflects his return to Catholicism. Who but the French could have produced a Paul Verlaine?

See also RIMBAUD, ARTHUR.

'Vers de Société.' *See* ABODE; CRAPS, A CROWD OF; 'FRIEND, IN A PIG'S ARSE'; LARKIN, PHILIP; MEET THERE SOMETIME, WE MUST.

Very real sense, in a. *See* AUTHORS.

Vets, wildlife. Forever knocking rhinoceroses unconscious with a valium dart.

'The car is their home, the wilderness their office.'

Victim, the. 'It's the mother of the victim who has the life sentence, that's what I always say.'

'Has Rebekah Wade perceived this?'

'Without a doubt.'

See also NEWS OF THE WORLD, THE; PRISON OFFICERS; TURNING ANGUISH INTO MONEY; WADE, REBEKAH.

Victors. There are always two sets of victors. Those who won, and those who lost.

'Another such victory and we are lost!'

Villeneuve, Jacques (1971–). Formula One racing driver. The question is, does the little Canadian still want it enough to succeed at this level? Is he *hungry* enough?

Villon, François (1431–c.1465). Poet, brawler and thief. He spent time at the court of the duke of Orléans until sentenced to death for an unknown offence, from which he was saved by the amnesty of a public holiday. On mention of his name, murmur *'Mais où sont les neiges d'antan?'*

See also GENET, JEAN.

VIPs, busty. Forever announcing their marital difficulties by posing in their underwear and revealing that their fellas are 'failing on the nookie front'.

'Leaving them unhappy with their body image, I imagine.'

'Indeed. Hence the underwear pictures in *GQ* magazine.'

See also BEAUTIES, SHATTERED.

Virtuoso. The modern virtuoso literally lives out of a suitcase. Isaac Stern once dreamt that he was playing Brahms in Budapest and woke to find he was playing Mendelssohn in Minnesota.

Vivaldi, Antonio (1678–1741). If Bach was the Beatles of his time was Vivaldi the Rolling Stones? Refer to him as *il prete rosso* as he was a red-headed priest.

Vogue. It's about offering its readers a little package holiday away from themselves and their lives.

'Thank you, Alexandra.'

See also LUXURIES, LIFE'S LITTLE; SHULMAN, ALEXANDRA.

Voice-overs. A source of tremendous wealth. An actor can earn in excess of £500,000 a year doing voice-overs. That said, doing a voice-over is harder than you might suppose.

Volatile. They have talent to spare, but the volatile Pakistanis tend to be their own worst enemies both on and off the cricket field.

'If the Rawalpindi express bowls with any sort of control, England could be all out by lunchtime. Over to you, Richie.'

'Good morning, everyone.'

See also MARKETS.

Volcano. Of a distinguished author who has not published for many years it might be amusing to remark, 'Is the volcano dead, or does it merely sleep?'

Vole, the water. The race is on to protect the water vole.
See also OSPREY.

Vulgarity. Always 'healthy'. We British are not afraid of healthy vulgarity.
See also WEST, MAE.

Vulture. A vulture can pick out a piece of decaying flesh no bigger than a sixpence at a distance of five miles.

Wade, Rebekah (1968–). Flame-haired editor of pornographic tabloids. She understands newspapers.

'I agree. Who has a better understanding of how to turn anguish into money?'

See also ELEPHANTS; FAME, THE PAIN BEHIND THE; FINALISTS, REALITY SHOW; *NEWS OF THE WORLD, THE*; TURNING ANGUISH INTO MONEY; VICTIM, THE.

Wales. When giving an idea of the size of a geographical area, always say 'an area the size of Wales'.

'Forest fires are raging over an area the size of Wales.'

Wales, Diana, Princess of (1961–97). Like many people with a full address book, she found there were times when no one was in.

See also BYRON, LORD GEORGE; CASS, MAMA; GUILTY, WE ARE ALL; MARGARET, PRINCESS; TOULOUSE-LAUTREC, HENRI.

Walsingham, Sir Francis (1530–90). Elizabethan statesman and spy-catcher. Contrary to received opinion, Professor Simon Schama really did say, 'Walsingham watched Elizabeth's enemies the full 24/7' in one of his popular television lectures.

See also CASE, ON THE.

Wannabes. Forever 'stunned', in 'a frenzy of speculation' or 'sent reeling' by the latest news from Planet Pop.

'Should they burst out laughing at each other's zany antics?'

'Not until they themselves have been catapulted to pop superstardom.'

'Of course.'

See also BUBBLY PERSONALITIES; BURST OUT LAUGHING; CELEBS.

Want it. If you didn't get it it's because you didn't want it enough.
'Or because you didn't have a bubbly personality.'
'Thank you, Geri.'
See also PERSONALITIES.

Wants, the wicket that everyone. *See* TENDULKAR, SACHIN.

Watchable, never less than. *See* COLONIAL FAÇADE.

Waterhouse, Keith (1929–). 'Surely the funniest and wisest writer in England now that "Plum" Wodehouse is no longer with us.'
'I'd second that.'

Waterman, Pete (1946–). Record producer (*see also* AMBITION; DESCRIPTIONS, THEORY OF; GET, WHAT YOU SEE IS WHAT YOU).

Waugh, Evelyn (1903–66). He narrowed his eyes in order to widen his gaze.

Way to go! *See* ALCOHOLIC.

Weather, the. Only worth a quick look. 'And now for a quick look at the weather.'

Weaver, Sigourney (1949–). Actress (*see* EROTICISM IN THE CINEMA; HEROINES, KICK-ARSE).

We British. We British bend over backwards to be a soft touch.
See also ASYLUM-SEEKERS; BRITISH; BRITISH, WE; VULGARITY.

Week, the events of the past. Always 'disturbing'.

Wellington, the. *See* ALCOHOLIC; GR8 4 C N SOCCER TOSSERS B N B10 UP BY BAD RS DOORMEN.

Well trolleyed. It is not generally known that when lecturing on George IV, Dr David Starkey really did say, 'One look at his future bride and George got well trolleyed. He was off his tits during the marriage ceremony and spent his wedding night unconscious in the fireplace.'
See also MAN, THE NEW.

Welsh politicians. Forever fellating Rastafarians on Clapham Common.

Welsh stunners. *See* BEAUTIES, BIG-SCREEN.

West, Mae (1893–1980). Actress and comedienne. In a period of sophistication, she brought a healthy vulgarity to the American cinema. Her name is synonymous with the famous inflatable life-jacket.

Westbrook, Daniella (1973–). Actress. The troubled soap babe sacrificed a leading role in *Crossroads* to get a new nose for Christmas. There may be a lesson here. That said, she's been to hell and back.

What it means to be human. *See* POPULAR SONG, THE AMERICAN.

Wheelbarrowful of notes to buy a loaf of bread. *See* INFLATION.

Whitfield, June. *See* COMEDY, UNSUNG HEROES OF BRITISH.

Wicked!, no peace for the. *See* AGE, THE VICTORIAN.

Widdecombe, Anne (1947–). British politician.
   'Surely it was Anne Widdecombe of whom it has been said that she dresses as if she'd had a fit in a charity shop?'
   'Boris Johnson, in fact, but the point holds.'

Widmark, Richard (1914–). There's an engaging irony in the fact that this legendary 'psychopath' of so many classic *films noirs* should in real life be a cultured, sensitive man who writes agreeably unpretentious verses and has assembled the finest collection of French impressionists outside France.
See also CAGNEY, JAMES; EASTWOOD, CLINT; MARVIN, LEE; PESCI, JOE; ROBINSON, EDWARD G.

William I ('the Conqueror') (1027–87). King of England from 1066. Like so many English monarchs, his last words were, 'Bugger Bognor!'
See also LAST WORDS; MOTHER, THE QUEEN.

Williams, Robbie (1974–). Pop singer. Who knows what he will come up with next!

Wiltshire, people who live in. Forever ringing up people who live in Shropshire and saying: 'What's your news?' A mystery.
See also SALISBURY, PEOPLE WHO LIVE IN.

Windsor, Barbara (1937–). Actress. It is too easily forgotten, perhaps, that this cheery cockney sparrow has been to hell and back.

Wisden Cricketers' Almanack. If the proverbial man from Mars were to read *Wisden Cricketers' Almanack* he'd be none the wiser about cricket, but he'd learn a great deal about English social history.

Wit. Always 'sparkling'.

Wittgenstein, Ludwig (1889–1951). He never appreciated that accessibility of thought is largely a question of good manners, but then he was notorious in his lifetime for his cultivated social awkwardness.

'Unlike David Starkey, hardly the ideal guest on the Michael Parkinson Show, then!'

See also ACCESSIBLE.

Women. Women have won the right to define and validate themselves in relation to reality – but are they any happier?

Women's intuition. A myth. It has been estimated that 97% of women who found their husbands at the base of a priapic pyramid consisting of the Swedish au pair, their best friend, Melissa, six table dancers from Spearmint Rhino and their fag master at Charterhouse would be totally satisfied by his explanation that he was auditioning them for a television commercial.

'I wdnt bet on it.'

'Nor wld i. Im leavin' u, Simon, u disgust me.'

'Dear God, now shes doin it.'

'So r u.'

'Its 2 late n e way. Hes gon.'

'Who?'

'Simon.'

'Do wot? Where?'

'He left an our ago wiv Dawn Airey. Or perhaps it woz Mickey Skinner. Me 'n shar r gonna swing by the Wellington. U comin, sue?'

'U bet!'

'Well, well, well. What a strange evening, Daphne. Daphne! DAPHNE! Damn me, Where's the woman gone?'

'She left with Roberto. Your bill, Mr Pratley.'

See also INTUITION, WOMEN'S.